THE EDINBURGH FRINGE
SURVIVAL GUIDE
HOW TO MAKE YOUR SHOW A SUCCESS

MARK FISHER performed in a student-written play called *Shubunkin* at the YWCA in Randolph Place, Edinburgh in 1983. Tickets cost £1.75 and the start time was 4.15 p.m. The play has not been heard of since, but the reviewer for the *Scotsman* said it wove a '*Coronation Street* idiom on a Miltonian frame' which helped attract a few people to see the last of its four performances. In the summer of 1986, Mark returned to Edinburgh to work in the Fringe Office and has not missed a festival since.

Today, he is one of Scotland's foremost commentators on the arts. He is the Scottish theatre critic for the *Guardian* and *Variety*, a former editor of *The List* and a freelance writer. Every August, he is one of the judges for the *Scotsman* Fringe Firsts and an adviser for the Carol Tambor Award. He has also been on the panel for the *Herald* Angels and the Amnesty International Freedom of Expression Award.

For Jane, Archie and Lotte
who see so little of me in August.

'The Edinburgh Fringe is a place to really test yourself out. There's a dynamic atmosphere of competition, which is very productive and because it's very much performance-led, there's a great camaraderie and some fantastic shows surface that you might not see anywhere else.'

Steven Berkoff

'Ah! The Fringe! I can't think of a more delightful way of putting my liver, bank account, relationship, complexion, and mental stability under the greatest strain they've ever known!'

Mel Giedroyc of Mel and Sue

Acknowledgements

This book would not have been possible without Anna Brewer, my ever-patient editor, whose idea it was, and without the actors, directors, producers, administrators and publicists who so generously shared their time and experience in my interviews with them. If your name is in the Index, I owe you a big thank you. A round of applause in particular to Kath Mainland and her ever-enthusiastic team in the Fringe Office. Their work is often unsung, but Edinburgh would be a poorer place without their expertise, dedication and level-headedness. Thanks, indeed, to all the people who make the Scottish capital the only city worth being in every August. If you are not yet one of them, I hope you soon will be.

Mark Fisher

Foreword

I AM FIRMLY CONVINCED that everybody should take a show to the Edinburgh Fringe at least once in their lives. Sometimes when you look at the packed Fringe brochure it seems as though everybody has. But, incredibly, there are still many men and women who have never been in a Fringe show. How much better our public life would be if every politician, civil servant and council worker had been part of a show that plays three weeks in a Scottish church hall during a rainy August. And how much better the world of business would be if every tycoon, chairman of the board and trade union official had taken part in a devised piece of physical theatre playing at just after midnight in a gloomy room in the Old Town. Performing at the Edinburgh festival makes you a better neighbour, better teacher, better friend, better parent. For a few, it even makes them better performers.

Taking a show to the Edinburgh festival is an essential rite of passage. It's an experience that teaches you the intense communality of sharing a drive in a broken van packed with cast, set and costumes and of living in a small Edinburgh flat with a large cast and visiting friends and their friends. It teaches you the dedication of waking up every day and hitting the streets with a pile of leaflets to persuade the public that your show, out of the thousands on offer, is the one they want to see in the next hour. And you develop an incredible optimism that today there will be more people in the audience than there are on stage and that, by the end of the week, your audience will reach healthy double figures.

I first went with a company of student actors performing two shows to the Fringe in 1985. We were presenting a children's show at 10 a.m. every morning. This meant we were leafleting outside our venue at 8.30 every morning. Once we'd finished performing our morning show, we would then carry our set, which was used for both shows, along the full length of Princes Street to the venue where we were performing our afternoon show, a piece based on the salacious poetry of the Earl of Rochester. Once the heavy set had been carried to this second venue, we'd start leafleting all over again. The Rochester show started at 3 p.m., finished by 4 p.m. and then the fun really began. I would hurry off into the streets of Edinburgh trying to see as much theatre as I could. I saw an incredible range of work – everything from densely metaphorical pieces from visiting Polish companies through to an early incarnation of John Godber's Fringe smash hit *Bouncers*. This was more theatre than I had seen in my life before and I was learning quickly about the infinite possibilities of what you put on a stage. Not only this – all these shows were part of the same festival; they were being listed in the same brochure as the piece that I was performing in. For the first time I didn't feel like an outsider wanting to be part of the world of theatre. Now I'd been let in and was part of the dialogue, part of the experience.

I went as part of a student production for each of the three years of my undergraduate life. During those few feverish weeks every August I learnt more about working and living with other people, more about making my finances stretch beyond what seemed possible and more about the joys and perils of drink and sex than I did the whole of the rest of my time as a student.

Now that I'm a working playwright, the Fringe is still a great place to premiere a new piece. Fringe-goers are an enthusiastic, risk-taking audience. Away from the Fringe, audiences are often looking for the reassuring and the familiar. But in the midst of the noise and clamour of the festival, the audience embraces the new, the innovative and the downright weird. There's nothing quite like the thrill of finding that word of mouth has spread through the bars and backstages of Edinburgh and that the audience want to see your performance: a diverse collection of Edinburgh locals, undergraduates from across the country and a smattering of tourists in rainwear, all eager to discover what is special about your show.

With this book in your hand, you'll have a head start on the incredible adventure of taking a show to the Edinburgh Fringe. Good luck and – before you go – can I give you a leaflet for my show?

Mark Ravenhill
July 2011

1. The City and its Festivals
Welcome to the Greatest Show on Earth

THE EDINBURGH FESTIVAL FRINGE likes statistics. As each festival approaches, you will hear all manner of head-spinning facts. If you are putting on a show, you will learn there are perhaps 2,500 companies doing exactly the same thing. You will be one of 21,000 participants and collectively you will be giving 40,000 performances. Throw in the cultural tourists who flock to the Scottish capital with the express purpose of seeing shows and you will be responsible for doubling the city's population. Your efforts, along with those of the Edinburgh International Festival, the Edinburgh International Book Festival, the Edinburgh Mela, the Royal Edinburgh Military Tattoo, the Edinburgh Art Festival and the Edinburgh Jazz and Blues Festival (now starting in July), will bring over £200m to the local economy.

You will read these statistics and you will get a sense of something big, exciting and a little bit unusual. Nothing, however, will prepare you for what these numbers mean in practice. 'It's like sex, it's like having children; there's no way to explain it to anybody,' says John Clancy, a visitor to the Fringe as director, playwright and producer since 2000. Clancy is a founding artistic director of the New York International Fringe Festival so he knows the territory, but that event, despite being the largest multi-arts festival in North America, fields only a tenth as many companies as Edinburgh. 'The Edinburgh Fringe is the arts Olympics of the world,' he says.

Even in the thick of the action, you will find it difficult to get the measure of the event. If you stop for a drink in one of the popular venues – perhaps at the Pleasance Courtyard or the Urban Garden at C Venue – it will feel as if you are at the heart of the festival. All around you will be audiences, performers, technicians, reviewers, promoters and people handing out flyers advertising their shows. Within spitting distance will be more performances than you could see, even if you did nothing else for a fortnight. Yet even then, you should remember that all over this city are people thinking they too are at the centre of the Fringe universe, whether they are seeing back-to-back dance at Dance Base, round-the-clock theatre at the Traverse, non-stop comedy at the Stand Comedy Club, nightly folk songs at the Acoustic Music Centre at St Bride's or all-day student theatre at the Bedlam. 'Embarrassingly, in my first three years working at the Pleasance, I didn't see a single show outside of the Pleasance,' says one box-office worker at one of the biggest multiplex venues. 'And I probably didn't see even ten per cent of what was on there.'

In 2010, first-time Fringe-goer Matthew Somerville, a web developer from Birmingham, managed to see 136 shows in just under four weeks. Despite this awesome achievement, he calculated he had seen only 5.54 per cent of what was on offer. The phenomenon is no more manageable for a dedicated theatre critic such as the *Guardian*'s Lyn Gardner, who sees as many shows as anyone yet still returns to London hungry for more. 'Even when I've done a year when I have consistently seen five, six, seven shows every single day over a period of three weeks, I always leave Edinburgh knowing there are shows I would have liked to have seen,' she says.

Some venues present only one show, others programme a dizzying number. 'We create something twice the size of the Edinburgh International Festival,' says William Burdett-Coutts, talking not about the whole Fringe but about his one organisation, Assembly. His programme routinely exceeds 130 shows and plays to 290,000 people: the equivalent of the BBC Proms. 'People outside of Edinburgh just don't get the scale of it at all,' he says. 'The Fringe is an incredible seedbed of opportunity.'

Assume nothing

When you perform in your home town or university, you will take certain things for granted. The start time will be 7.30 p.m., the room will be available all day for setting up and a predictable number of people will turn up to see the show. On the Edinburgh Fringe, there is no such certainty. If your show is scheduled to start at noon, it will not be the first performance of the day. Neither will it be the only show starting at noon; on a typical weekday, your potential audience might have fifty productions to choose from between 12 p.m. and 1 p.m. And that is in the theatre programme alone. Starting around 1 p.m. will be fifty more – not to mention around ten dance, five music and forty comedy shows, in a city not short of restaurants, museums and tourist attractions to lure people away. With such fierce competition for spectators – even when the city is full of spectators – it is common for performances to go ahead with the audience numbering in single figures.

Until you see this for yourself – see what it means to have every basement, lecture hall, Masonic lodge and back room turned into a performing space; to have your way blocked on the Royal Mile because of the sheer volume of people; to come out of a show at 10 p.m. knowing there is still time to catch a couple more before bedtime – it is impossible to appreciate the scale, relentlessness and energy of the Edinburgh Fringe. Today, there are fringes all over the world, in Dublin, Adelaide, New York and Johannesburg. Each has its own qualities, but none even remotely compares to the all-consuming intensity of this three-week event in August. 'When I think of "fringe", I think of the Halifax Fringe, which is a very small festival that has never included itself on the Canadian fringe circuit,' says Anthony Black of Nova Scotia's 2b Theatre Company:

Obviously the Edinburgh Fringe is huge, but it's just mayhem. When I arrived I was amazed at how many people were around, anxious at not getting any reviewers and anxious at not getting any audience.

'Until you get here you have no idea,' says Black's producer Sarah Rogers of Montreal theatre agent Menno Plukker:

We arrived here on 2 August and you could see the company were looking round thinking, 'What's the big deal?' But the population just surged in a day and a half and by 4 August we couldn't move. It's been a challenge just seeing how big it is. For the company, it's become a great challenge, like a puzzle that they have to solve.

If you are a first-timer, there are still many things you can do to increase the odds of success. Reading this book is one of them. Finding a Fringe veteran to help you is another. Keeping in close contact with the staff at the Fringe Office should be a given. The more information you can gather in advance, the more realistic you will be about the adventure that awaits you and the more enjoyable time you will have in the world's greatest arts festival. 'Coming from Sweden, the thought of Edinburgh is quite intimidating,' says first-time visitor Emil Lager of physical theatre company Scandimaniacs.

When you get here it's like being on a bus where you feel alone but you discover everyone else feels alone too. That's the feeling.

So climb aboard the bus, befriend your fellow passengers and enjoy the ride. Even if it's standing room only, you'll have a thrilling journey.

In the beginning

Because of the unprecedented size of the Edinburgh Festival Fringe, it is easy to assume it is the central event in the city's summer calendar. Technically, this is not the case. The clue is in the name. It is the fringe of the Edinburgh International Festival, sometimes referred to as the 'official' festival, an event that began on 24 August 1947 as a gesture of renewal and reconciliation for a Europe still reeling from the devastation of the Second World War. Inviting companies such as Glyndebourne Opera, the Hallé Orchestra and Sadler's Wells Ballet, the Edinburgh International Festival was founded on high-minded ideals. The city's Lord Provost wrote that he hoped the new festival would give audiences 'a sense of peace and inspiration with which to refresh their souls and reaffirm their belief in things other than material'.

These were rousing principles and they caught the imaginations of more than just the artists who had been invited by artistic director Rudolph Bing to perform in the inaugural programme. In that same year, eight companies who had not received a call from Bing decided they would come anyway. Companies including the radical Glasgow Unity Theatre, the amateur Christine Orr Players from Edinburgh and the Manchester Marionette Theatre took over four theatres not being used by the International Festival – plus Dunfermline Abbey 17 miles away – and presented a programme that included Shakespeare's *Macbeth*, Gorky's *The Lower Depths* and Bridie's *The Anatomist*. Inadvertently, they established the core principle of open access that characterises the Fringe to this day. While the director of the Edinburgh International Festival continues to invite the world's great orchestras, opera companies and theatre troupes, aided by a public subsidy covering about half of its £9.5m budget, the chief executive of the Edinburgh Festival Fringe issues no invitations. Anyone who can afford it is free to perform. You do not need to wait to be asked.

Initially, this spontaneous artistic movement was known, rather clumsily, as 'Festival adjuncts' or the 'semi-official' festival, but in 1948, Robert Kemp, a journalist on the *Scotsman* newspaper, wrote that 'round the fringe of official Festival drama there seems to be more private enterprise than before' and the name we know today was coined. Although the word 'fringe' has connotations of being alternative, underground and low-budget, it need not be any of these things. Just as the first programme in 1947 featured two plays by T. S. Eliot by the professional Pilgrim Players from London's Mercury Theatre as well as *Thunder Rock* (a wartime allegory by Robert Ardrey) by local amateurs the Edinburgh People's Theatre (a Fringe regular to this day), today's line-up is a broad church that embraces television comedians, leading classical actors, commercial musicals, student revues, Edinburgh amdram companies, African dancers, Korean musicians and experimental theatre-makers from Eastern Europe.

A select number of artists including Steven Berkoff, Anthony Neilson, David Greig, Frank Woodley and Martyn Jacques have had work in both the Fringe and the International Festival; indeed, since 2007, the International Festival has offered a prize that allows Fringe companies to present works-in-progress as part of its programme. In other words, a company's presence on the Fringe tells you nothing about its quality, professionalism or ambition, merely that it is appearing in Edinburgh under its own steam as part of a vast, unregulated artistic explosion.

Even though the Fringe has eclipsed the International Festival in size several times over and even though, since 1998, the Fringe has started and finished a week earlier, there remains an important symbolic connection between the two events. One provides vitality, exuberance and a maverick energy; the other celebrates world-class accomplishment and artistic innovation. They are two sides of the same coin and it is part of the explanation for the Fringe's rapid expansion.

After the spontaneous invention of the Fringe in 1947, the idea caught on. From 8 companies in the first year, the total rose to 19 in 1959. Ten years after that, it had risen to 57 and, after another ten years, it was at 324. Two years later, in 1981, it shot up to 494. At this stage, people thought the city had reached saturation point, especially as the numbers stabilised for a few years. But they were wrong. In the 1999 Fringe, more than 600 companies gave over 15,000 performances. In 2010, more than 1,900 companies gave over 40,000 performances. You can only imagine how that would have made a certain Gerard Slevin feel: in 1961, the theatre director complained that the Fringe had grown too big and made a serious proposal that it would be 'much better if only ten halls were licensed'.

Throw in the Military Tattoo, initiated in 1950 and playing to a total audience of over 200,000 each year on the esplanade of Edinburgh Castle, the Jazz and Blues Festival, which has been on the go since 1980 (but moved into July in 2011), the International Book Festival, increasing steadily in size since 1983, and the Art Festival, launched in 2004, and you start to get an inkling of the cultural magnet the city becomes every summer. The moving of the Edinburgh International Film Festival back to June in 2008 after sixty-one years scarcely makes the city feel any less busy.

A capital atmosphere

Once bitten by the Fringe bug, it is very hard to resist. The cultural and social riches are just too tempting. 'I was there this year with the intention of popping in for a couple of nights, going Munroe-bagging for a week, then coming back for a couple of nights,' says comedian Ed Byrne, a frequent visitor since the early 1990s. 'I did it exactly the other way around: three or four jaunts into the Highlands and the rest of the time in Edinburgh. There are all these people there who I only get to see in Edinburgh. People from all over the world that I haven't seen for years and won't see again until the next festival.'

Historically, you can reel off the famous names who have got their first break in Edinburgh or simply performed there for the love of it once their reputation was sealed. They include Rowan Atkinson, Steven Berkoff, Jo Brand, Billy Connolly, Ben Elton, Eddie Izzard, Sir Derek Jacobi, Tadeusz Kantor, Jude Law, Dannii Minogue, Michael Palin, Christian Slater and Tom Stoppard. It was here we first saw global hits including *Stomp, Black Watch* and *Jerry Springer: The Opera*. However impressive this may be, it is not in the nature of the Fringe to trade on past glories. It is a festival that hungers for the new, thriving on the unexpected and the unpredictable, making every one of its participants feel their contribution is valuable. For this reason, the Fringe is forever reinventing itself and its energy constantly shifting. 'For something that is fairly old and huge, the Fringe is incredibly light on its feet,' says the Fringe's chief executive Kath Mainland. 'Things will develop in response to something else.'

It means the Fringe has its own micro-culture with a set of impresarios, performers and faces-about-town who are celebrities nowhere else but in this one city for this one month. The spotlight falls on the directors of the biggest venues, such as Karen Koren of the Gilded Balloon, William Burdett-Coutts of Assembly, Anthony Alderson of the Pleasance and Charlie Wood and Ed Bartlam of the Underbelly. It falls on the generation responsible for key moments in Fringe history, people such as Richard Demarco (a conduit for avant-garde Eastern European theatre and art through his own gallery), Jim Haynes (co-founder of the Traverse Theatre) and Christopher Richardson (founder of the Pleasance), as well as their modern-day equivalents. It falls on a select group of comedians who rarely trouble the headlines for the rest of the year but have steadfastly built up a following here. It even falls on a handful of prominent critics who, after eleven months in the cultural wilderness, find an uncommonly engaged audience hanging on their every word.

'It's an extraordinary festival,' says producer Kate McGrath, director of Fuel:

I have an emotional relationship with it, not just because I am from Edinburgh and have been there probably every year of my life, but also because I've seen incredible work there, I've had amazing experiences of things that we've done going well and it feels as though everything is possible.

Director Toby Gough agrees. Despite working all over the world, from Cuba to Malawi, he cannot resist being at the Fringe in August. 'I haven't seen the passion that you can find at the Edinburgh festival anywhere else in the world,' he says. 'People are risking everything to get here and making huge personal sacrifices, because they are believing in their work and they are saying that Edinburgh is where the benchmark for new work is being set.'

You can perform in places that are more economically viable, where there are decent get-in times and a fraction of the competition, but no arts event on the planet will give you such a buzz. Even people whose fame and reputation is assured are not immune to the Fringe's charms. 'I've become Edinburgh's publicity agent,' says magician Paul Daniels, who first performed on the Fringe in 2003, long after establishing himself as a household name on television. 'I tell everybody, "You've got to be in it."'

Finding your way around

Quite why Edinburgh has been the site of such an artistic flowering is open for speculation. The city itself has something to do with it. Built around a volcanic rock at the top of which sits the castle with buildings dating back to the twelfth century, it is one of the most beautiful cities in Europe. The medieval atmosphere of the Old Town, with its warren of closes, cobbled streets and tottering tenements, plays against the cool Georgian elegance of the New Town, laid out in neat parallel roads. Meanwhile the imposing silhouette of Arthur's Seat – the 832-foot peak to the east of the city centre – and the occasional views across to Fife remind you of a world beyond the city. As well as being picturesque, it is also compact. Usually home to a population of less than half a million, it is built on a human scale. Not only does that mean it is easy to get around, but also that the Fringe has an uncommonly visible presence on the streets. Whether you are an arts lover or not, you always know when the Fringe is in full swing.

'Edinburgh has that unique alchemy,' says Eugene Downes, chief executive of Culture Ireland, who uses the city's festivals to promote his nation's artists:

> Seamus Heaney may bump into two Irish visual artists or a young comedy dance troupe on George Street. It's the serendipity of these radically different kinds of artists and work all co-existing which gives Edinburgh its special magic.

Edinburgh is a compact city and the majority of Fringe venues are within walking distance of the centre. It is relatively easy to orientate yourself, although you can be confused by the different levels of the Old Town, which is built on a steep-sided volcanic hill. Roads that look close together on a map can actually be at very different heights. Apart from that, the venue map in the Fringe Programme should be all you need to get your bearings.

The two most familiar roads run west to east in parallel. In the Old Town is the Royal Mile which connects Edinburgh Castle with the Palace of Holyroodhouse, official residence of the Queen. Like several Edinburgh roads, the Royal Mile is known by different names along its length, including the Lawnmarket, the High Street and the Canongate. A short distance to the north, in the New Town, is Princes Street, with chain stores on one side and public gardens on the other. It is common for venues and shows to advertise themselves in terms of how close they are to the Royal Mile and Princes Street; nearly all of them are just minutes away.

The biggest cluster of venues is in property owned by the University of Edinburgh in the area around Bristo Square to the south of the Royal Mile. Here the Gilded Balloon, the Pleasance, Assembly and the Underbelly all run multi-room venues. You will find venues throughout the city, however, stretching out to Leith in the north, Murrayfield in the west and, indeed, beyond the city in Traquair House in the Scottish Borders and Rosslyn Chapel in Roslin. See Chapter 6 for more about venues.

Using this guide

Whether you are a veteran or a first-timer, the Fringe can be an overwhelming experience. The better prepared you are, the more smoothly you will be able to ride the highs and lows, deal with the pressure and savour the moment. For it is also a tremendously enjoyable experience and, by outlining the Fringe's demands, challenges and opportunities, this book will help you plan ahead and enjoy it all the more.

Drawing on the knowledge of actors, comedians, directors, producers and publicists, it takes you through the crucial decisions about what, where, when and why you should perform. On the way, it signals the pitfalls to look out for and the great opportunities that can come your way. Starting with a snapshot of the Fringe Office, the nerve centre of the festival, it runs through the twelve months of the Fringe calendar before looking in more detail at everything you'll have to deal with, from flyering to finance, from publicity to parties, from opening night to coming back for more.

For more details and to share your own experiences go to: www.edinburghfringesurvivalguide.com

2. The Fringe Office
The Festival Nerve Centre

TURN UP IN EDINBURGH to visit the Fringe Office in the middle of August and you will find yourself battling through crowds. Positioned in the heart of the city's Old Town, the shop, box office and administration centre at 180 High Street is on a pedestrianised section of the Royal Mile, the historic road that connects Edinburgh Castle with Holyrood Palace. Come the festival, this is where street-theatre performers do their juggling, acrobatics and fire-eating while Fringe companies act out extracts from their shows, strike poses in their stage costumes and hand out flyer after flyer in the hope of drumming up an audience. Lured by the promise of free entertainment and a taste of the festival spirit, everyone from resident to tourist joins the throng. It is the most visible symbol of Edinburgh's transformation from genteel capital to carnival city and, for anyone in a hurry, it requires extra reserves of patience to navigate.

Off-season, it is a different story. The shop, which in the summer buzzes with people looking for souvenir posters, postcards and T-shirts – and, of course, a copy of the Fringe Programme – is likely to be closed and you have to ring the doorbell in order to get in. The basement-level box office with its entrance down Old Assembly Close, a typical Old Town alleyway, is deserted where in August you can't move for the queues. The quiet, however, is deceptive. In the offices here and in a neighbouring building in Old Fishmarket

Close, a team works year round to sustain the Fringe's position as the largest arts festival in the world. In this chapter, we will meet some of that team and find out how they can play a part in making your Fringe show a success.

First, though, a question. If the Fringe trades on being an open-access festival, why does the Fringe Society need to exist at all? Would it not be more in the spirit of such a free-wheeling, independent and unprogrammed event to resist the idea of a controlling body and just leave everyone to do their own thing? For the first twelve years of the Fringe's life, that is exactly what did happen. Emerging spontaneously in 1947, the Fringe had no central organisation. It was simply a collection of performances taking place in the shadow of the Edinburgh International Festival. Each company made its own arrangements and sold its own tickets, much as it would at any other time of the year.

As ex-Fringe administrator Alistair Moffat explains in his book *The Edinburgh Fringe* (long since out of print), a group of companies got together in 1954 to change this. Responding to the increasing size of the event, which was now attracting a dozen or so companies, they held a meeting to discuss the creation of what one of them called a 'small organisation to act as a brain for the Fringe'. As the *Scotsman* newspaper put it, they wanted to create an 'official unofficial festival'. You can always rely on the Fringe to produce differences of opinion, however, and the idea did not convince everybody. When a group of students from Edinburgh University lost money running a central box office the following year, they blamed it on those companies that had not joined in. All the same, the move towards cooperation had begun.

This development was helped along by an Edinburgh printer with an eye for a commercial opportunity. In 1954, C.J. Cousland published a listings guide called *Additional Entertainments* – the term 'Fringe' was still to take hold – which was funded by companies advertising their shows. As this was the only such round-up, it became the most important place for companies to be listed. To miss out was to risk losing audiences. Some companies did miss out, including the prominent actor-manager Donald Wolfit, who declared 'there is no such thing as the fringe of art' and managed to attract an audience regardless. Not every company was as fortunate.

Things continued in the same ad hoc way until 1958, when the Oxford Theatre Group's director Michael Imison led the charge to establish the Festival Fringe Society. Launched in the festival of 1959, the organisation had a brief to run a central box office, publish a programme of everything that was not in the International Festival and organise a club where participants could socialise. The founder members recognised the self-selecting sprit of 1947 and agreed not to impose artistic controls on participating companies. It cost £10 to join (£11 for first-timers), a fee that guaranteed inclusion in the published programme.

For the next decade, volunteers held the key administrative roles, taking on an increasing workload as the festival tripled in size. The pressure grew to take on professional staff and, in January 1971, John Milligan became the first paid administrator, his part-time job soon expanding to full-time. It gives you an idea of the exponential growth of the festival that as recently as the late 1980s, the Fringe employed only two full-time year-round staff. Today, there are fifteen permanent employees, plus others who take up six-month contracts and, as has long been the case, a small army of summer workers.

True to the vision of Imison and his fellow founders, the Fringe Society exists to serve the performers. The organisation is a registered charity governed by a board of trustees who are elected by the society's members. Any interested party can become a member and, since November 2010 when the organisation voted in favour of a new constitution, any participant can choose to become a member. Aided by a twelve-member participants' council, also introduced with the new constitution, the Fringe Society is designed to be responsive to your needs. To think of it merely as a box office and a programme publisher is to underestimate what else it can do for you. Drawing on decades of experience, it will help you step by step from your earliest half-formed thoughts about putting on a show to the excitement of your first performance and, should you prove popular, beyond Edinburgh too.

Before we take a closer look at the way the Fringe Society works, let's head to London where we find Nica Burns in her office on the Strand. In London, Burns is a major West End producer and the chief executive of Nimax Theatres. On the morning we meet, she is celebrating the previous night's opening of Samuel Beckett's *Krapp's Last Tape* starring Michael Gambon. This makes her a formidable force, but Edinburgh plays by its own rules and in the Scottish capital Burns is famous for different reasons. Here she is the powerhouse behind the Edinburgh Comedy Awards, established in 1981 as the Perrier Awards and renamed when Perrier pulled out in 2005 (the current sponsor is Foster's). To get an idea of the significance of these awards, you need look no further than the inaugural winner. The Cambridge Footlights took home the first Perrier Award, having introduced the world to Stephen Fry, Emma Thompson, Hugh Laurie and Tony Slattery. Subsequent winners include Jeremy Hardy, Sean Hughes, Frank Skinner, Steve Coogan, Jenny Eclair and Al Murray. The list of runners-up, most of them virtual unknowns before their Edinburgh triumphs, is hardly less impressive.

Burns took over the running of the awards in 1984, but it is her Fringe experience a couple of years earlier that was her real turning point. In 1982, she starred in *Dulcimer*, a one-woman show that played at 8 p.m. in the Celtic Lodge, a Masonic hall at the top of the Royal Mile. She took the stage immediately after *Dusty and Dick and their Struggle Against the Bosch,* a double-act starring the undiscovered TV writer Bryan Elsley and comedian Harry Enfield. 'My show got great reviews in the *Scotsman* and sold out,' she says. 'It changed my life coming to Edinburgh. To this day, it's the thing I'm most proud of, spending £600 – which was my entire savings from working three years constantly in rep as a leading lady – and we got £33 profit. We were thrilled. Then we were invited to the Finborough Theatre and we couldn't have been more delighted. We got a whole tour out of going to Edinburgh.'

For Fringe performers today, her advice, borne of thirty years' experience, is clear and to the point: 'Start early, think it through and do get advice from the Festival Fringe Office.' She insists the Fringe Office should be the first port of call, not only for newcomers but established artists too:

> That's what they do, that's what they're there for and they're very good. You shouldn't be afraid to pick up the phone and send emails. They will help you. If you've got no one else to help you, book your cheap advance train ticket and go to the Fringe Office and talk to them. It is time well spent.

It is indeed, but before you book your train ticket, spend time on the dedicated participants' pages at www.edfringe.com. Here you will find information about current fees, venues and accommodation, as well as practical advice on such topics as publicity, marketing and budgeting. It costs nothing to download *The Fringe Guide to Choosing a Venue*, *The Fringe Guide to Selling a Show* and, if you're feeling ambitious, the *Fringe Guide to Running a Venue*. The fee you pay to the Fringe Society is in the region of £400 including VAT. It is a big sum, but it buys a lot. Not only does it guarantee you a place in the 340-page programme and the chance to sell your tickets through a major box office, but also it opens up the services of a media office and a professional development department, as well as free entry to talks, workshops and networking events at Fringe Central, the university-owned building between Bristo Square and George Square that serves as a festival hub for participants.

The Fringe's chief executive Kath Mainland, an unflappable festival veteran with a calming Orkney accent, explains that the organisation's work falls into three broad areas:

The first is to support, advise and encourage anybody and everybody who wants to take part, from before they decide to come to the festival, during their visit and beyond.

The second is to provide up-to-date, accurate and comprehensive information, including ticketing, to get the word out about what they're doing. The third is to do with profile-building for the event as a whole, to tell people this is the world's greatest arts festival and they should get involved in it.

The staff structure you will find today has a lot to do with the Fringe's *annus horribilis* of 2008. That was the year a £350,000 box office system crashed on its first day of operation. Subsequent technical hitches included a failure to print tickets as well as the overselling of some shows and the underselling of others. It precipitated a financial crisis and led to questions being asked about the organisation's management. As a consequence, the board commissioned a review which recommended a new staff structure as well as changes to the business and financial operation. The top job which, in the early days, was simply called 'administrator' and, since the mid-1990s, had been known as 'director', would now be called 'chief executive'. There would be a new departmental structure with a head of external affairs overseeing relationships with the media, funders and other interested parties, a head of participant services responsible for helping performers and venues and a head of marketing and sponsorship charged with generating additional income for the organisation.

Let's take a closer look at the jobs that will most directly affect you and get a sense of the people who do them.

Chief Executive

The change of title from director to chief executive is not just a question of semantics. The person with the top job at the world's biggest arts festival is in an unusual position. On the one hand, they are in charge of a massive cultural event, they are called upon as a high-profile spokesperson and, at least for one month in the year, they are regarded as a figurehead. On the other hand, they have no control over the content of that event. There are fringe festivals in other places in the world, such as Dublin, New York and Sydney, where the person in charge is a curator, selecting the shows that get staged and making sure their favourite work is seen to the best advantage. The Edinburgh Fringe has never been like that. It was built on the principles of open access, which means the people who decide what you see on stage are the artists themselves. In that sense, the name 'chief executive' better reflects the nature of the job than 'director' and sounds more authoritative than mere 'administrator'. Far from 'directing' the participants, the chief executive is working for them, although doing a little more than just administering. The role is to make the artists' experience as satisfactory as possible, while having no say in the artistic content of their work, their length of stay or their choice of venue.

This is how it has been as the baton was passed from John Milligan (1971–1977) to Alistair Moffat (1977–81), Michael Dale (1981–86), Mhairi Mackenzie-Robinson (1986–94), Hilary Strong (1994–99), Paul Gudgin (1999–2007), Jon Morgan (2007–08) and Kath Mainland (2009–).

Mainland has a long association with the Fringe and has loved it ever since her first visit as a student at the University of Glasgow when she had a great day seeing her flatmate's brother in an amdram production in a distant church hall, before calling in on the Pleasance, one of the original multiplex venues, for a night of revelry. She first worked in the Fringe Office as an administrative assistant in 1991 before stints at Edinburgh's Hogmanay, the Assembly Rooms and the Edinburgh International Book Festival where she was administrative director. She returned to the Fringe to become chief executive in 2009, beating more than 100 applicants to the post.

What, then, are her first principles? 'We always start with the participants,' she says:

> That's where all our work begins. I think the Edinburgh Festival Fringe is the greatest thing. As a cultural entertainment experience it is absolutely the best. It grew up by itself and developed organically alongside the other festivals and it is completely open access. Therefore it is not our job to say, 'Next year's Fringe should be made up of these people or should be this size.' But it is our job to create and maintain an environment where people want to bring work.

In doing this, she is as likely to exert influence over decision-makers as she is to put decisions into practice herself. If, for example, she thought it was in the interests of the Fringe for the city to have a bigger stock of sprung floors for dancers or a bigger pool of cheap accommodation for performers, she would be in no position to build theatres or subsidise landlords herself, but she would be able to talk to people who could. 'If we thought there was a barrier preventing people coming to the Fringe, then we would be able to share that belief with our Fringe constituency,' she says. 'That may encourage something to develop, but we don't run the venues ourselves. We have a very good relationship with the venues and we talk to them all the time about things like that. It's all about influence and not decision-making power.'

She can also exert influence on artists, encouraging them to consider performing on the Fringe and generally spreading the word, not least through the Fringe's regular roadshows in Edinburgh, London and further afield. Once artists have signed up to come to the Fringe, she sees it as the organisation's role to support them in what is the most competitive cultural environment on the planet.

Her advice to Fringe companies echoes that of Nica Burns:

> Sign up and get all the information from us. Have a scan over
> it at least once and focus on the bits you need. The way to
> use the Fringe Office is to ask as many questions as you can.
> Think about the things that we haven't told you or ask us to
> put you in touch with people who might be able to give you
> first-hand information. The more direct advice you can get,
> the more informed you will be.

Head of External Affairs

Much like Mainland, Neil Mackinnon's earliest memories of the
Fringe date from when he was a university student. He recalls
visiting on a day trip from Stirling in the early 1990s, having lunch in
the City Café, packing in as many shows as possible and getting the
last coach back. Before he took the job of head of external affairs in
2009, he was working as a PR for the Scottish Liberal Democrats,
an ideal post for a secret Fringe junkie who could take time off to
see shows while the Scottish parliament was in recess. 'The brief
time in my adult life when I haven't lived in Edinburgh, the Fringe
is one of the things I've missed most about it,' he says, as he gets
ready to join an end-of-festival staff meeting at Fringe Central.

His job is to safeguard the reputation of the Fringe Society,
talking to funders, public agencies and the media to ensure they
have a proper understanding of the organisation. 'Quite often you
can only see a partial vision that can be quite misleading,' he says.
His audience is anyone who has a vested interest in the Fringe, be
they performers, audiences, journalists or the government, all of
whom benefit from knowing what is going on. This can mean going
back to basics to explain the fundamentals of the Fringe to someone
unfamiliar with the organisation, helping foreign film crews get
footage of the festival in full swing or working out how a Fringe

company should make the most of their good reviews.

'The standard misconception is to do with us selecting artists to come here,' he says:

> The single most important facet of the Fringe is that it is open access. That is probably what has driven it, in terms of its growth and its attractiveness to performers and the media. People tend not to know that. One of the things that's nice about the Fringe is that it's still tied to its founding principles in 1947.

As well as being responsible for the media office (see below) and being a spokesperson for the Fringe when a news story arises, the head of external affairs will have discussions with the council about the location of poster boards, deal with complaints from the public (often to do with levels of noise) and ensure companies make the most of their run in Edinburgh. 'One of the key things we do is to encourage performers to think about how they sell their shows,' says Mackinnon:

> Performers can come in and get really strong advice, good tips on how to sell their show to the point where it will make a difference in terms of bringing people in. We encourage performers to come in and see us – and as soon as possible – to get hold of that advice.

Media Manager

Reporting to the head of external affairs, the media manager has two main roles. One is to support Fringe participants as they run their own press campaigns, the other is to assist the world's media when they arrive in Edinburgh and try to get their heads round an event of such gargantuan proportions.

Like many people who have chosen to make Edinburgh their home, Miriam Attwood fell in love with the Fringe at a formative point in her life. 'I was eighteen, broke up with a boy and my sister was coming to the Fringe to do the PR for a friend's show,' she says:

I missed the Wimbledon final, went to the pub, broke up with this boy, and came back to the house and said to my mum, 'Can I go to Edinburgh to visit my sister in August?' She said yes, so I came up to the festival, didn't sleep for five days, went to see all kinds of random stuff, went to see Daniel Kitson at the Stand, had this absolutely crazy five days, traipsing across the Meadows, going to shows at three in the morning . . . I just thought this was the coolest place in the world.

So taken was she with the experience that, a year later, she applied for a place at Edinburgh's Queen Margaret University: 'Nothing about the course, it was just that I wanted to be near the Fringe.' She got closer still in 2007 when she took a job as press assistant with the Fringe, eventually becoming media manager on a six-month contract and returning every year until 2011.

If you are one of the many participants who do not employ a professional press relations (PR) officer and who are not performing at a venue that offers its own press services, then the Fringe media office is an invaluable resource. Attwood says:

We will help the performer that doesn't have any of that infrastructure, but who has that great show to sell. We have a media officer who sits and talks to performers all day every day of the Fringe. We know who's about and who's covering what; we have that relationship with the media at large. When that person comes in and tells us about their show and it does sound genuinely fascinating, we can make sure they're getting in touch with the right people.

The media manager is employed from April to September. In the first months, the job is about helping participants write their press releases, working out what is special about their show and coming up with images that will strike a chord with press and audiences. Once June comes around and the Fringe Programme is published, so the media manager is increasingly involved with talking to journalists and generating interest in August's event, which is newsworthy for its sheer enormity alone. During July, there is still more work to be done helping companies on their press campaigns. For August, the media office moves from its High Street base to the spacious Fringe Central on Crichton Street where it can give equal attention to journalists and performers, acting as a kind of match-making service between those looking for stories and those with stories.

On many occasions this will lead to happy marriages. She says:

> The best part about the media office is performers flooding in and telling us about their shows. Then two minutes later the exact right person might come in to pick up their press pass. That central brain with all the information is invaluable. We won't recommend or push anyone, but we'll get stupid calls like 'What shows this year have a dog in them?' and we'll know which shows.

As well as ideas for stories, the media office provides journalists with photographs, statistics, contact information for Fringe participants and news about launches and photocalls. To qualify for a media pass, applicants must produce letters from their editors or producers confirming their plans to cover the Fringe, as well as showing evidence of their work, be that as a writer, photographer, presenter or researcher. If issued with a media pass, journalists can request tickets – usually only one per show – which are issued at the discretion of the performing company. The media office rejects roughly 8 per cent of applicants, although those people are still at liberty to request tickets directly from Fringe participants. 'The impetus has to be on performers getting the right treatment,' she says. 'If journalists are writing well, critically and coherently, then they deserve a free ticket. If they are writing a blog that is poorly put together, then that's no use to a company.'

'We're very aware that we don't actually own the tickets,' adds Neil Mackinnon:

> They are owned by the producers who run the venues that are staging those shows. We have a responsibility to ensure we can deliver something that is valuable to them, such as a review that will help sell tickets for their show. So we look very carefully at who we are accrediting, we look at their work and their track record, and we try to make sure the system has some integrity to it.

There will be something in the region of 1,100 accredited journalists, of whom around 600 will be writing reviews. If that sounds a lot, remember there is an enormous number of shows to get round and, as Mackinnon points out, no one has ever complained about being over-reviewed. The remainder will be made up of cameramen, photographers, podcasters, presenters, diarists, news reporters, feature writers and researchers. Any one of them could turn out to be beneficial to your show or, in the longer term, your career. The media, however, is not always benign and, particularly when it comes to reviews, the marriage can turn sour. The media office is on hand to help you through your trial separation. 'The Fringe is so big and terrifying, and the important thing for me is making sure performers know there is support and advice here,' says Attwood.

The degree to which you use the media office's services depends on you. Some people make contact in April, provide a press release and leave it at that. Others may check in on day one even though they have employed a PR agency, because they want to cover all bases. Some might need more hands-on input for their posters, flyers and press releases and be regular visitors. Others might have handed responsibility to a professional PR or may simply have no interest in attracting media attention. Except in these last cases, you should make the most of what the media office has to offer.

See Chapter 10 for more about your media campaign.

Head of Participant Services

The participant services department provides support for anyone who takes part in the Fringe, whether as a performer, producer, technician, stage manager or venue manager. It also runs the arts industry office which caters to the many national and international bookers, promoters and agents who come to Edinburgh in August in search of new talent. Just as the media office acts as a liaison between performers and journalists, so the participant services department brings performers and promoters together. There are about 1,000 arts industry professionals, who go through a similar accreditation process to journalists. They can pick up and book tickets through the Fringe Office although, unlike journalists, they often pay for their own unless the venue has agreed to issue complimentary tickets.

The head of participant services is Christabel Anderson, whose first experience of the Fringe was in 1991, just after she had sat her GCSEs. With a family from Edinburgh and an interest in theatre, she wanted to know what the event was all about. 'I had a great time,' she says. 'I got the programme, wandered around, saw random things, didn't really plan it.' She returned with friends the following year on a similar trip and, the year after that, worked at the South Bridge Resource Centre selling tickets and operating the lighting board for a play her sister was doing with a university group. 'That was amazing,' she says, admitting that the Fringe played a big part in her decision to study at the University of Edinburgh.

In subsequent years, she worked as an administrator for the

National Student Theatre Company, as a house manager at C Too and as front-of-house manager at the Pleasance, before moving to *ThreeWeeks*, a newspaper dedicated to covering the Fringe, where she was a reviewer and subeditor. For the rest of the year, she worked as a freelance stage manager before joining the Fringe in 2009.

In the early part of the year, much of her job is focused on the roadshows staged by the Fringe Society in Edinburgh and London – and as far afield as New York and Poland. These are a chance for prospective performers to find out more about the Fringe, listen to insider experts and guest speakers and ask questions. Each event generates considerable interest, which the participant services department responds to in the following weeks. Questions can vary from how to find a venue to how to get a visa. The department produces bulletins, which increase in frequency from monthly to weekly as the festival draws near, keeping participants up to date with news and reminding them of tasks that need to be completed. It also publishes separate bulletins for venue managers, keeping them up to date with issues such as licence changes.

By August, the attention has shifted to the programme of events at Fringe Central, a social and professional hub for participants where there are networking sessions and talks on topics such as selling a show and getting media attention. Anderson says:

> The festival itself is really interesting for us. It's a lot about running our events and offering support, but it's also really unpredictable. We have lots of meetings with other festivals and groups who might want to come – it's a time when lots of people come to Edinburgh just to see, so I spend a lot of time doing general outreach.

Venues and Companies Manager

Working in the participant services department, the venues and companies manager is an intermediary between performers and the people who run the spaces. Offering an impartial match-making service, the manager knows who has the shows and who has the places to perform them and helps bring the two together. Companies often call on the manager to look over contracts for them and, if it turns out not to be a match made in heaven, to support them in a dispute with a venue. On rare occasions, a venue will close after running into financial trouble before the festival begins, at which point the manager will step in to help re-house the homeless companies.

The manager is heavily involved in the Fringe roadshows that explain about performing in Edinburgh and, later, how to attract audiences. Once those are out of the way, the focus shifts to organising the seminars at Fringe Central during the festival itself. After the festival, it is the venues and companies manager who ends up mediating between companies and venues in those few cases where the two disagree about the revenue due from ticket sales. The manager also has a remit to look after education, equalities and the environment, which can mean outreach work to get local young people to engage with the Fringe, encouraging signed performances for people with hearing difficulties and helping venues and companies reduce their carbon footprint.

Barry Church-Woods grew up in Livingston and made his earliest visits to the Fringe as a child. It was as a student in Fife that he journeyed to Edinburgh under his own steam. 'I'd spend all my money in August over four days,' he laughs. He joined the Fringe Office in 2007, initially running an education project on a freelance basis before becoming venues and companies manager. He says:

It's kind of match-making. It's giving people information about how to participate as companies and as potential venue managers. Because we're impartial, you can't say, 'Well, you should go here with your show,' but when you've got a document with three hundred venues on it and someone is saying they want a forty-seater that is good for physical theatre, you can wade through the soup with them and say, 'These are the twelve venues that fit your criteria.'

See Chapter 6 for more about your venue.

Participant Development Coordinator

Working in the same department, the participant development coordinator focuses on the professional and creative lives of Fringe performers. Not only is it about making the most of the Fringe itself, it is also about the company's life beyond August. One part of the job is to offer advice on subjects such as fund-raising, networking and touring that will help performers in a career in the arts. The other part is to run the arts industry office, a service for around 1,000 professional promoters and producers. The coordinator also programmes talks, networking events and discussions in Fringe Central. In this way, the coordinator acts as a go-between for companies and producers, helping match the right work with the right promoter. During August the coordinator can meet as many as 300 companies, ranging from newcomers to old hands, all trying to capitalise on the opportunity of performing at the world's largest arts festival.

The first person to do the job in this form is Louise Oliver. Her memories of the Fringe go back to 2005 when she and her fellow graduates from the University of Glasgow brought a show they had created as a final-year project to a newly converted venue in a hotel. 'It was like guerrilla theatre,' she laughs. 'We were in a hotel suite with no dressing room. But we had a really good time. We only did a week but we had the full Fringe experience: great reviews, terrible reviews, full house, nobody turning up . . .'

Bitten by the bug, she returned every year and, at the start of 2010, began working in the Fringe Office. The job brings her into contact with a wide range of companies, primarily those on a professional footing, but theoretically student companies as well. The range of industry professionals is no less broad. She says:

> There are a thousand people and a thousand different types. It's comprised mainly of venue programmers, tour bookers, freelance producers, comedy scouts, TV and radio people, actors' agents . . . and they're all looking for different things and they're all at different levels. There are some who don't have much budget but create really good opportunities, such as the Contact Theatre in Manchester, then there is a big promoter, such as Avalon, that all the comedians want to be seen by.

It could be that you see performing on the Fringe as an end in itself, in which case you are likely to have little need of this service. If, however, you regard your time in Edinburgh as a stepping stone on a longer artistic career, you would do well to make early contact with the participant development coordinator.

See Chapter 13 for more about taking your show beyond the Edinburgh Fringe.

Box Office Manager

It is the first job of the box office manager to ensure the computer system is up to date with times, prices and venues, as well as the bank details of the participating companies. Participants enter into a standard deal, supplying at least 25 per cent of their tickets to the Fringe box office, which takes a 6 per cent commission on sales. With that in hand, the manager's attention switches to the customers, making sure audiences can buy tickets reliably and efficiently. After the box office meltdown of 2008, the Fringe Society has put a lot of effort into courting audiences, improving the sales service for them while sharpening up the efficiency of its own internal systems.

Once the festival is over, it is time to coordinate the payout for Fringe companies. This is made at the end of September and involves balancing ticket sales against deductions such as PRS (see Chapter 8), fees owing for other Fringe services and, in some cases, VAT. This is a major job, with payments having to be made to perhaps 1,000 companies in addition to the big venues, which for accounting purposes count as a single company. Since 2010, the Fringe has paid every company by bank transfer.

José Ferran first encountered the Edinburgh Fringe in 1998. He was working for the Pleasance in London and headed north to be an assistant box office manager at the organisation's Edinburgh branch. 'The love affair grew from there,' he says. He worked his way through the Pleasance hierarchy, becoming general manager for four years. In 2006, he joined a ticketing software company, before landing the job of box office manager at the Fringe in 2008.

Sitting at his desk in the deserted out-of-season box office, he says:

A lot of companies, regardless of whether it's their first year or their twentieth year, make quite a lot of assumptions. Every year there's a slight change to the way things happen or there's something new. If they continue communicating, we will be in a better position to serve them. Regardless of the magnitude of what this festival now stands for, there is still quite a small organisation that helps put this event on. We're striving for that better communication and over the years I've been here, the communication with the venues has been a lot better.

Going it alone

It is early afternoon and the applause is dying down on a midday show at Hill Street Theatre. Actor Anthony Black has taken his curtain call after his one-man show, *Invisible Atom*, but he has remained on stage. When the room goes quiet, he speaks directly to the audience. 'We are not in the printed Fringe programme,' he says. 'So we'd appreciate it if you could spread the word.'

In the case of Black and his 2b company from Canada, he made the decision to come to Edinburgh in June, well past the Fringe Office's deadline to get in the programme. It was a question of last-minute planning rather than deliberately trying to circumvent the Fringe, but it gives an indication of the challenges faced by anyone who tries to go it alone. As we shall see later in the book, there is a happy ending to Black's story, thanks to having good connections and a great show, but he might easily have sunk without trace. There is competition enough without making your show even harder for an audience to find.

All the same, there is no obligation for you to take the conventional Fringe Society route. If you can find a venue and have a way of selling tickets, there is nothing to stop you doing it independently. The question you need to ask is whether there would be an advantage in it. 'If we are essentially a service organisation then we're only as useful as the services we provide,' says Kath Mainland. 'They need to be the right services in order for people to use us. For the broad majority of people coming here, they do need those services. If people don't want those services, we shouldn't be protectionist about it.'

One organisation that decided it did not want those services was Forest Fringe. Set up by Debbie Pearson in 2007, it was conceived as a venue unlike any other in town. Invited to run a performance programme by the Forest Café, a bohemian hang-out on Bristo Place, Pearson created a venue where artists could experiment, play and try things out. Money was not an object. She made the shows free (although she encouraged audience donations), but she also kept costs to a minimum so artists could contain their losses.

One of the artists in that first year was Andy Field who put on a hastily devised piece called *Exposures*, which sent the audience onto the streets with disposable cameras. In subsequent years, Field joined Pearson as co-director and watched the venue gain cult status. He makes clear, however, it was a pragmatic decision not to join the Fringe Society, because of the particular nature of what they wanted to do, and no reflection on the Fringe itself.

'We want to be a home in Edinburgh for projects that couldn't happen anywhere else,' says Field, who has also worked in C Venues, the now defunct Aurora Nova and for producer James Seabright:

> Forest Fringe came out of a need to construct a space that functioned in a different way. We always get called up by the newspapers whenever there's a Fringe story to be the people who say, 'The Fringe is shit.' But it's not. Forest Fringe came about not in opposition to the Fringe but out of the Fringe's failure to provide a space that is more informal, that provides the process and development of work, a space for talking and experimenting with new ideas, and also a space that is more flexible in terms of those very unusual practices that border on live art and visual art. These things are very hard to do in Edinburgh.
>
> Not being in the Fringe was not a philosophical choice, but a pragmatic choice. If we wanted to do one-off events, unusual performance models that don't normally fit in Edinburgh, things that aren't three-week runs, we had to unpick all of the architecture that was built up in order to facilitate that. Paying your money to be in the Fringe programme has a real value if you're paying for an entire

run. If you're doing a one-off twenty-minute experiment, it's of no value whatsoever. No one's going to find you that way. We're not trying to do what the Underbelly and the Pleasance already do very well, we're trying to do something else.

We will return to Forest Fringe later in the book, but for the most part, we will assume you are following the established Fringe pattern like hundreds, if not thousands, of companies before you. To do this, you must have a sense of what you want to do, where you want to do it, how much it will all cost and how you can achieve your artistic and professional goals as effectively as possible. In the next chapters, we will consider each of those questions in turn.

3. The Timing
Month by Month through the Fringe Year

'IN THE SAME WAY that April to April is the financial year, comics go Edinburgh to Edinburgh,' says publicist Claire Walker. It is true not only of comics; for all manner of performers, producers, technicians, press officers and arts journalists, the Fringe is the fulcrum of the calendar, a secular Christmas around which the rest of the year revolves. As with Christmas, the more carefully you plan, the more you can enjoy the big day when it arrives. We'll go into more detail in the following chapters, but here is an outline of what you should be doing when.

August: twelve months to go

If you have never been to the Edinburgh Fringe as a spectator, you should think seriously about delaying your arrival as a performer. Treat the forthcoming festival as a research opportunity. Stay for a week or two, see a load of shows, observe what works and what doesn't, get an idea of the venues, figure out how other performers generate audiences, enjoy yourself, stay up late, talk to as many people as you can and, when it is all over, make a level-headed plan for bringing your show next year. 'Come and see one festival first,' agrees William Burdett-Coutts, Assembly's artistic director who has been producing Fringe shows for over thirty years. 'Edinburgh confounds expectation. It's not like touring a show anywhere else. It is an entire experience.'

Even if you are familiar with the city at other times of year, you can be taken aback at the transformation that occurs in August. Sedate lecture theatres are suddenly heaving with crowds. Rooms you hardly knew existed have queues round the block. Inauspicious car parks become raucous outdoor drinking dens. Seeing how this works in practice can help you decide where you should perform and who you should work with. In some cases, you might even make early contact with a prospective venue manager. 'People are quite happy to show you round if they can rent you the space next year,' says Nick Read, head of hire and events at Northern Light, an Edinburgh-based stage equipment hire company. 'If you're thinking about it seriously, go and see a few shows in there. Do some research.'

It is not just a matter of coming to terms with the enormity of the event. It is also a question of being ready. The Fringe gives professional companies – and those with professional ambitions – an opportunity to present work in what is effectively the world's largest performing arts market. If that work is substandard, it is an opportunity lost. Some people might think it worth biding their time for even longer. Claire Walker gives the example of Micky Flanagan, who was nominated for the Edinburgh Comedy Award's newcomer at the age of 43:

> He'd been schlepping around the circuit in London quite happily, had a wealth of material, was a fantastic comedian and the first time he went to Edinburgh, he was an old-timer who qualified for the newcomer. It's important not to rush your first go. Do a split bill and do half an hour with somebody else. Get up and do a few spots here and there. And go with your first hour when you really feel you're ready.

Such a measured approach may fly in the face of the let's-do-the-show-right-here spirit. If you ignore this advice, you will not be alone. Fuelled by self-belief, impatience and excitement, countless performers throw themselves in at the deep end every year. Some are overwhelmed by the cultural tsunami, others thrive on the crazy exhilaration of it all. Either way, they will not forget the experience. The Fringe has a history of rash behaviour – it is part of what makes it exciting – and, as *Scotsman* theatre critic Joyce McMillan argues, the spontaneous approach has much to recommend it. 'Saying you should scope it out a year in advance is excellent practical advice,' she says:

> But one of the really good things about the Fringe is it can be quick. It's one of the good things about live performance anyway – it can respond to things quickly. The important thing is to be doing something that you really want to do and you really believe in and that gives you the energy to solve all the practical problems. And part of the joy of the thing is you don't have to be preparing it for two or three years – you can, and sometimes it's a good thing, but it's not essential.

A case in point is Anthony Black. When the Canadian actor decided to break with conventional wisdom about Fringe timing, it was half-calculated risk and half-step into the unknown. His company, 2b from Nova Scotia, had been awarded some funding from the Canada Council for the Arts to tour and, after some dates fell through, it had the choice between returning the money or putting it towards a trip to Edinburgh. On the plus side, 2b knew it had a good show in *Invisible Atom*; on the down side, it was already June and the Fringe deadline had passed. Once the company arrived in Edinburgh, it had to get the show up and running in Hill Street Theatre and it had little time for last-minute publicity.

'We have had a kind of a miracle,' says Black over mid-morning coffee in the Grassmarket, crediting his venue publicist, Dani Rae, and his producer, Sarah Rogers, for getting a reviewer in from the *Herald*, which led to a *Herald* Angel Award which, in turn, precipitated interest from other media. 'We had really good people working for the show, both formally and informally.' Because of this, the story has a happy ending, but it is despite the odds. The show attracted relatively healthy audiences, which ranged from 6 to 76 in a 108-seat venue, but as Black says, it was not 'full to the rafters' and when he changed to a different time of day after extending his run in the final week, the figures plunged as low as 24. 'If you use the audience as a measure, it's not an unqualified hit,' he says. 'If you use the reviews as a measure, yes, it's a wonderful success. If you use the future touring prospects of the show, it's exceeded our wildest expectations.'

His producer Sarah Rogers, who knew she was taking a calculated risk, says she would willingly bring another company to the Fringe, although perhaps not in quite the same way: 'I would be in the Fringe Programme and I would do all those things earlier so we had a little bit more of a fair chance. 2b is already thinking, "How can we do this better next time?"'

For every story of triumph in the face of disaster, there are many more stories of straightforward disaster. Flyering on the Royal Mile for a production of *Waiting for Lefty*, student actor Daniel Smith recalls a disastrous trip to Edinburgh. 'Last year I did a show that was pretty terrible,' he says:

We weren't even in the Fringe Programme. We weren't in any listings. When we came to do the tech run, the techies in our venue actually said, 'We didn't know you existed until today.' That was really hard to sell because it was almost like we weren't even here. We were just on the periphery and the audiences were far worse. We'd get five people in a day and we'd have to give out a lot of free tickets. It's all about the deadlines, getting everything in and getting things done well. This year, everybody thought, 'I could have done a much better job,' and got involved again to prove ourselves right. It has worked out a lot better this year; we're in a better venue [the Pleasance], they've worked really hard for us getting reviewers in and we feel like we owe them for taking us on.

So let's assume you're resisting the spontaneous approach and we'll go through month by month ticking off what to do when.

September: eleven months to go

'Sleep in September,' recommends Sam Gough, venue manager at the Edinburgh International Conference Centre (EICC). After the round-the-clock rollercoaster of August, it is sound advice. September is also a month of stocktaking and financial reconciliation. Box-office managers are matching income to expenditure and calculating who owes what to whom. Press officers are writing reports for venues and producers, letting them know how the media campaign went. The Fringe box office is preparing for the big payout for tickets sold at the end of the month.

Having recuperated from August, you can start to map out the year ahead. In September, you should have at least a notional plan about when the creative work will take place. The detail of the plan will vary. There are no rules. Ella Hickson wrote her state-of-the-nation play *Eight* in the six weeks between her university finals and the start of rehearsals, and it went on to win several awards. Some comedians, such as Sarah Millican, begin writing their show in September; others, such as Phil Nichol, hold off until May.

However much you intend to give yourself time, you can easily find yourself diverted by more pressing concerns. Now is the best time to look at the year ahead and make a realistic assessment of what you can achieve. 'There was one performer who is really talented who had been so busy working during the year that they hadn't had enough time to prepare their show properly,' says Nica Burns:

They started the festival and they weren't happy with the show, they got a couple of bad reviews and their confidence fell on the floor. They were so distressed by the whole thing, they could barely get on the stage to do it. As a comedian, you're putting yourself on stage every night, so make sure you've got enough time to prepare. You can't wing a show in Edinburgh.

September, then, is the month to start asking yourself questions both about the nature of your show and about how much time you can dedicate to it over the coming months. No need to panic just yet – time is still on your side – but good to start thinking about it before the pressure mounts.

Autumn: ten ... nine ... eight months to go

'Bringing something to the Fringe is a huge decision because you have to plan so far in advance and, in this business, even knowing what you're doing next week is difficult,' says Renny Krupinski, a Manchester-based actor, director, playwright and fight director. In October he made the decision to come to the Fringe and, after consulting the Fringe Office, considered a number of venues that would be suitable for his play *Bare*, a physical drama set in an underworld of illegal fighting. Eventually, he booked a slot in one of the Space UK's venues at the Radisson Hotel. Straight away, he booked accommodation for seven actors and a stage manager through the university and, because he was booking early, got the rooms at the current year's prices. 'If you book in advance, you get the pick of what you want,' he says.

Krupinski was quicker off the mark than many, so don't panic if you are not ready to commit. Venues don't need to register with the Fringe Office straight away, so you might even miss out on some options if you are too early, and a lot of them wait until January before processing applications (see below). For those dealing with larger-scale shows and work from abroad, however, October is when significant decisions are starting to be made.

If you are thinking about running your own venue or performing in an unusual location, you should consult the Fringe's venues and companies manager and the City of Edinburgh Council's public entertainment licensing department as soon as you can to discuss safety issues.

Sign up for the Fringe's mailing list at www.edfringe.com. These regular bulletins will keep you focused, bring you up to date with news and alert you when deadlines are approaching.

January: seven months to go

Conversations between participants and venues may have been going on for the last few months, but for many, January is the month when applications begin in earnest. Keep an eye on venue websites for the exact dates and be ready to supply whatever materials you have to in order to persuade them to prioritise your show. If you want to get a prime slot, especially in a smaller venue, the sooner you can get your application in the better. If you have not already done so, get in touch with the Fringe Society's venues and companies manager to make sure you have a full sense of the range of spaces available to you.

'Planning is really important,' says Nica Burns:

> With a lot of first-timers, it's about making sure they start early enough. To get the best venues and the best slots, they've got to be approaching people in January. I get letters from people asking for money in June or July: I think, 'What are you doing?' You need to get in early before the venues are inundated with masses of product, so you can start a bit of a dialogue. Get on a train and go and meet them.

Meanwhile, the Fringe Society is stimulating interest in the forthcoming festival with its programme of roadshows, allowing would-be participants to ask questions of the staff and other guest speakers. These take place in Edinburgh, London and selected cities abroad and continue into February and are well worth attending, even if your planning is under way.

If you book display advertising in the Fringe Programme by the end of the month, you should qualify for a discounted rate. It won't be necessary to provide the artwork yet, so you still have time to work on your design.

February: six months to go

It is Saturday lunchtime early in February at the Edinburgh International Conference Centre (EICC), where a meeting room is full of would-be Fringe participants looking nervous as they hear what is in store for them. It is the latest in a string of Fringe roadshows and they are listening to a panel of festival veterans: Christabel Anderson, the Fringe Society's head of participant services; Frodo McDaniel of the long-standing Bongo Club cabaret; Mhari Hetherington, arts administrator; Kath Mainland, the Fringe Society's chief executive; Sam Gough, the EICC's venue manager and Marlene Zwickler, an artist manager for acts including comedian Daniel Sloss.

They are full of good advice:

Don't assume you'll sell as many seats as you do normally . . . Remember, things can and do go wrong . . . Have a rehearsed pitch for your show that you can use no matter how many beers you've had . . . Meet another performer and share costs . . . Don't forget the artistic side: you'll come out of it a better performer . . .

After audience questions, it is time to make way for the venue managers, a long line of them who each take to the stage for thirty seconds to make a pitch. Some offer straight hires, others do a box-office split; some have dozens of rooms, others a single space; some are in dedicated buildings, others are in hotels, offices and churches. Keeping all this in mind, the audience moves next door for individual meetings with the venue managers, many of whom are offering guided tours later in the afternoon. The romantic idea of performing on the Fringe is starting to become a reality.

It is now that venue managers will want to start allocating slots. The Fringe's early-bird deadline is a matter of weeks away, so participants need time to consider their options and decide on the best deal. At the Pleasance in London, things are heating up for artistic director Anthony Alderson. 'In February the theatre really starts to hit,' he says. 'We get a lot of theatre companies coming then. We're lucky because of this space in London, the rehearsal space and the development work we do, we see a lot of them throughout the year.'

The sooner your deal with the venue is agreed, the sooner you can start making other practical arrangements such as signing up a publicist, if required, and booking any technical equipment that you might need to hire. Nick Read at Northern Light says:

> We always have a number of people who phone up and say, 'We're coming to Edinburgh next week and we'd like to do this.' Everyone gets very busy during the festival and if you're given too short notice, you can't do deals and discounts, and often there isn't a lot of equipment left. The earlier people start talking the better. If they're talking about specific effects, even if they're not too sure about how to use them, getting a price and a quote in February/March is a lot better than waiting to the end of June.

Online registration with the Fringe Society opens in the last week of the month.

March: five months to go

Anthony Alderson says:

> March is when it gets really hairy because it is really about locking the programme down. Then you realise the theatre company has actually booked into Assembly, Underbelly, Gilded Balloon and the Pleasance and hasn't told you. We all find out because we do talk to each other. Then there's a bit of a squabble about who can actually land the deal.

The closer it gets to making your final decisions, the more crucial it is you have no legal obstacles in your way. Make sure, for example, that you have the performing rights for your show if it is under copyright and if you want to perform in a new or unusual venue, you need to know it is fit for purpose.

The early-bird deadline for registration with the Fringe Society is at the end of the month: get in before the advertised date and you will save around £100. Although it might seem you are in good time for the mid-April copy deadline for the Fringe Programme, now is the time you should be conceiving and commissioning the images around which your marketing campaign will revolve.

If your show might be of interest to magazines with a long lead time, you should get in touch with the appropriate editors or contributors. But beware: if you contact an editor too early, they are likely to have lost interest in the show by the time the festival comes around. Sending out a press release in June is more likely to work in your favour.

If you are a Fringe participant from outside the EU, you will need to apply for a visa and to get your venue manager to write a supporting letter.

April: four months to go

The Fringe Programme deadline is in the middle of the month, the last chance to get your show listed in the printed edition. It is possible to register after this date, but audiences will find it harder to know you are performing. Make sure your entry in the Fringe Programme is as good as it can be and when the Fringe sends out proofs, you should make any corrections by the end of the month – any mistake could cost you sales.

The media manager at the Fringe begins a six-month contract, so this is a good time to work on your press release and to make the most of the Fringe Office's resources. The same applies if your venue has its own press office. Once press officers are contracted, they will start telling the media informally about the bigger shows.

Once your show is booked in to the venue, you can begin the search for accommodation. Remember, the city's population doubles in August, so competition for the best rooms is fierce. 'July isn't too late to book, but it can be a little bit fraught, particularly for the larger flats,' says Chris Boisseau of Factotum Letting.

May: three months to go

The Fringe Programme is published next month, so use May to get your press and publicity material ready. Send copies to the Fringe press office and your venue press office. Some publications, including the *List*'s Festival Preview supplement and the *Edinburgh Festivals Magazine*, come out well in advance of the festival and should be approached now with editorial ideas and to book advertising.

Your venue might need to know more about the practical aspects of your show, so make yourself available to answer questions.

If you are travelling to Edinburgh by train, the cheapest tickets go on sale about twelve weeks before the departure date. The cost of a single fare between London and Edinburgh can vary by as much as £100 depending on availability and how far in advance you book. At www.thetrainline.com/ticketalert, you can sign up to receive an email telling you when tickets go on sale. If you can be flexible with your time of travel, www.thetrainline.com/farefinder will show you the cheapest tickets. You will have to wait three or four weeks before your return tickets go on sale.

Registration opens for performing on one of the special stages erected on the Royal Mile and the Mound. It isn't appropriate for every show, but it can be a good way of drumming up audiences. Book early with the Fringe Office to ensure a good slot.

June: two months to go

It's a weekday morning in the middle of June and people are starting to gather outside one of the halls of the Edinburgh International Conference Centre. Staff from the Fringe office are arranging the cloth bags they will give out to the day's guests, each containing a copy of the 344-page Fringe Programme – published today – as well as a press release and a can of beer from one of the sponsors. Waiters are standing by with tea and coffee.

Kath Mainland is there, wearing a smart frock for the occasion. As chief executive of the world's biggest arts festival, she knows this is a crucial day in the Fringe's calendar. Now the room is filling up. Neil Mackinnon, the Fringe's head of external affairs, welcomes the arriving journalists such as *Scotsman* theatre critic Joyce McMillan; the *Herald*'s Neil Cooper, who is about to get an early view of a couple of Fringe shows on a press trip to Poland; the *Stage*'s Thom Dibdin, a noted chronicler of the local amdram scene in his *Annals of the Edinburgh Stage* blog; and *Scotsman* feature writer Susan Mansfield, who'll be sniffing out story ideas to fill the newspaper's pages. In another corner, Jonny Ensall, editor of the *List*, the Scottish arts and events magazine, chats to former editors Alan Morrison, now arts editor on the *Sunday Herald*, and Nick

Barley, now director of the Edinburgh International Book Festival. Across the increasingly busy room, you can spot Dana MacLeod, a senior adviser at the British Council Scotland, greeting Faith Liddell, director of Festivals Edinburgh, the body responsible for coordinating the city's twelve major festivals, seven of which take place in the summer.

Actor and Fringe board member Pip Utton takes to the stage and reminds us in a very direct way why we are here. He is a veteran of Edinburgh Fringes since the mid-1990s, having launched a series of international tours here, and loves it too much to stop. After a welcome from the leader of Edinburgh City Council, it is Mainland's turn on stage and, with a smile and a glow of satisfaction, she celebrates a festival in which 'first-time performers arrive in the same spirit of hope and determination as seasoned celebrities'.

The journalists head off to file their copy. Within hours there will be blogs, news reports and comment pieces everywhere from industry magazine *Variety* to the BBC, from the *Guardian*'s high-hitting website to the smallest local newspaper. The launch is the trigger for much activity. The Fringe box office experiences its first sales peak as audiences snap up tickets for well-known names, live BBC radio recordings and companies familiar from previous festivals. The venues' own box offices also swing into action. The Fringe Office begins the accreditation process for arts industry professionals and the media, many of whom are setting to work on making sense of what August will bring.

In the days following the launch, there will be a number of news and comment pieces in the media, so if there is something striking or unusual about your show, you should flag it up to the right journalists a couple of days in advance. Companies generally observe an embargo on releasing information to the press until the programme is launched. 'We encourage performers to use that hype that we try to create and to get in touch with the world at large and tell them about their show,' says Miriam Attwood.

As arts editors are beginning to plan their festival coverage, it is an ideal time to get your press release to them. 'You need to write to me in plenty of time – maybe round about the time that the Fringe Programme is going to come out in June,' says *Guardian* theatre critic Lyn Gardner. 'A lot of us will be doing some kind of pick-of-the-Fringe things immediately round about that time, so what would be really good is to have some kind of letter, not too detailed and not giving me their life story, but just a little bit about this production.'

At the *List* magazine, editor Jonny Ensall is thinking in earnest about the shape of his festival coverage. 'We'll be deciding the type of features we want to include and what our interview formats are going to look like,' he says. 'It's never too early to start pitching.'

July: one month to go

While you are getting your show ready and taking time out to attend the Fringe's networking meetings, the various venue managers will be in Edinburgh converting their spaces into usable theatres. Towards the end of the month and at the start of August, there is another surge of ticket sales as audiences start thinking seriously about the Fringe.

If you have missed the first wave of media attention, it is not too late to get your press release together and drum up interest in your August performances. Keep in touch with the Fringe media office to ensure you are on the right lines. If your show has changed since the programme deadline, perhaps because it was still to be devised, you can update your online entry. If you have a budget for advertising, you should book space in newspapers and magazines with August publication dates.

All your publicity material – posters, flyers, company sweatshirts – should be printed before the start of your run so you are ready to start selling immediately. Allow your printer plenty of time to turn the job around – the presses are likely to be busy with everyone else's flyers.

If you have professional ambitions and want to be seen by promoters, agents or programmers, you should let them know about your show. 'What's really annoying is when people call you in the third week of the festival and say, "Will you come and see our show?" and that's the first you're hearing from them,' says Mark Godfrey, executive director of London's Soho Theatre. 'If you're desperate for someone to see you, get in touch in July.'

Companies travelling from abroad must file FEU forms with HM Revenue and Customs in case you are liable to pay foreign entertainers' tax.

August: the Fringe begins

It takes a couple of days for the festival to grind into action. At one venue, the woman behind the bar pulls her first pint and has to draft in the bar manager for help. She forgets the sandwich order as soon as she has taken it. At another venue, the Spanish ushers appear to have a shaky grasp of English and an even shakier grasp of where the performances are taking place. In Bristo Square, a woman tries to attract an audience for a show starting in twenty minutes – a passer-by goes to take a flyer only to be told it is the only one she has and she wants to hang on to it. In another venue, the press-office printer is not working and neither is the coffee machine.

Such teething troubles are soon remedied. The party is not yet in full swing and the atmosphere is still relatively peaceful. Come the opening weekend, the crowds will appear and there will be no turning back. Although you have been planning your appearance on the Fringe for months, many audiences, critics and promoters prefer to be spontaneous. This means that no sooner have you got your show settled into the venue than you must go all out to attract an audience.

Your press campaign moves from long-term planning to more immediate concerns. Diary stories, photo calls and news events can all draw extra attention to your show – although you are likely to get more direct results with a couple of hours' flyering each day. Call in to the Fringe media office to make sure the staff are aware of your show and to get advice on publicity.

What happens next is covered in more detail elsewhere in this book, but if you work hard, play hard, see shows and meet people, you cannot fail but to have an extraordinary experience. Anthony Alderson says:

> We have twenty-eight days of mayhem then on that last Monday night, they all disappear again. Then there are two manic days of taking everything down and then my favourite moment in the whole festival when we have a sit-down dinner for the entire technical crew – we sit 220 people in a marquee at the back of the Pleasance. Then on Thursday morning, they leave and we're left with ten or twelve people who basically spend two days carrying the same pieces of wood around the courtyard looking vaguely for somewhere to put it.

A lot has to happen before you get to that point. Before anything else you need to have the right idea about why you want to perform on the Fringe in the first place. That's what the next chapter is about. It looks at the philosophy that will underpin all your efforts to make your show a success. Because of that, it is the most crucial chapter of all.

4. The Motivation
Getting in the Right Frame of Mind

EVERYONE WANTS THEIR RUN on the Fringe to be successful. But not everyone has the same idea of success. For one company it might be playing to a decent-sized audience; to another it might be a booking for an international tour. A top comedian might be content with a healthy pay cheque; the performers in a student revue might be happy to have partied every night. Some want to leave with a set of positive newspaper reviews, others hope to be spotted by an agent. Some care only about developing their performing skills over twenty-five consecutive nights; others will not rest easy until they have won a major award.

There is no right or wrong answer. The Fringe is a mix of amateur and professional, mainstream and avant garde, local and international, serious and frivolous. One of its glories is that it takes all comers, each with their own reason for being there. It really doesn't matter what your reason is.

What does matter is you understand that reason and have a realistic idea of the kind of success you want. The clearer you are about your goals, the better able you will be to deal with the choices that present themselves to you. Questions such as where to perform, whether to advertise and how much to spend on marketing will have very different answers depending on whether you are part of a youth theatre company that wants to see lots of shows or the conductor of a Polish choir hoping for an autumn tour of Europe. If you start off by knowing what you want, then you can attempt to go out and get it. 'Goals are important,' says Laura Mackenzie Stuart of Universal Arts. 'They are how you will measure whether you had a good Fringe or not.'

Kath Mainland, the Fringe Society's chief executive says:

> The companies that have a good experience generally have a good idea of what they are doing it for and what they expect to get out of it. What they expect to get out of it might be entirely different, but people have a good experience if they understand what it is that they're trying to do. Everything else follows from that.

It is a philosophy that underscores the Fringe Office's work with participants. If you identify what you want to get out of the experience, the staff will be able to guide you through every subsequent question. 'Whatever they say will inform the answer to their original question,' says Christabel Anderson, head of participant services:

> If they say, 'Should I spend £4,000 on getting a PR person?' we can say, 'What are you trying to do? If you're coming up for a laugh, then no.' The key to success is knowing what you want to achieve and doing everything with that in mind.

Kate McGrath, a producer with her company Fuel, agrees:

> The advice I give people most often about Edinburgh is really think about why you want to go. Make sure you have good reasons and then understand the consequences of those reasons. Almost every company has a different set of reasons for going and it's worth understanding those reasons – whether it's to see lots of shows and meet people, to tour the work afterwards, to get national press to come and see

it, to get British Council delegates to see it or a combination of reasons – because it will have an impact on the decisions you make and where you put your resources. Most people's experience of Edinburgh is being a bit short of time and a bit short of money to make it all happen, so you've got to be really on the ball with where you're going to put your time and money.

Director Toby Gough, whose *Children of the Sea* was performed by teenagers orphaned by the Asian tsunami of 2004, argues that everything follows from having a clear idea of why you are coming to the Fringe and what you want to achieve:

I was running workshops after the tsunami in Sri Lanka without thinking at all that I was going to do a show for the Edinburgh festival. You work there, for whatever reason, and you go, 'Well, actually, there are people here with talent on an international level who could impress the world by the fact that after this calamity, they can still sing, act and show off a culture that is profoundly rich.' If you've got something that is powerful and sacred, it is a flame that can make it. That's what I look for. People will be convinced by you, because you'll be more passionate. That will help you getting your passports, finding potential funders, getting on that plane, getting through immigration and convincing the audience to come and watch the show. You need passion.

Being realistic

If you have never performed on the Fringe before, it is likely your expectations will be coloured by Edinburgh success stories. There is a long and impressive list of well-known names and high-profile shows that first came to attention in Edinburgh. It was a crucial stepping stone for Tom Stoppard in 1966 with *Rosencrantz and Guildenstern Are Dead*, for the bin-lid crashing musical spectacular *Stomp* in 1991 and for Stewart Lee's *Jerry Springer:The Opera* in 2002. Bob Golding's *Morecambe* played to sell-out crowds in Edinburgh before transferring to London and picking up an Olivier Award for best entertainment. Winners of the Edinburgh Comedy Awards, previously known as the Perrier Award, include Al Murray, the League of Gentlemen and Frank Skinner. It was here that Gregory Burke made his name with *Gagarin Way* and cemented it with *Black Watch*; here too that Enda Walsh made a splash with *Disco Pigs*, the first of many Fringe hits; and here that Belgium's Ontroerend Goed, Poland's Teatr Biuro Podrozy and Russia's Derevo enhanced their international profile.

But even though there are similar success stories every year, it would be foolhardy to plan your run in Edinburgh on the assumption that the same thing will happen to you. By all means dream about it, by all means have it as your aspiration, but when it comes to practical decision-making, you need to be realistic. For every Eddie Izzard, Soweto Gospel Choir and Mark Watson, there will be many talented artists who return home not just empty-handed but out of pocket. To avoid disappointment, you should set yourself achievable targets. 'I always try and put people off before they come,' says producer Dana MacLeod. 'I know that doesn't sound very encouraging, but they've got to have a solution to all the problems, so they can manage their expectations.'

'When people don't fulfil their dreams it's normally because those dreams are fairly wild,' says Miriam Attwood, the Fringe's former media manager:

You read about the Cambridge Footlights in 1981 [a Perrier Award-winning line-up that included Stephen Fry, Hugh Laurie and Emma Thompson] now being some of the biggest names in British entertainment and you think, 'I can go to the Fringe, I'm quite funny, I'll be made famous.' But it doesn't work like that. If you are a brand new stand-up doing your first one-hour show or if you are a theatre company and this is your second piece, and you know your show is good and you start thinking about it in March and come back to it every week, developing all areas of your plan, then it's totally possible to achieve all of your goals. It's hard work and you have to fully commit yourself, but the more structured everything is, the more likely you are to succeed.

You gotta have faith

Having identified what success would look like – whether it be full houses, critical acclaim or just a new set of Facebook friends – you need a strategy to achieve it. Fundamental to that is a belief in your show. The Fringe can be dispiriting as well as exhilarating ('It's a very stressful and highly competitive environment and it's no place for the paranoid or the faint of heart,' says Tommy Sheppard, director of the Stand Comedy Club), but if you have faith in what you are doing you will be able not only to cope with setbacks such as low attendance and negative reviews, but also to persuade everyone you work with, from box-office staff to flyering teams, that your show is worth backing. The best way to have faith in it is to make it as good as you possibly can. 'In a programme of 2,500 shows and all the noise of marketing and publicity, if you don't believe in what you're doing, why would you bother?' says Mainland.

Fringe First-winning playwright Ella Hickson agrees:

Believe in what you're doing even if the rest of the world turns round and says they don't like it. There is nowhere like the Fringe in the world for kicking the shit out of you if you're unsure. You've really got to believe in what you're doing and why you're doing it.

Anyone who has seen the look of incredulity on the face of a rejected contest on a TV talent show will know how the arts world can attract people with more ego than ability. You will be competing for audiences with those deluded people as well as with the truly gifted, so you need to make sure your whole team is committed to your show. 'The best advice I could give anybody is just sheer determination,' says Karen Koren, artistic director of the Gilded Balloon. 'It doesn't matter how you do it, it is your determination to do it.'

'Edinburgh is a difficult undertaking,' agrees William Burdett-Coutts, artistic director of Assembly:

> You've got to be committed if you want to do it and, if you're not, you're not going to succeed. And you've got to be passionate about what you're doing. It's a complex, difficult, challenging, stupid thing to do, but when it works, it's the most exhilarating thing there is.

Beyond belief

From commitment will emerge the drive to work hard. The Fringe is not a TV talent show offering a fast track to fame and fortune. It might take several return journeys before you hit your target. 'There is no such thing as an overnight success,' says artist manager Marlene Zwickler:

> It doesn't make a lot of sense to go to all that effort to get to the Fringe and then not be ready with your show. The common denominator is that the so-called overnight successes, like Michael McIntyre, have been working pretty hard for quite a long time, found their voice, stuck at it, got better at it. Don't be scared of hard work.

Anthony Alderson, artistic director of the Pleasance, says luck plays a part, but so too does dedication:

> There are also those companies that go out and just fight for it, they work really hard and won't give up, fighting for that last ticket.

For all your graft and commitment, however, you need to know where your strengths and weaknesses lie. Success on the Edinburgh Fringe requires a team effort and, especially if you have a weak spot, you need to call in all the favours you can.

Producer Nica Burns, director of the Edinburgh Comedy Awards, says you shouldn't be ashamed to ask for help:

> If you're a performer who's following your life's dream and you aren't very good at getting organised, find somebody who can help you. If you haven't got any money, see if you've got a relative who is happy to come and do the organising side. Be realistic: someone has got to produce the show, to make sure all the bits and pieces are there, who gets a press release written and sent out, who understands the timetables and the Fringe's deadlines which you miss at your peril. Why not get that side of things right? It's just silly not to. You have to make sure that you've done everything you can so that when you walk on stage, the conditions are at their optimum. That's your responsibility to yourself as an artist. Don't compromise on that.

Having articulated your reasons for coming to the Fringe (and remember, there is no wrong answer), you can work out a goal to aim for. If you are passionate about your show and your goal is realistic, you will find it easy to enthuse everyone you work with, from company members to venue managers to flyering teams and, eventually, to audiences. The more people who share in your goal, the more you will spread the load. And the more you draw on other people's talents, the better chance you have of enjoying the success you dream of.

In the next chapter, we will look in more detail at the kind of shows that proliferate on the Edinburgh Fringe and the various challenges they face. We will see that as long as your motivation is right, there should be nothing you can't do.

5. The Show
Making a Spectacle of Yourself

WHAT KIND OF SHOWS do well on the Fringe? The simple answer is good ones. It sounds flippant but, on one level, there is no mystery. Audiences like being entertained: it is your job to entertain them. The same applies whether your show is mainstream or highbrow, tragic or comic, musical or silent – you should aspire to be the best you can be. This is true whenever you perform, but in Edinburgh, it has special relevance. As we established in the last chapter, if you believe you have a good show, you will find everything else you do on the Fringe so much easier.

That was the experience of Canadian actor Anthony Black as he struggled to find audiences after missing the Fringe Programme deadline (see Chapter 3). 'Right now I'm enjoying playing the show and people are telling me they enjoy it,' he says in the middle of the run of *Invisible Atom*, winner of a *Herald* Angel award. 'That makes it all do-able. If we were flopping, it would be very hard to keep my morale up.'

It is one reason director John Clancy and actor Nancy Walsh have made the journey from New York to Edinburgh most years but not every single year since scoring a Fringe First-winning hit with David Calvito's *Americana Absurdum* in 2000. They love the Fringe and have come back repeatedly – one year with four productions – but they have never returned just for the sake of returning. 'You should only go when you have a show you feel is worthy,' says Clancy:

It's true any time you're producing theatre, but especially in Edinburgh, not just because of the physical toll, but because you find the most discerning, intelligent critics, audience members and fellow artists. If there are ten people in and those ten people are seeing your best work, it's worth it. There's nothing more heartbreaking than being there and realising this is not your best.

The shock of the new

This is why William Burdett-Coutts, artistic director of Assembly, suggests a 'basic rule' is only to bring tried and tested shows to the Fringe. 'I break that rule every year – and every year, I come out thinking I was right,' he says:

> You need to turn up in Edinburgh with a show that is in good working order before you get there. You don't have time to learn. You need to hit the ground running and be open to the press from the beginning.

It is not only Burdett-Coutts who breaks this rule. In practice, the Fringe is a celebration of the new. The *Scotsman* Fringe Firsts and the Edinburgh Comedy Awards champion originality, the media is hungry for fresh stories and there is an active part of the audience that goes in search of novel experiences. Having a show in good working order is certainly an advantage, but it is not enough on its own. 'If your show is ordinary, mediocre or just good, it's not enough,' says producer Nica Burns, director of the Edinburgh Comedy Awards. 'You have to be very, very good to get noticed.'

Not everyone wants to be noticed, of course. All kinds of work finds an audience in Edinburgh and much of it manages to do so without any media profile. Sadly, the reverse can also be true: there are perfectly good shows that somehow don't catch on. 'I don't understand why sometimes some of the greatest pieces of work just fall underneath the radar,' says Anthony Alderson, artistic director of the Pleasance:

> The amount of times when a reviewer hasn't quite made it or they've loved it and, for whatever reason, the newspaper didn't review it until the last day . . . there are lots of unlucky things that happen. And there are those lucky companies where everything just happens to hit them at the right time.

Catching the zeitgeist

How, then, can you improve your luck? One way is to have a sense of the kind of shows that do well in Edinburgh and what kind of people go to see them. A trip to the Fringe the year before you perform will help you understand these distinctions. 'You need to know your audience,' says director Toby Gough:

> If you're performing in the Botanic Gardens, you know what kind of audience will come and watch a show there. An outdoor Shakespeare with an interesting angle to it, an interesting social background, is going to get that type of audience. And if you do a show at the Underbelly at 7 p.m., you're going to get a certain audience who have been drinking in the beer tent.

In Chapter 12, Suzanne Andrade explains how her company 1927 created its multi-award winning *Between the Devil and the Deep Blue Sea* after undertaking a serious study of the Fringe the previous year. Playwright Ella Hickson took a similar approach when she came to write *Eight*, a state-of-the-nation series of monologues that went on to win a Fringe First, the Carol Tambor Award and an NSDF Emerging Artists Award. 'The Fringe is wonderful,' says

Hickson, who has missed only three festivals since she was twelve:

> Without it I would not be doing what I do and a job that
> I love. But it sometimes celebrates zeitgeist more than it
> celebrates real worth. You've got to be new, you've got to be
> political, as well as being good.

She points to the 2010 Fringe when there was a glut of shows
about sex trafficking at the same time as the press had been
focusing on female sexuality and the rise of raunch culture. While
she was writing *Eight*, she had observed the popularity of audience
participation programmes such as *Big Brother* and *X Factor* and felt
theatre could capitalise on it. On the way into the Bedlam Theatre,
the audience was given a list of eight monologues and asked to vote
for the four they would like to see. The poll determined the show.
She says:

> Everybody was voting, but no one seemed to have done
> it on the Fringe and I reckoned that would probably get
> newspapers going, 'Ooh' – and lo and behold, they did.
> You have to know the Fringe is not a meritocracy. Doing
> the best you can do, working the hardest you can work and
> producing the best show you can produce is but the first
> hurdle. Get that down, tick that box, but don't believe it's
> enough. You've got to be making the same headlines that
> have been making the headlines for the past six months. It's
> every theatre practitioner's responsibility to be as wired to
> their culture as they possibly can.

Cutting corners

If your definition of success is not losing money, you will be tempted
to minimise the number of performers you need. Stand-up comedy

has proliferated on the Fringe not only because it is popular, but also because it requires nothing more than one performer, a spotlight and a microphone. As well as being cheap to stage, it has a format that suits the one-hour time slot. For similar reasons, the theatre programme is rife with one-person plays and many of them, such as Daniel Kitson's series of monologues at the Traverse Theatre, Matthew Zajac's Fringe First-winning *The Tailor of Inverness* and many Guy Masterson productions, have gone on to international acclaim. Saving on actors, however, can present its own problems. 'A one-person show is economically great but it's not a selling point because audiences worry they might be bored,' says producer Dana MacLeod.

Although there are many examples of successful one-person plays on the Fringe, there are many more examples of larger-cast hits. Audiences love the colour and drama that a big company can provide. By all means put on a one-person show if that's what you want to do, but think carefully about your reasons if money has been a decisive factor. The important thing, says Barry Church-Woods, the Fringe's venues and companies manager, is to do the work you want to do and to resist as much as possible being restricted by conditions on the Fringe. 'Don't compromise your work,' he says. 'The reason you're in Edinburgh is to show yourself off.'

The question to ask yourself, therefore, is what is the best way to show yourself off. If, for example, your elaborate set is fundamental to what you do, then you should try to find a way of constructing that set. If it is not fundamental, then it might make more sense to cut back. 'If you've got a very heavy production with lots of sets and lights that need setting, that's a bit of a disaster for the Fringe unless you've got a circus marquee or something where you can do your own show,' says Dana MacLeod. Fringe First-winning director and playwright Renny Krupinski agrees: 'No set is very important. You've got very little get-in time, so you have to be practical about it.'

You can have the same kind of debate about how long your show

69

should be. Comedian Mark Watson has performed marathon shows lasting twenty-four hours and thirty-six hours (he proposed to his wife at the end of one of them), so any length is possible. It is also true, however, that the Fringe average is somewhere between an hour and ninety minutes. If you choose to exceed that, you could find yourself not only spending more on venue hire but also having to work harder to attract audiences and reviewers. Producer James Seabright sometimes chooses not to launch a show in Edinburgh, especially if it is longer than the Fringe average. 'It's always a challenge if you're trying to push above that seventy/eighty-minute barrier,' he says. 'It pushes the barrier of comfort for Fringe venues that aren't designed for people to be sitting in a seat for much more than an hour.'

Again, Barry Church-Woods would say the decisive factor should be not length, cast size or set, but your passion for the show. Even though your venue is operating on a commercial basis, it can still be swayed by its love of the art:

> The main thing is a piece of work that they can be committed to selling from the run-up to the Fringe and right up to the last day. They want the quality of work so they can be passionate about it.

Getting programmed

We will look in more detail at venues in the next chapter, but while you are thinking about your show, you should think about where it will go on, not only in terms of the physical requirements of the building but also the likely commitment of the venue staff. Some managers will do no more than rent you the room and will not care about the nature of your show, but others want to present a distinct programme and will take a particular interest if your show helps them do that.

As with all the major programmers, Alex Rochford aimed for a balance. He worked for Assembly as programmer and producer in 2009 and 2010 after working for several years as a scout and booker for the Comedy Store in London. Part of his job was to find around 130 shows from the 700 applications that Assembly receives. The spaces in his jurisdiction went from 60 seats to 840. It you wanted to perform outdoors, around cabaret tables, under canvas, in the round or end-on, he would almost certainly have a room to suit. If he did not, the other big venues would offer you as many choices again.

A typical mix at Assembly would include a large-scale clowning spectacular, a TV comic, a polemical drama, an off-beat American stand-up and an African choir. If you are lucky, your show will fill a programming gap; if you are unlucky, another similar-sounding show will have got there first. 'That's not to say that you won't find somewhere else within the festival,' he says, explaining that venues will often suggest good shows to each other if they do not have room for them. The majority of Assembly's 700 applications do find a home somewhere in the city.

In common with many venue programmers, Rochford says the start of January is the best time to make contact. If you have a world premiere, he suggests you send the programmer a script and, if possible, an invitation to a workshop reading. 'There was a lovely one-woman show called *Long Live the King* by Ansuya Nathan,' he says:

> I saw a ten-minute presentation at Hampstead Theatre on a new reading night and I said, 'Please keep in touch.' Then there was a twenty-five-minute preview at the end of February and she got on board with producer Guy Masterson who has a track record for doing great one-woman shows. I thought, 'Well, I've seen twenty-five minutes and it's good.' They sent me all the supporting materials and how the project was going to be and it was a good world premiere.

Although having Masterson on board worked in Nathan's favour, Rochford made his decision on the strength of the material. Masterson has a relationship with Assembly that goes back to 1994, but even he cannot take his presence in the programme for granted. 'He brought six or seven things that he thought we might want this year and I think we took four that fitted with what we wanted to do,' says Rochford. At the Pleasance, artistic director Anthony Alderson has a similar commitment to putting together a programme that is artistically satisfying as well as financially successful. His small programming team spends a lot of time in comedy clubs and London fringe theatres, keeping an eye open for up-and-coming talent. Come January, they have two months to whittle down around 2,000 applications to 200 slots in the theatre programme alone, making judgements on the basis of synopses, scripts, DVDs, familiarity with the company, personal contacts and scratch performances as short as five minutes long. 'There are a million and one ways that we find stuff,' says Alderson, who grew up in Edinburgh and dates his earliest memory of the Fringe to 1979 when his mother casually suggested they see a show:

> But it's always done on the merit of the company or the work, the artistry, the writing, reputation from other festivals. You get quite quick at spotting the ones that you think are Pleasance shows. We know instinctively what works with us.

It is the same thing at the Underbelly. Concentrating on programming in earnest from February, co-artistic director Charlie Wood encourages companies to send in scripts, DVDs and photographs from as early as October. Online registration opens in the new year. 'The best way is to encourage us to see the show, either a scratch performance or just to have a meeting if it's not written yet,' says Wood, whose first trip to the Fringe was in 1991 as a seventeen-year-old pupil at Eton College, where he helped set up Double Edge Drama and directed a production of Edward

Albee's *The Zoo Story* in a community centre on Montgomery Street. All these years later, he and Ed Bartam field in the region of 600 applications for 120 Underbelly slots. Of those, they will take around 60 shows and will go out and find a further 60 themselves. He gives the example of musical comedy double act Frisky and Mannish who invited them to see a five-minute routine in a pub:

> We went to see it and thought it was great and their first full hour-long show they ever did was with us. It was the same with 1927's *Between the Devil and the Deep Blue Sea*. Again, they'd never done a full hour show before.

As 1927's Suzanne Andrade explains in Chapter 13, that show turned into the hit of the Fringe, winning several awards and going on to tour the world. So what kind of thing is the Underbelly looking for? 'We're looking something that will suit the space,' says Wood:

> From a theatre point of view, we really like taking on new writing from young people; not just students, but young professional companies. The fun for us is taking that kind of company and guiding them through the process. I don't want to come up here and just produce big shows. Producing really good theatre by young companies is just as exciting for us as producing a big show like *Five Guys Named Moe* or Flawless.

The approach of Rochford, Alderson and Wood is repeated at venues around the Fringe, so if you believe in your show, it should be possible to find a venue manager who will share in your belief. The important thing is to do the show you want to do rather than trying to second-guess what venues, audiences, critics or producers will be interested in. That being the case, let's take a look at the various types of show and consider the particular challenges they face.

Amdram

Claire Wood grew up in Nottingham and always had a sense of the Edinburgh Fringe as a 'buzzing hub of cool stuff happening up north'. She came as a visitor in her 20s and later moved to the city, where she works for an advertising agency. 'Suddenly the possibility of doing a show on the Fringe miraculously fell on to my doorstep,' she says. 'It seems amazing to me when I think back to what I thought when I was little and here I am doing it.'

She joined the Edinburgh Graduate Theatre Group, which has been putting on four shows a year since 1954. Becoming a central player, she spent ten years as president and has also been secretary, treasurer, director and actor. The company has a year-round local audience, so in one respect, it has no need to play the Fringe. Like several amateur groups in Edinburgh, however, the Grads make August a fixture. 'It's purely for love of the Fringe,' says Wood over a lunchtime cup of tea in the Leith branch of the Scotch Malt Whisky Society.

Unlike many Edinburgh amdram groups which always perform in the same place, the company has appeared in a number of venues around town, including the Quaker Meeting House and Diverse Attractions, and in 2010 made the unusual step of performing *The Tempest* on a barge moored in Leith. Her employer, the Leith Agency, had rented the boat as extra office space and suggested she might use it to put on a show. The agency even picked up the bill for licensing it with the council as a festival venue, which was a big help in balancing the books, not least because the audience capacity was just thirty.

'I thought there was no point doing it on a boat if it wasn't vaguely nautical,' says Wood, who chose *The Tempest* for that reason, staging it promenade-style to cope with the small space. The show got a fair amount of advance publicity because of the novelty of the venue. It went on to sell out, attracting a broader audience than the friends and family you expect at an amdram show. It was an adventurous choice and one very much in the spirit of the Fringe.

Not everyone is comfortable taking such risks, however, she says:

> Other amateur groups tend to do the stuff they know will be popular in the Fringe, as a calculated decision to sell tickets. It's traditional to do Scots comedies on the grounds that it attracts people. I've tried very hard to do stuff that was cool and interesting. In amateur theatre, contemporary plays aren't done very often. I'm very disparaging about these drawing-room dramas that are done endlessly by amateur groups because I wonder what new wisdom they shed on the world.

Once you break from standard amdram fare, you are faced with the inexact science of figuring out what audiences will go to see. Wood had a sell-out success with Sarah Kane's *Crave* as well as with *The Tempest* and *Antigone*, but did less well with Mark Ravenhill's *Some Explicit Polaroids* and Abi Morgan's *Tiny Dynamite*. 'Maybe amateur plus well-known classic is better than amateur plus uneasy avant-garde thing,' she speculates.

Artistically ambitious

The average Fringe experience involves a sixty-minute time slot, an incredibly quick get-in and a show in a space never intended for performance. It is reasonable, therefore, to question whether it is worth staging anything with high production standards. For all the excitement of performances going on all around you, there are undoubted disadvantages. 'Very few venues can accommodate a show that needs absolute silence,' says Marlene Zwickler as an example.

The Fringe, however, is a broad church, big enough to embrace everything from no-budget student revues to sophisticated pieces of professional theatre. You are likely to have to work harder the more technically demanding your show is, but you should hold out for the best conditions. For a select few companies, that could mean performing at the Traverse, a year-round two-studio theatre with a commitment to presenting polished full-length productions. Dance companies are similarly well served at Dance Base, another year-round venue. Several Fringe venues, such as Zoo and the New Town Theatre, make efforts to match those standards and some companies take control by finding and running the venue themselves.

Barry Church-Woods, the Fringe's venues and companies manager, believes you should not compromise your artistic standards. 'Everyone is here, so the best technicians are here,' he says. It is a sentiment shared by Sam Gough, venue manager at the Edinburgh International Conference Centre: 'If you've got two pieces of work, make sure you bring the best one; don't just bring the easiest one.'

Wolfgang Hoffman is the producer who brilliantly demonstrated the merit of this argument with Aurora Nova, a venue that ran in St Stephens Church in Stockbridge from 2001 to 2007. Hoffman first came to the Fringe in 1989 as tour manager and performer in *Hopeless Games*, a dance-theatre collaboration between Potsdam's Fabrik and St Petersburg's Do-Theatre. After the buzz of excitement wore off, he became dissatisfied with the artistic conditions on the Fringe. It did not seem conducive to good work when performers had no place to warm up and every show had the pressure of a fast turn-around. At the same time, friends in Europe were asking him how to come to Edinburgh, so he resolved to set up his own venue that would be built in a spirit of artistic cooperation:

I thought maybe if we did a venue ourselves that communicated through quality, it could work as a festival within a festival. We had a technical team that was dedicated to making the show look as good-looking as it needed to be, even with seven or eight shows in a day. Because of the solidarity ethics, everything was easier in terms of the change over. It became a huge critical success because of its artistic integrity. Sharing meant that much more was going to be achieved with less effort.

Aurora Nova ran for eight seasons, after which Hoffman switched his focus to the Dublin Fringe Festival, for which he was artistic director. He now works as artistic director for the Berlin-based Circle of Eleven. Despite his success bringing physical theatre and dance to Edinburgh, and despite his love of the 'appreciative' audience, he sounds a note of caution. 'There's a lot of work that I respect very much that I definitely wouldn't recommend going to Edinburgh,' he says. 'Work needs to have a certain sexiness in Edinburgh. Work of a more contemplative nature will find it very hard and there are better festivals to go to and be appreciated by.'

He does, however, acknowledge the Fringe's value as a trade fair for professional companies with artistic ambition, something Kate McGrath agrees about. With her London-based producing organisation Fuel, she has brought shows such as the Perrier Award-winning *Jackson's Way*, the site-specific submarine drama *Kursk* and the museum-like *Under Glass* performed in the basement of the McEwan Hall (only after they had laid carpet and blacked out the walls). Some of her shows have done well with a simple presentation and a strong concept; more challenging is to present work with high production values. 'For us the key has been finding spaces that are right for the work and finding a way to escape the fifteen-minute get-in and get-out cycle,' says McGrath, who was born and brought up in the city. 'It is possible. It requires an incredible amount of hard work. You either need to spend quite a lot of money or work like maniacs – which is what we've done.'

Cabaret

Introduced as an independent section in the Fringe Programme as recently as 2011, cabaret has gained in prominence with the renewed interest in the form. It is a broad church that includes burlesque, vaudeville, torch singers, comedy, music, dance, magic, drag, circus and performance art. Such an eclectic range, when served up on a variety bill, goes down well with a festival crowd in search of novelty, entertainment and the suggestion of something risqué.

Children's

In a round-the-clock festival there are plenty of daytime slots taken up by shows for younger audiences. As well as visits from established children's theatre companies, the programme attracts magicians, circus acts and comedians who have realised it doesn't take much to strip out the rude words from their adult shows. A big plus is that audiences are actively seeking to see things. 'You're more likely to get the complete family together, as opposed to Dad being on the golf course,' says Iain Johnstone, artistic director of Edinburgh's Wee Stories theatre company. 'They're in the mood to have a good time because it's festival city.'

The pressures of quick turn-around times and high competition apply to children's shows as much as any other type of work, but there is one particular problem the sector faces. State schools in Scotland begin their autumn term in the middle of August, which means the audience you have steadily built up in the first week or two disappears overnight. 'Programming is very different because suddenly you are totally reliant on tourists who have come with family to the Fringe,' says Johnstone.

That audience, as well as private school students and pre-schoolers, might be enough to sustain you, but you are likely to find it harder work as the festival goes on. 'A good show like *Stickman* by Julia Donaldson sold out its first ten days, then down a bit, sold out at weekends and probably averaged about 320 tickets a day,' says Charlie Wood, co-director of the Underbelly, about one of the bigger children's shows.

If you are used to attracting a schools audience, you have to plan a long way ahead to have any hope of getting them to the Fringe. If your venue does a schools mail-out, make sure you are in it, but bear in mind the schools will be on holiday at the start of the festival and focusing on the new school year at the end of it. Once the Fringe Programme is launched there are only about three weeks until the end of the summer term, so you have to move fast to get teachers on board. If you are looking for opportunities for cross-selling, the Edinburgh International Book Festival attracts big audiences to its children's programme and you could find the pavement outside the tented village in Charlotte Square is a good place to do your flyering.

Comedy

There was a time when theatre was the biggest category in the Fringe Programme, but over the last two decades stand-up comedy has grown to take up at least as many pages and earn a lot more at the box office. Audiences generally understand 'comedy' to mean stand-up, sketch shows and revues, and do not expect to find comic plays or amusing musicals listed in that section of the Fringe Programme. If you choose to do that – and some people do – you might attract a new audience but you run the risk of being overlooked by people searching for theatre and of disappointing comedy fans expecting punchlines.

For dedicated comedians, however, the Fringe is a central part of the professional calendar. 'You're going to be a better comic at the end of the month than when you started and it's worth doing for that reason alone,' says Claire Walker, publicist for several big-name comedians. Tommy Sheppard, artistic director of the Stand Comedy Club, is quick to agree:

> I don't think there's anywhere else in the world where you can do twenty-four nights on the trot and, as a comedian, to get the material honed, get confidence in it, in a very short space of time, it's an unparalleled opportunity. I've seen shows that are entirely different on the last day than the first.

For many comedians, the Fringe is a catalyst to up their game or to try something new. To play to an audience of dedicated comedy fans every night for three weeks gives many of them the freedom to break away from the lowest-common-denominator material they need to entertain the hen parties and stag nights for the rest of the year. Being in one city for so long also inspires many to put their free time to good use – perhaps a play in the afternoon or open spots at late-night comedy gigs.

In 1997, Ed Byrne teamed up with Brendon Burns to perform *The Act,* a play that, naturally enough, was about two comedians living together at the Edinburgh Fringe. Byrne admits it had its shortcomings as a piece of drama, but without the Fringe, he would not have done it at all. The same could be said of the regular stand-up gig he did every evening in the same 120-seater space. 'It was called *Psychobabble* and I had a chaise longue on the stage,' says Byrne, who was nominated for the Perrier Award the following year:

> I would sit on the chaise longue and pretend to talk to my therapist. There was a mixture of light and dark in the whole thing. I would never have attempted that anywhere else than Edinburgh and I never did that show anywhere else.

Nick Doody's first appearance on the Fringe was in 1992, when he appeared in a three-hander student sketch show from Oxford

University. Subsequently, he appeared in mixed bills such as the *Big Value Comedy Show*. In 1997, he reached the final of the So You Think You're Funny? competition and, in 2006, he did his first solo show:

> You have more time, you have more freedom, you don't have the same pressures of somebody having to follow you and somebody having to build you up in the right way. They're yours for an hour and you can take more time. You can do stuff that doesn't punch up a laugh every ten seconds because it has a bigger pay-off or it gives something extra to what you're doing.

This is a privilege Phil Nichol thrives on. He has been appearing on the Fringe since the early 1990s when he was part of the hit musical comedy trio Corky and the Juice Pigs. Returning nearly every year since, he has appeared not only in his acclaimed solo stand-up shows, but also as the driving force behind the Comedians Theatre Company. 'Go for it,' he says:

> The sooner you start working on a long-form show, the better your life will be. If you do a brand-new hour of comedy, even if it's not a great hour, you should be very pleased with yourself.

A note to comedians travelling from North America: you are likely to find British audiences quieter than those you are used to. Don't take it personally. Karen Koren, artistic director of the Gilded Balloon, says:

> Caroline Rhea kept saying, 'Why are you all so quiet?' I would say, 'They weren't quiet. They were good. They liked you.' Because in America they all slap their thighs, she could not help talking to them and wanting something back from them the whole time.

81

Dance and physical theatre

If it is important for a theatre company to find the right venue, it is doubly important for a dance company. Hastily constructed Fringe theatres are not known for their sprung floors and perfect sight lines. And although a dance company might not want a huge audience capacity, it is likely to want a large stage – a combination that can be hard to find. 'The challenge is getting suitable spaces that are affordable or where you can get enough box office in order to pay the rent,' says dancer Frank McConnell, who has been appearing on the Fringe since the 1980s. 'I would say to people to try and create pieces for small spaces and a small auditorium in order that it doesn't feel like a really bare experience.'

For a recent Fringe run, McConnell chose the St Bride's Centre, deciding that the facilities it offered, including the opportunity to be in the space an hour before the performance, outweighed the problem of being a short but significant distance away from most Fringe traffic. He was not spoilt for choice, however, and even the venues that sounded promising sometimes proved impractical. The stage at one, for example, was being made from hardboard placed over a tiled floor. 'At the age of forty-eight, I thought I'll just wreck my body,' he says. 'I can't perform without a sprung floor any more. It would be detrimental to trying to do quality work.'

Eugene Downes of Culture Ireland agrees that finding the right space is one of the greatest challenges:

> We have found that with dance and physical theatre it's been a question of finding offsite venues, converting them and using them for the duration so you can have a standing set. There's a very significant expense with that, although there are some shows where you can lose the set and present the piece in more of a showcase environment.

In a festival that attracts so many people, there is a substantial dance audience, although it is hard work attracting them and even harder reaching a cross-over audience. As many artists find, however, the Fringe has unique artistic advantages. 'The benefits are really getting under the skin of the material,' says McConnell:

It's very difficult when you're doing one-night stands; you're always in a different space. No dance company would get more than two nights in Scotland, so it is an opportunity to allow the material to grow and develop in front of interested audiences. Also, you never know who is in that audience. Without knowing it, we had five senior officers from Creative Scotland who appeared on five successive nights.

For these reasons, McConnell believes the Fringe is a good place for dance companies as long as they are 'clever and imaginative' with their budgets and marketing. They also need to make special efforts to find a place for the dancers to get ready. 'There are places like Dance Base or maybe a yoga centre where you can warm up pretty thoroughly before you get your twenty minutes' allocation before your show starts,' he says. 'It's terribly important – and just time to clear your head, chill out and think about what you're doing.'

Experimental

Although there is an image of the Fringe as a hotbed of weird and wonderful underground performance art, there is actually relatively little left-field work around. The costs of a three-week run and the ubiquity of the fixed-length time slot are not conducive to scratch performances or free-form experiments. That does not mean it cannot be done, however, and if you do want to stage work of this type, the Fringe has the advantage of a curious audience primed for new and unusual performances.

By its nature, the work appears in different forms and in different

83

places from year to year, but you should be able to find somewhere sympathetic. In years gone by it might have been the Demarco European Art Foundation, where you could see Hungarian dancer Yvette Bozsik writhing in a glass coffin in a performance that lasted until her air supply ran out. A few years ago, it might have been the Routemaster bus parked on the Meadows where Anthony Roberts programmed a series of shows under the banner 'Never knowingly understood'. More recently, it was in Forest Fringe, which occupied a space on Bristo Place, and featured everything from one-to-one poetry encounters to James Baker climbing a six-foot ladder 43,710 times until he reached the height of outer space.

Andy Field, co-director of Forest Fringe, says if you can find the right place to perform, there is a ready audience for such work. 'There is a healthy number of critics who will have quite large chunks of time when they deliberately want to see left-field things,' he says. 'I've got two hours to kill: surprise me.' It's the only time of the year that's going to happen. Similarly with promoters: everybody is here to check stuff out.'

International

The principles of universal friendship that led to the establishment of the Edinburgh International Festival in 1947 are shared by the Fringe. Thanks to pioneers such as Richard Demarco, who was instrumental in bringing key names from the Eastern European avant garde to Edinburgh, and to today's promoters such as Tomek Borkowy, Wolfgang Hoffman and Toby Gough, the Fringe draws much of its energy from the influx of global cultures. It is a place where Australian comedians rub shoulders with New York actors, Brazilian dancers and Ukrainian musicians. For artistic reasons alone, this makes the Fringe an alluring proposition. 'Edinburgh is remarkable for the international relationships you build and the quality of international work,' says William Burdett-Coutts, artistic director of Assembly who has a particular history of bringing theatre from Georgia, as well as everywhere from the USA to South Korea.

Many professional companies believe the cost of performing in Edinburgh can be offset by the opportunities the Fringe presents. By the time you have paid for international travel, it is virtually impossible to make money, but you can regard it as a long-term investment. 'There isn't any other festival where you have that much variety of work going on and that exposure to the worldwide arts industry,' says Wolfgang Hoffman.

New York director John Clancy has returned repeatedly to the Fringe with shows such as *Americana Absurdum, Fatboy, Cincinnati, Horse Country* and *The Event*, because of the business and artistic doors it opens:

Most of the income in the last eight years that we've got out of theatre can be directly traced to shows that premiered in Edinburgh and then have gone on to have tours. That's the business side. The other side is the artistic. It's the Olympics. When we opened *Americana Absurdum* in New York in 1997, I remember listening to the writing by Brian Parks, watching the performances and the ensemble work, and thinking 'This has got to be some of the best work going on in the world.' I wanted the opportunity to put it in Edinburgh where all the rest of that work was going on. It was an opportunity and a challenge that I thought the work was up for.

Any company arriving in Edinburgh from abroad without adequate preparation risks suffering serious culture shock. Once you have understood the principle that the Fringe does not invite participants, you have to accept that, whatever status you have in your own country, in Edinburgh you have to fight for audiences as much as everyone else. 'A lot of them will be coming from a country where they've had a lot of success,' says Tomek Borkowy of

Universal Arts, who made his first visit to the Fringe in 1983:

> They come here and suddenly, everything is much tighter
> and the audiences are very choosy and very often something
> that is successful in one country is not necessarily successful
> in another.

Much as the Fringe is receptive to international work, it can
be tough to sell shows in a language other than English unless
they have a strong visual or musical appeal. There are people in
Edinburgh who are willing to experience different cultures and
different languages, but there are also those who are more resistant.
'I advise people not to do it in their own languages because it's
very difficult,' says Borkowy. 'Although we can have a translation,
the audience shrinks.' The alternatives are not necessarily better,
however. The actors of one Polish company went to the trouble of
learning their script in English, but they had such a poor command
of the language that audiences still did not understand them and by
the end of the run, they reverted to Polish.

With five Fringe Firsts and several other awards under his belt,
director Toby Gough has brought large companies from Sri Lanka,
Malawi, Cuba and Tibet to Edinburgh, often performing exuberant
promenade shows in the Royal Botanic Garden. As well as enlivening
the city, such work feeds back into the cultures and communities it
has come from. 'People go to the Edinburgh Festival because they
want to see what theatre can achieve,' says Gough:

> The Edinburgh audience has an expanded appetite to know
> the different uses of theatre around the world. You see the
> effect it can have on the world you're living in. The young
> children from Sri Lanka I worked with went back with a
> greater sense of the world, of English and of Shakespeare and
> were writing stories about Shakespeare in their exams that
> the teachers felt were unbelievable. Being in an international

situation, meeting people you would never normally meet, going to award ceremonies, being recognised for dances you've been doing all your life and feeling acknowledged and having your voices heard – that is something that will have an unbelievable transformative power on these young souls.

Music

Youth orchestras, chart-topping bands, folk acts, jazz singers, choirs and performers from across the musical spectrum find a place on the Fringe. For many, the challenges are little different from playing in any other city at any other time of year: they perform one or two concerts – often in dedicated music venues such as the Queen's Hall and the Jazz Bar – then move on to their next gig in a different town. Some choose to stay for a longer run, however, and they must deal with all the issues of performing rights, publicity, accommodation and venues in just the same way as other artists.

There are no rules about the kind of music that can sustain a three-week run, but it helps to have cross-over appeal. It would be unusual for a straightforward pop band or a conventional orchestra to do a long run, but quite common for an act that has an extra twist. That could be a theatrical element, a bit of musical comedy or some kind of spectacle. Cabaret-style performers find a ready audience, as do African drummers and Cuban choirs – anything with a touch of the exotic. What the successful acts have in common is a capacity to reach out to a wider audience than just dedicated music lovers.

The Tiger Lillies are one British band that matches this description. Fronted by the larger-than-life figure of Martyn Jacques, they specialise in blackly comic tales of the seamy side of life, performed in an atmosphere somewhere between Berlin cabaret and punk circus.

They first played on the Fringe in 1995 at a point when they were still playing in bars and building a name for themselves. They subsequently played at St Stephen's Church, Pod Deco (the former Odeon cinema) and, one year, at the Usher Hall in the Edinburgh International Festival. Steadily, they have built an audience – some drawn in from the band's central role to Improbable Theatre's *Shockheaded Peter* – so that, today, they can be reasonably assured of selling out a 150-seat venue for a two-week run, earning a living in the process. Covering costs is one thing, but Jacques values the experience from an artistic point of view. 'We do lots of long runs, but those are circus shows: *The Tiger Lillies' Freak Show,*' he says. 'To do a three-week run just as the Tiger Lillies is a good opportunity for us. It's healthy for us as a band.'

His tip for any band planning a run on the Fringe is to work with someone who appreciates what you are trying to do and has a good knowledge of the festival. 'You really need a good promoter,' he says. 'Someone who understands you and who knows how many people you're going to attract, knows how to promote you and what to do with you.'

Musicals

You have only to look at the trajectory of *Jerry Springer: The Opera*, which premiered in Edinburgh before runs at the National Theatre and in the West End before a UK tour and international stagings, to know there is a place for musicals on the Fringe. But it can be especially tough to put on a show that will typically involve not only a large cast but also musicians and the stage space to accommodate them all. 'You're trying to blend the book, the drama, high quality music and musicianship, dance and often unusual staging and in many cases technical effects,' says Chris Grady, who ran a festival of musicals at George Square Theatre until 2009 and set up the MTM:UK Musical Theatre Awards. 'And you have an hour and ten minutes, or whatever, to deliver that.'

The problem is compounded by the average musical being a

two or three-hour affair. Squeezing such a show into a short Fringe slot risks cutting out its heart. 'It is almost that you have to write another show,' says Grady:

> You have to structure it so that it has an arc in its own right in the Fringe slot. That is a real challenge because it means you have to throw out glorious tunes and to change the arc of the show. Cutting corners in musical theatre is a dangerous game.

His recommendation is to keep it simple. He gives the example of a show that had eighteen people on stage. That meant so much time had to be spent getting the sound balance right and installing a large sound rig that other aspects of the production, such as the way it looked, were rushed. Although costs can be high, they are not necessarily higher than putting on a showcase production in London, with the added advantage that in Edinburgh you might come across the producer, the publisher or the collaborator who will help you make the next step. 'It's completely lunatic to imagine you can break even, but it might be very good money spent in terms of development,' he says.

> For example, the company that put on a show called *Only the Brave* reckoned they lost as much on doing the show in Edinburgh as they would have spent on a studio recording and a showcase performance in London. What they got was three weeks of playing the show, the opportunity to look at it in real detail and the chance for critics and producers from all over the world to look at it. Had they spent the same amount of money on a West End cast for a showcase in London they would have generated less impact.

Site specific

In a festival with such an appetite for unusual experiences, there is always a buzz around shows in non-theatre spaces. There have been performances on a double-decker bus, in a car, in an out-of-hours department store, in a pub, on the streets, in a rented flat, in public toilets, on a boat and in a children's playground. More than one of these have been created by Grid Iron, an Edinburgh theatre company that specialises in site-specific performances. For a company struggling to find the right conventional venue for its show, it might be tempting to imagine an alternative space would be an easier option, but that, says producer Judith Doherty, would be a mistake:

> It's by no means a straightforward way of producing theatre. If anyone thinks it is cheaper or simpler then, to my mind, that's wrong. Quite often we have to look at putting in running water, re-plumbing toilets, getting the electricity supply connected, putting in emergency lighting. It takes an awful lot of attention to detail even to make it look like you aren't there.

Edinburgh, with its rich architectural history, has many potentially fascinating locations to perform in. Staging site-specific shows, however, requires a responsive and flexible approach that can take some adjusting to. 'In the same way you shouldn't force a show into a site it doesn't belong in, you shouldn't force a site to behave in a way that it can't,' says Doherty. 'If there aren't enough fire exits, if there are too many stairs, you just have to accept it. As our director Ben Harrison always says, "You can't argue with a brick wall."'

A building might be perfect for your show, but if – as is likely – it has another use, you will need to find a way of allowing for that. When producer Kate McGrath put on *Must* by Peggy Shaw and

Clod Ensemble in the university's medical lecture theatre, it was the perfect place for a medically themed show:

> They have these amazing elephant skeletons outside and there's a whole bit in the show about this, so it was an amazing venue, but it is obviously used by medical students until 5 p.m. every day for lectures and dissections. The show was at 7.30 p.m. so we had to get in very quickly and we couldn't leave a lot of stuff because it was a public space and there are issues about insurance. So it's not straightforward using those spaces.

For more detail about working in non-theatre spaces see Chapter 6.

Student

It is as a student that many people get their first taste of the Fringe and, indeed, the stories of early sightings of future stars – from Emma Thompson to Matt Lucas – are legion. For many participants, supported by their college drama society or student union, it is simply a tremendous event to be part of, an exciting activity for the summer vacation. For those with professional ambitions, it is a valuable chance to develop performing skills in front of a non-student audience.

Although there are times when an actor will be spotted by an agent or a playwright will pick up a film commission, for the vast majority of students the Fringe is a chance to gain experience. 'It's playing in front of a diverse audience and working out how they react to you,' says Holly Kendrick of the National Student Drama Festival, whose first experience of the Fringe was as a 16-year-old working in the crew for Hull Truck theatre company. 'Doing a show seven times a week is a lot to ask of an untrained voice and body. It's mentally and physically difficult, so it makes you realise what it might be like.'

What the Fringe can provide is a kind of halfway house between the student and professional worlds, a chance to experiment and learn in a relatively safe environment. Kendrick says:

> I've seen companies develop in confidence and realise the direction they were going in was either right or wrong – and both of them being a very positive thing. It's also about networking and using more of the industry that's there, going to the Equity workshops, going to the Spotlight workshops, hanging around with Masterclass or us or Ideas Tap and using those things to meet people.

Theatre

When theatre fans complain about comedy taking over the Fringe, it rather suggests they are not satisfied with a choice of several hundred plays in a day. The rise of stand-up over the past twenty years means the theatre section is no longer the biggest category, but it is still vast and you need only factor in physical theatre, children's theatre and musicals to see how present the dramatic form is. That being the case, it is impossible to make any rules about the kind of theatre that proliferates. Not only will you find an example of pretty much any genre or subgenre you can think of, but you are likely to find certain plays cropping up in as many as five different productions in any given year.

Incidentally, if you do find you are not the only one to have chosen a particular play, don't panic. The Fringe is almost certainly big enough for all of you and, if you get in touch with your rival companies, you might even be able to make a marketing feature of the coincidence by encouraging audiences to see all of them.

Having secured the performing rights (see Chapter 8), you should aim to do the play you want to do and deal with the various challenges as you come to them. With a piece of serious drama, for example, one of those challenges is how to sell it. To a casual audience member, your tragedy about domestic abuse might seem less enticing than someone else's sketch show about speed dating. One solution is to take a different approach to marketing and reach your audience in other ways (see Chapter 9 for ideas). Doing the kind of show that goes down well on a Royal Mile stage might get you audiences – and if that's what you want, then great – but it won't necessarily make you artistically happy or get you the critical attention you feel you deserve. As we saw in Chapter 4, if you believe in your show, everything else becomes easier, so if you choose a show with a cynical eye to the market, you could live to regret it. In any case, audiences are unpredictable and if you try to second-guess what they want, there is no guarantee you will get it right. Better to do what you want to do than what you think you ought to do.

If you want to make your mark professionally and critically, however, you should bear in mind the high value placed on originality. When the late Allen Wright, arts editor of the *Scotsman*, set up the Fringe Firsts in 1973, it was to encourage new writing. So successful have the awards become, however, there are now almost too many new plays for the newspaper's reviewing team to see, especially when there are so many other demands on their time. The ethos of discovering the new has spread throughout the media, not least because new ideas make more interesting journalism. Every year you will read feature articles inspired by the themes preoccupying Fringe playwrights, and those themes will go on to set the agenda for the review schedules.

That means it is very hard to stand out from the crowd with a production of an established play unless it has a star-name actor, an intriguing track record from abroad or an interpretation of shocking originality. You are more likely to attract attention with an original idea. Not all audiences, however, are as hung up about the new as journalists, so if media attention is not your priority, you can put on anything from the Ancient Greeks to the modern classics with impunity.

All this should give you the idea that the type of show you bring matters less than your belief in it. As long as it is ready and it is the best you can do, your show can take pretty much any form. Yes, it helps if it captures the moment, yes, it helps if you understand the audience, but equally important is that you remain true to your artistic aspirations. The less you compromise, the happier you'll be.

In the next chapter, we'll look at venues; you should try to find one that suits your show, rather than shaping the show to fit the venue. This means holding out for the right conditions. If you cut corners, you could risk losing what was good about your show in the first place.

One last word about shows: do go and see as much as you can of other people's work. You'll never have a chance to see such a quantity, quality and diversity in such a short period again. At least, not until you come back next year . . .

6. The Venue
Enter Stage Right

ON ITS INCEPTION IN 1947, the Fringe took place in small and unconventional spaces. The International Festival had laid claim to the city's major theatres and concert halls, so the uninvited companies had to make do with wherever they could find. In the first year, that meant a YMCA theatre in South St Andrew Street, somewhere called the Little Theatre on the Pleasance, the now defunct Gateway Theatre on Leith Walk, the restaurant of the New Victoria Cinema on Clerk Street and, seventeen miles away, Dunfermline Abbey. They established a template that is little changed to this day. Hardly any Fringe performances take place in permanent purpose-built theatres. Unless you are appearing at the Traverse Theatre, the Stand Comedy Club, Dance Base or one of a small number of music venues, you are likely to be in a space that has a completely different function for the rest of the year. There are rooms in pubs, temporary tents, Masonic lodges, university classrooms and church halls.

Up to the 1970s, Fringe companies behaved as they would in any other city and occupied one venue each. As numbers rose, it became practical for a couple of companies to share the same space and perform at different times. That process continued so that today the majority of the 250-odd venues operate like multiplex cinemas, staging new shows in a choice of spaces every ninety minutes. Some companies do still get a venue all to themselves – local amdram companies, for example, might have a longstanding relationship with a particular theatre and, by definition, a company staging a site-specific performance will be somewhere unique – but in all likelihood, you will be performing on an artistic conveyor belt, sharing the same space with anything up to ten companies.

When a medium-sized city hosts a festival with 2,500 shows, something has to give. In Edinburgh, that something is almost always the conditions of production. If a venue is hosting eight shows between midday and midnight, it has to demand an inordinately fast turn-around time of each company. Trying to be as fair and efficient as possible, many venue managers rent their spaces in units of an hour or ninety minutes – and rarely more than that – making it expensive to present shows that are any longer. If you are a stand-up comedian who needs only a spotlight and a microphone, this is unlikely to be a problem. If, however, you are a band used to having a sound-check, a theatre company with a complex set or a dancer who needs space and time to warm up, you could find yourself making serious artistic compromises.

The immediate consequence is that backstage and onstage conditions are rarely what you would expect when performing elsewhere. Even in the better equipped venues, things will not be exactly as you would like them. 'You're sharing dressing rooms, lighting rigs, sound equipment . . . it's amazing what people accomplish,' says Christabel Anderson, the Fringe Office's head of participant services.

Surveying the market

It is through the Fringe Office that you are likely to begin your search for somewhere to perform. Venues register with the organisation, which provides participants with detailed lists of what is available. From www.edfringe.com you can download *The Fringe Guide to Choosing a Venue*, a document itemising all the available spaces with details of the typical programme, audience capacity, stage dimensions, get-in time, backstage facilities, disability access, technical equipment, box office, marketing and the standard financial deal. Many venues provide more detail on their websites, which you should take time to study. It is not the role of the Fringe Office to recommend venues, but it will help you narrow down your search. 'People come to us and say, "I've got to choose between C Venues and the Pleasance,"' says Anderson. 'We always say, we cannot make that decision for you, but we can talk you through the decisions.'

A call to the Fringe Office's venues and companies manager could save you a lot of time. So could paying a visit to Edinburgh the year before you plan to perform; seeing the venues in action and talking to the venue managers will give you a much fuller picture than downloading a form from the internet. This is not a rule only for first-timers: the year before *Ten Plagues* played at the Traverse Theatre, you could see playwright Mark Ravenhill, director Stewart Laing and producer David Johnson – with many years of Fringe experience between them – taking a break in the Pleasance Courtyard as they scoured the city for an appropriate space. 'It was at that moment that we decided that the only place to do the show was Traverse One – the only place we hadn't visited that day,' recalls Johnson later.

'Because of the temporary nature of the venues, you're not going to see the space working as a space outside of August,' says Barry Church-Woods, the Fringe Office's venues and companies manager:

It's a big investment, so we do recommend people come to Edinburgh, look for the venues that are programming a similar type of work, see what their technical capabilities actually are (rather than what they say they are) and check out the noise pollution and footfall.

Your choice will be informed by the financial package, the technical facilities, the location, the time slot and the venue's character and reputation. The more you investigate one venue's deal, the more attractive a rival venue might become. It is in the interests of your show that you explore the options and resist the temptation to accept the first offer that comes your way. 'A lot of people, particularly new companies, are just thrilled to have any venue,' says Church-Woods:

> But they should also be asking what support they'll get, about the venue's press office, their marketing campaigns, the infrastructure when you are in the building, how long your get-in is, how long your get-out is, if the company before you will be penalised if they run over and stop your show from starting at the advertised time . . .

As discussed in Chapter 4, the clearer an idea you have of what you want to achieve, the easier it will be to weigh up these factors and decide which venue is right for your show. Let's look at each aspect in turn.

Financial package

Most venues charge either a one-off hire fee or a box-office split, which means you share the net revenue from ticket sales at an agreed percentage, typically 60 per cent to the artist and 40 per cent to the venue. We will return to these deals in more detail when we consider budgets in Chapter 14 and it is important to have a clear understanding of what they are likely to cost you. Equally important is knowing what you will get for your money. With a straight hire, you would not expect the venue to provide media and marketing support, for example, nor would you expect to find a collegiate atmosphere among the other companies sharing the space with you. With a box-office split, the venue has a financial stake in your success (although you will probably have to pay a minimum guarantee) and is more likely to offer additional services.

Anthony Alderson, artistic director of the Pleasance, says:

> We take 40 per cent because we have to build the entire theatre from scratch, staff it with 600 people, pay all the wages and we do things with all the bells and whistles. You get a standard black-box theatre, fully working grid and sound system. We recharge things like smoke machines, radio microphones, lasers, moving lights . . . stuff that is out of the ordinary. We have a technician you can pay for or you can bring your own. We have a press office that works for everyone. You can buy hours of our street team or bring your own.

Whatever arrangement you have, you should read the small print to make sure you get the services to which you are entitled, while not paying for services you don't want. Keep your eyes peeled for hidden costs such as commission on ticket sales, the printing of tickets and entry into the venue's own printed programme. Equally, look out for hidden benefits: a venue, for example, might offer you a cut of bar sales or revenue from programme sales. 'You should make use of every resource your venue offers you and push them for more,' says producer Aneke McCulloch.

'Venues have become much more shrewd at protecting themselves,' says producer Dana MacLeod, who routinely works with companies in a dozen different venues:

> Their contracts guarantee their costs will be covered – the lighting the artists will be using, the technicians' wages, price per metre of a lockable storeroom or a percentage of table space to sell your merchandise on. The culture of the different venues and what people care about is very interesting. In

some, it's a one-and-a-half-page contract and it's all about the money and nothing else. In others, it's all about space – 'You cannot leave any instrument here and you can't leave any CDs there' – going into quite ridiculous detail. Others are much more altruistic and there are no contracts; it's just an agreement. Finding your venue is crucial. Because your venue is really your co-producer.

Just as a venue needs to trust in you, you need to trust in the venue. Running a venue is financially risky – a great amount of money is at stake and the upfront costs are high – and it happens occasionally that a venue, usually a new one, will fold before the festival has even begun. There is no certain way of predicting this, but it pays to be prepared. 'Be cautious about it and make sure there's a cancellation clause in your contract,' says Church-Woods.

The Fringe Society has a good track record of rehousing companies that have lost their venue in this way. A generous venue that steps in to rescue a company might even match the original financial deal, although it is unlikely to have the same time slot available or be able to do much about notifying audiences of the change.

That scenario could be preferable, however, to a venue running into financial trouble later in the festival and leaving you out of pocket. On the other end of the scale, there are successful venues, such as the Stand Comedy Club, that make a special effort to help performers. 'It's the best deal on offer for some people, not necessarily for everyone,' says artistic director Tommy Sheppard, sitting in his basement club on York Place. 'Because we are a commercial organisation with principles, we take the view that we should take the financial risk. So we take the financial burden away from the performer.'

In recent years, some Fringe entrepreneurs have found a way to sidestep the question of money almost altogether. Peter Buckley Hill's Free Fringe, the Laughing Horse Free Festival and Forest Fringe charge performers little or nothing and, in turn, the performers do not charge audiences (although they welcome donations). The system is possible because the venues, which are usually pubs, agree not to charge rent in return for getting increased custom at the bar, bringing as much as £10,000 across the month at a time of year when many people are being lured away to the many temporary bars around town. By 2011, Laughing Horse Free Festival was running 32 spaces in 15 venues and presenting over 300 shows and PBH's Free Fringe was operating on a similar scale.

Laughing Horse charges performers only a relatively small fee – around £40 – to cover administration, publicity and equipment hire. You still have to pay for your regular production costs, such as entry into the Fringe Programme, but saving upwards of £2,000 on venue hire can be very attractive. There is no administration fee for PBH's Free Fringe, but you are responsible for your own equipment, usually sharing the costs with the performers who are in the same room.

'We've been full – most days there have been people standing at the back,' says director and actor David Fynn as he drums up an audience for *Thunderer!* appearing at the Voodoo Rooms as part of PBH's Free Fringe:

> The capacity is 110 and we've not had an empty seat for a week. They've been very generous with their donations. We've been really lucky: we've not had to spend any money in our bank accounts because of the money from the pot. The writer gave us a bit of a budget that covered accommodation and travel, then the pot is good for spending money.

Appearing in the same venue, Sweden's Emil Lager and Sara Lewerth of Scandimaniacs performed *Take Me to Hollywood*, a physical theatre comedy. Choosing the Free Fringe, they say, meant risking £2,000 rather than £4,000. With an average audience of 60, they were on course to cover their £1,400 costs (mainly accommodation), although if they made more than that, it would quickly disappear. 'We tend to spend it on beer in the evening,' says Lager. 'We even went clothes shopping yesterday.'

Technical facilities

The combination of temporary venues and fast turn-arounds means there is tremendous pressure on technical presentation. It is, however, worth being vigilant and holding out for the conditions that best suit your show. 'There are so many options with venues that you should never compromise your work,' says Church-Woods:

> You see these people with beautiful three-hour pieces and they completely bastardise them to get them down to sixty minutes and then present them in front of the world's press. If your work is good and the venue manager has seen you and wants you, they will do everything they can to make sure you get the ideal conditions. Where it is important that you get a perfect black-out and excellent lighting, you can find it if you look hard enough and you ask for it. Generally, if they're not offering you something, it's about budget and not availability.

The best policy is to take nothing for granted and to double-check all your requirements with each venue manager you talk to. There might not be space, for example, to store your set and props, and even if there is, it might not be possible to guarantee they will be looked after. 'Don't assume there'll be a piano,' says Sam Gough, venue manager of the Edinburgh International Conference Centre, speaking at a Fringe roadshow. 'And don't assume you won't have to pay for a piano if they hire one.'

If you consider these questions at the point when you are looking for a venue, you could save yourself a headache come August. Draw up a checklist of your requirements – everything from the size of the stage to special lighting effects – and talk to venue managers about what they can offer. Ask them how much time you will get for your technical rehearsal and how fast will be the turn-around time between shows. Find out if the venue's technical crew will be working with you and, if so, how experienced they are.

'Think about the type of show you're doing and look at all the venue operators, because some of the spaces may suit your particular style better,' says Nick Read, head of hire and events at Northern Light, the Edinburgh-based stage equipment hire company:

Try to find a venue that is going to do more of your sort of thing, because the chances are the lighting will be set better and designed for your specific type of performance. For dance, for example, you often have a lot of side lighting that doesn't touch the floor because you get lovely shadows and it lights the people not the set. So for dance, you need space in the wings and lots of side lighting, whereas a comedian will probably have a small stage and a couple of spots on the front. A comedian probably wouldn't want to be in a dance space because they'll be paying for the venue with that lighting system in it. If you've got a venue that works already for you, you're half-way there because you're not battling against an impossible space.

Some things you can learn only from seeing the venue in operation in August. Eugene Downes, of Culture Ireland, recalls an internationally successful Irish show that got a slot in one of the major venues only to find the space was adjacent to a bar. 'It was a very delicate piece and the sound bleeding in from the bar area was very disruptive of the piece,' he says. 'It just didn't serve it. When presenters see the show in an unsuitable venue, you're not doing yourself any favours.'

A downside of the free festivals is that rooms in pubs generally do not have the technical specifications of a purpose-built theatre.

There may be no proper stage, it might be hard to get a blackout and you could be competing with noise from the bar. Laughing Horse Free Festival ensures each space has, at the very least, a mixer, two CD players, two microphones, general lighting, a backdrop and seating; and in a couple of venues, it has bigger stages and lighting rigs. PBH's Free Fringe promises a 'basic PA' and 'basic lights' and leaves it to the performers to provide anything else. You need to be confident your show will work in these conditions or be prepared to spend money on additional equipment.

You need also to make a level-headed judgement about the size of the room you want to play in. The bigger the capacity, the more potential to make money at the box office, but also the greater the likelihood of killing the atmosphere when tickets don't sell. 'The venue we were playing in held 150 people, it was a small venue, but it was full every night and that's nice,' says Martyn Jacques:

> It doesn't matter if you play to 1,000 people, which we do in big cities, or 200 people in a small city, the most important thing is it's full. It's a psychological thing: if the audience feel they're in a packed space, they get a sense of occasion, something special and there's an excitement. If you're playing in a half-full space it's horrible. In 2009, we got great reviews, everything was really good, but we were playing in a venue that held 320 people and it wasn't full.

Location

Although the very first Fringe included an event seventeen miles away in Dunfermline Abbey and, even today, shows go on in venues such as Rosslyn Chapel eight miles out of town, most activity is concentrated in a compact area in the centre. Edinburgh is a small place and it would be nice to argue that no venue is remote by the standards of a bigger city. Psychologically, however, a venue need only be a short way from the main flow of Fringe traffic to seem peripheral. Unless you have been in the city at festival time, it is hard to comprehend the significance of a few streets: a walk of fifteen minutes is all it takes to go from all-encompassing hubbub to a festival-free zone. This means the further away you are, the harder you must work to attract audiences.

In recent years, there has been a shift towards the south of the city, in particular the university-owned area around Bristo Square where the Pleasance, Underbelly, Gilded Balloon and Assembly all have major operations. Edinburgh has a phenomenal capacity to produce new venues and no doubt the energy will shift elsewhere in future years, but for the moment, this is where you will find the greatest numbers of interested audiences ready to make snap decisions about what to see. The further away you are from these crowds, the less confident you will be about drawing in passing trade.

There are no rules, however. If a venue acquires a reputation for a certain sort of work, be it contemporary dance, international theatre or world music, it will attract fans of that work almost regardless of its location. Equally, if people are intrigued enough by your show, they will come and find you. Claire Wood staged a production of *The Tempest* on a barge in Leith, a fifteen-minute bus ride from the town centre, and it sold out with an audience capacity of thirty. 'It didn't feel like a problem, but probably because we were so small,' she says:

If we had been bigger and been reliant on passing footfall, we would have really struggled. Having an unusual venue probably got people down to Leith. If we were just in the community centre down in Leith, nobody would have been interested.

To get a clearer idea, you need to see the venue in operation and to ask questions of your venue manager. Having found the perfectly located venue, however, you should not assume you can sit back and watch the audiences flow in. 'Select your venue carefully and don't get complacent if you think you've got the hottest venue in town: you need to work really hard every day,' says Aneke McCulloch, who produced *Controlled Falling Project* in the prime site of the Udderbelly. The only day the company didn't flyer was the very last day.

Time slot

Even if you secure the venue you want, you might not be able to get your ideal time slot. There is no science to choosing the best time of day to perform, but there are a number of factors you should take into account. First, it is worth getting a sense of what other companies do. There is a tendency for children's shows to take place earlier in the day, say between 10 a.m. and 2 p.m., theatre, dance and musicals are popular in the afternoon, and the evenings are dominated by stand-up comedy and music. This is a very broad generalisation – you will find sketch shows at midday and philosophical tragedy at midnight – but as it is what most companies choose to do, it should at least influence your thinking.

The battle for audiences is at its most intense in the evenings and it is a battle being won by stand-up comedians. In a recent festival you could see popular television names such as Ardal O'Hanlon at 7.25 p.m., Chris Addison at 8.20 p.m., Jimmy Carr at 9.30 p.m. and Mark Watson at 10.30 p.m. (but note, there are always exceptions: Al Murray played at 12.30 p.m. with the 'ultimate lunchtime pub quiz'). You can come to different conclusions about this depending on the nature of your show. If you are a comedian, you might deduce that most audiences for comedy are around in the evening and so that must be the best time for you to perform. If, however, you are relatively unknown, you could decide it is futile to compete against the biggest names on the comedy circuit and you would have more chance of attracting audiences and talent scouts earlier in the day.

A theatre company might use similar reasoning to aim for an evening slot, taking a gamble that it is more likely to attract an audience when there are fewer straight plays to choose from. There is merit in this argument, but there are other factors to consider. One is that the Fringe is not the only event in town and, in the evening, your audience might be drawn towards the Edinburgh International Festival which usually programmes drama at 7.30 p.m. or 8 p.m. Another factor is the difficulty of categorising audiences: a person who sees a straight play in the afternoon might be the same person who fancies something lighter in the evening, so might still miss your production.

There is no right or wrong answer, but although performing in the daytime would be box-office suicide in any other city, it is certainly not the case in Edinburgh. In a recent festival, you could see storytelling theatre by Daniel Kitson at 10 a.m., a piece of verbatim drama from Georgia at 11.35 a.m., Simon Callow doing a turn as Shakespeare at 2.30 p.m., a play about sex trafficking at 3.30 p.m. and the musical *Five Guys Named Moe* at 5.30 p.m. All of these had highly successful runs. 'Don't be offended if someone offers you a 4 p.m. slot,' says Church-Woods. 'That's a really good slot for theatre. You're not being insulted because you've not got a 7.45 p.m. curtain.'

Nica Burns agrees. 'For a theatre show and a young comedian, I would say avoid the 8 p.m. slot,' she says. 'All the big boys are performing somewhere between 7.30 p.m. and 10 p.m. If I was taking a young playwright, I would seek to perform between 4 p.m. and 6 p.m. A 6 p.m. slot is great because it doesn't compete with all the comedians and there's also the local audience, which is really important, because they can get to a show after work.'

That has also been the experience of comedian Nick Doody, who has always performed in the evening. 'In Edinburgh, as a stand-up, you want a time when people will have finished work,' he says:

If you're starting at 6 p.m. or earlier, you're losing quite a lot of your potential audience. You also don't want to be coming in too late, unless you have a very boozy offensive show and that's the vibe you want. If you're on at a prime-time slot, you will be people's tenth choice – and that's generous – but then you might also be the tenth choice because the first nine have sold out, which is also very likely if you're up against good-selling shows. It's not a bad thing for people to be in the Pleasance Courtyard, say, hoping to see Mark Watson but not able to because he's sold out, so then they say, 'Right, well, what else is on?' You sell a lot of tickets that way.

Because of the round-the-clock nature of the Fringe, you can also choose to perform much later than you would do normally. By around 10 p.m., you tend to see more theatre creeping in again. You will not be alone if you schedule your show for midnight. The later you start, however, the more likely your audience will be in the mood for a raucous night out, so you should consider how well your material would work, especially if it is in a venue known for its lively atmosphere.

One factor to consider is how much opportunity you have to flyer immediately before your show starts. Before a morning slot you will find the streets relatively quiet, which means you may have to rely more on flyering the previous day than on attracting passing trade. Similarly for a later show, you could find people have already made plans about how to spend their evening, so it could prove more profitable to flyer during the afternoon.

On a practical level, the time you are allotted by your venue includes your get-in and get-out, so if you have ninety minutes, don't assume you can do a ninety-minute show. Your venue is likely to penalise you if you over-run because of the inconvenience it causes to the companies that follow you and their audiences.

If only for reasons of efficiency, most venues will prefer you to do a full run. It is easier for them to deal with one company for three weeks than three companies for one week each. More importantly, there are also advantages for you. Yes, you have to raise extra funds for accommodation and subsistence, but your travel and production costs are likely to be fixed regardless of how many times you perform, so it could be a better investment to stay. With a longer run, you have the potential to build audiences on the strength of good reviews, to earn more at the box office and to be seen by agents and promoters. If you leave too soon, you can waste the momentum you have built up.

Brian Logan of Cartoon de Salvo experienced the drawback of doing too short a run when his company first played the Fringe in 2000 at Pleasance Two:

We were quite green, we had a bad time and we lost money. We did ten days and then another company replaced us in the same slot. That was partly because we couldn't afford to do longer. At the point at which we were building up momentum, it felt like the run stopped. So we went away with our fantasies that week three would have been a hit!

First-time producer Aneke McCulloch had similar misgivings when she came to book a run for Australia's *Controlled Falling Project* at the Underbelly. The company had a booking in France which meant it would not be able to play the first week of the Fringe:

I said if you can't be there the whole month then we can't do it. Ed Bartlam at the Underbelly said he knew what I meant but they'd had a few shows that didn't do the whole run and they'd sold really well. So I thought if he thinks it's still worthwhile, he's not going to waste his programming decisions, so we rethought and decided to do it.

Many companies perform every single day, others take one or two days off during the run, sometimes as part of a venue-wide policy. If you have a say in the matter, you need to weigh up the benefit of giving your performers a rest against the loss of income and should budget accordingly.

Reputation

Much is made about the open-access nature of the Fringe. A key reason the festival has flourished is nobody needs permission to perform. But look more closely and the picture is not quite so simple. Although the Fringe Society itself exerts no control over what, where and when you perform, the same is not necessarily true of the individual venues. Just because anybody can perform on the Fringe does not mean anybody can perform at, say, the Traverse, a publicly funded year-round theatre whose reputation rests on the artistic quality of its programme. 'The only thing we talk about for most of the year is the quality of the work we're putting on,' says William Burdett-Coutts, artistic director of Assembly, who first came to the Fringe in 1979 with a staging of *Paradise is Closing Down* by Pieter-Dirk Uys.

Such pride in the quality of the work is common among venue managers. 'I will not repeat the same show over and over,' says Karen Koren, artistic director of the Gilded Balloon, who has been running venues since 1985:

I'll programme the same performers, but not the same show. I want a very varied programme. I will not put on just one-hour stand-up. You want content with a beginning, middle and end, or you want pathos, you want something unique.

Laura Mackenzie Stuart, whose company Universal Arts runs the New Town Theatre, explains that programming is affected by three elements. 'One is the personal preference of what we would like to present,' she says:

Another is what's good for the companies as part of an overall programme. And third is what an audience is expecting to find from us. There are plenty we don't work with. The first thing is making sure people really know why they want to come and the second is whether we are the right venue in terms of the programme or the technical facilities that we've got. We probably take a quarter of what we potentially could.

When Alex Rochford was programme manager and producer at Assembly he estimated he received 700 applications for around 130 slots. Tommy Sheppard turns away roughly two in every three comedians for his 34 slots at the Stand Comedy Club. At the Pleasance, Anthony Alderson and his team have to whittle down 2,000 applicants to about 200. Programmers such as these are calling the shots and if you get through their selection process, you are already on your way to be taken seriously by audiences, promoters and critics. 'We try to get beyond the four big venues plus the Traverse and the Stand, but it's much harder to get noticed if you're not in those venues,' says Mark Godfrey, executive director of London's Soho Theatre, who scouts for work every year in Edinburgh. 'I would say you've got to choose your venue as well as you can.'

There is a similar pressure on reviewers. What they are looking for is very similar to what the venue managers are looking for – good shows by interesting artists – and the more they trust the venue, the more likely they are to go there first. 'The serious reviewers do tend to have to cover the programmes of the big main venues because they're the main focus of journalistic interest,' says Joyce McMillan, theatre critic on the *Scotsman*:

It is slightly difficult to get right away from the Traverse, Assembly, the Underbelly, the Gilded Balloon and Pleasance – these are the big venues that dominate the Fringe and it's difficult not to feel you have to cover all of their stuff first before you can start looking at other stuff. If you're not discussing their work, you can't be involved in the conversation about what's going on on the Fringe.

In his book *So You Want To Be a Theatre Producer?* (NHB, 2010), which is pitched at the professional market, James Seabright argues 'you should aim to get your show programmed into one of the five that make up the unofficial "Premier League".' He is right to say Assembly, Gilded Balloon, Pleasance, Traverse and Underbelly 'dominate the attentions of audiences and media alike' – if only in terms of quantity of shows, how could they not? – but the picture is a little more complex. Just as there are shows that do poorly at the better-known venues, so there are others that flourish in a first-time space. The creative energy in the city is fluid, word of mouth travels fast and venues can make or lose reputations quickly. 'You keep your ear very close to the ground and if you hear of anything that's happening in a smaller venue and getting a big buzz, you rush along and check it out,' says McMillan.

So although it makes sense to consider your venue's profile – and to pay particular attention to its reputation for presenting the kind of work you are doing – it need not be the decisive factor.

Lyn Gardner, theatre critic on the *Guardian,* says:

> If you were in London, you would know that you were either going to the West End or to the London fringe and, just from where it is, you would have a sense of what it is you might see. In Edinburgh, everything is a constant surprise. There is no answer to the question of where it is you should be. I try and get a spread of things at different venues, but if word gets out that there's a run of five good shows at the Pleasance Dome, then that's where you go. It's a difficult ecology to break into, but there are ways of breaking into it; the other venues do get shows, they do get audiences and they do get reviews.'

If there is a venue you particularly like, you should be creative about endearing yourself to the management. 'One person put a £1 coin on the back of their script and said, "Please!",' laughs Koren. 'Or they send me lollipops; lovely little things like that.'

All of this assumes you are beholden to the venues, but they need you as much as you need them. Well-known performers – or simply companies with shows that sound exciting – can find themselves courted by several venues, each trying to outbid the other. In such a case, you need to keep a level head and weigh up the pros and cons carefully.

But whether you are chasing the venues or the venues are chasing you, it makes sense to register your interest with several of them, ideally in January, so you can choose the one that suits you best. 'We recommend, certainly for first-timers who don't have a body of work to back them up, that they make their first round of applications to six or eight venues,' says Church-Woods:

> Let them all know that you're applying to different spaces, because they do speak to each other. Then you can start negotiating and if you've got three different offers, you can go for the most favourable slot or most favourable financial deal or the reputation of the venue.

There can be more to the package a venue offers than money. If it has a particular philosophy, such as a commitment to treat companies fairly, to encourage creative exchange, to be environmentally friendly or to be accessible to people with disabilities, it might appeal to you more than a well-located space with a favourable financial deal. Talking to venue managers and other artists in advance will give you a sense of whether you will get on with each other. 'We talk about a sense of community a lot and reinforce that among the artists right at the start,' says Forest Fringe's co-director Andy Field. 'Once the programme is confirmed, the first thing I do is send a group email out, with everyone's emails included, and say "Hi" to everyone. That is one of the values. It brings the artists together and improves the work through that dialogue.'

The Laughing Horse Free Festival and PBH's Free Fringe also try to engender a collective spirit among participants, but they are still establishing their reputation in the outside world. Both organisations have produced acclaimed shows – in 2010 for the first time a Laughing Horse Free Festival comedian, Imran Yusuf, was nominated for the Edinburgh Comedy Awards' newcomer gong – but audiences, press and promoters find it hard not to conflate the words 'free' and 'worthless'. Doing a free show might get you audiences and might cover your costs, but it might not get you credibility. 'Our rooms are not necessarily wonderful,' Peter Buckley Hill tells the audience at a Fringe roadshow in Edinburgh. 'But the whole thing works in a moneyless way. We take great pains to stop people thinking we are rubbish, so we don't book rubbish.'

Nica Burns confirms his claim. 'We've seen a lot of very good work on the Free Fringe,' she says.

> It takes a lot of the hot-house pressure off and that's a massive advantage. I went to see a comic on the Free Fringe and it was a really terrific show. As I came out, I was thinking, 'If I had been sitting at Assembly, what would I have paid for this?' There were loads of people going out and he was standing there with his hat and I put a tenner in. Half way up the stairs, I suddenly heard, 'A tenner! Wow!' because the performer felt that he had been judged as a pro. I was giggling all the way home. It made me feel good and I certainly had £10's worth of entertainment.

In this way, the free venues are reviving the let's-do-the-show-right-here spirit that characterised the Fringe in its formative years. They are a healthy antidote to the TV-name commercial exploitation that has been a feature of recent years. 'You can get everything you want by doing it for free that you can by doing it paid – and the opportunity of playing in front of big crowds,' says Alex Petty, who worked in conjunction with Peter Buckley-Hill for three years before developing the Laughing Horse Free Festival separately from 2007. He estimates his central venues routinely attract audiences of between sixty and eighty at any time of the day. Perhaps 20 per cent of those will have turned up simply to see a free show, but the majority will have made a more considered decision. Donations average somewhere between £1 and £2 a head but the downside is that, having made no financial investment in advance, audiences feel less obliged to stay if they are not enjoying themselves.

There is another downside. 'It's another kind of struggle with the Free Fringe because we don't have the big Underbelly or Pleasance name,' says Sara Lewerth of Scandimaniacs, who had a successful run in PBH's Free Fringe at the Voodoo Rooms. Her stage partner, Emil Lager, agrees: 'The negative aspect is that it doesn't sound as good. Reviewers don't want to come. People say, "Oh, you're doing the Free Fringe, your show must be really shit."'

Lewerth and Lager were generally happy with their experience, but performing for free does seem to change the relationship with the audience. 'If people think it's not what they expected, they'll just walk out,' says anthropologist Mark de Rond, who is studying the effects of pressure on Fringe comedians.

> You need to cope with that. People will feel free to heckle, because often it's in a pub and they've had a few drinks and they hang out at the back and think it's part of the fun. It can be very off-putting for somebody trying to put on something quasi-serious.

Even for the free festivals, however, reputation is important. With its tag line of 'putting the alternative back into the Fringe', Laughing Horse has done a lot to redress the perceived imbalance at the commercial end of the Fringe where television stars draw large mainstream audiences. At the same time, like any producer,

Laughing Horse has a reputation to protect and shapes its programme to give audiences as good an experience as possible. This means a free festival is not the same as a festival free-for-all. 'The Fringe is an open-access festival and I believe fully in it being a festival in which anyone can perform,' says Petty. 'But we do select as much as possible so we've got the best acts we can find.'

Running your own venue

If you cannot find the venue you want, if your show needs a very particular space or if you have an entrepreneurial flair, then taking charge of your own venue is a possibility. Take a look at *The Fringe Guide to Running a Venue*, one of the excellent downloads at www.edfringe.com, providing a thorough breakdown of what is involved. In a city with 250 venues – and potential for more – one of them could be run by you. 'My advice is to find a space to do it and have a reason for doing it,' says Andy Field, co-director of Forest Fringe:

> Mark Ravenhill says he started writing because no one was writing the kind of plays that he wanted to be in. It's the same thing here: if there's no opportunity in Edinburgh for you to do what you want, then you've discovered the perfect opportunity to make a venue of your own.

As with putting on a show in someone else's venue, you need to do your research. 'The first thing would be to get experience working inside a venue, not just during the Fringe but in the run-up, to see what the conversion process is,' says Laura Mackenzie Stuart of Universal Arts. 'It's very easy to arrive for staff training the day before the Fringe starts and all these places have been magically converted. You leave at the end of the run and have no concept of what it takes to put it all together.'

Having got your head round the finances, you will understand the importance of keeping costs – especially rent – to a minimum. The idea of finding a venue with a peppercorn rent might sound fanciful, but producer Dana MacLeod says it can be done. 'Often the way I've sold it to landlords is that it's shining a light on a site that is about to be developed,' she says:

> For example, Shrub Place at the top of Leith Walk, when No Fit State Circus was looking for somewhere, I had a chat with the landlord of the site and I happened to know he was fairly arts-sensitive. I said it would be great profile for him if a fantastic Fringe venue appeared and everyone would know where that site was.

For her third play, *Hot Mess*, Ella Hickson, who writes, directs and produces her own shows, had exclusive use of a bar area in the Hawke and Hunter nightclub. 'I chose it very carefully,' she says:

> It's closed all day and we rehearsed in the space for a month. No get-in, no get-out. They just wanted publicity for their venue. Because it was empty, there was no one in there. They get a few people at the bar before and after the show and they still open it as a club in the evening. You can go to any nightclub in the city and say, 'It's closed, I can make you more money than you're currently making.' It's so easy. People think it's harder than it is.

Hickson had found a venue that was geared up for public entertainment. In the case of site-specific work, the challenges can be greater. A couple of months before the Fringe starts, Cora Bissett is standing on the pavement at the top of London Road. She has decided to stage her play *Roadkill* in a real-life private flat; it is about sex trafficking and she wants to do it in the kind of place where an African girl might find herself forced into prostitution.

117

Right now, she is waiting for the landlady to give her a tour of the apartment. It is a risk, because the place she chooses will determine the character of the whole production. The landlady arrives and the viewing is successful. A few weeks later, *Roadkill* becomes a multi-award winning hit.

'It is difficult,' says Bissett, once the run has ended:

> You have to go through a lot of legal hoops and licensing hurdles to make it happen. If it's just a gimmick, I would say just use a theatre. There's a vogue for site-specific work and that's very exciting, but I would say you should have a very clear reason why. Is it really specific to your piece? Is it really serving your story? If not, you're probably going to waste a lot of energy, money and time making it happen.

As soon as you move into an untried space, you should take nothing for granted. Even if you don't need to make major changes such as the installation of a new power supply or the introduction of fire doors, both of which are perfectly possible, you will encounter many minor problems. You can find yourself installing fire exit signs, rewiring elderly fuse boards or discovering you cannot black out the windows. 'I worked harder on putting it all together than anything I've worked on in my life,' says Claire Wood, about her production of *The Tempest* on a barge in Leith:

> Normally, the venue would give you a plan of the space, what electricity points were available, what lights were already hanging, what lights you could bring in, what sound desk was available, what time you could get in for your technical rehearsal and what time for your performances, but here, all of that was up for negotiation.

Even when working in a park with *Decky Does a Bronco,* Judith Doherty of Grid Iron found there were lots of rules and regulations.

And even when staging *The Devil's Larder* in an out-of-hours Debenhams, she could make no assumptions. 'We had to make sure that building could still be a multi-floored department store during the daytime and be safe,' she says:

> That was a massive undertaking. You would think they would have all the fire extinguishers, fire escapes and emergency exit lighting you'd need, but never take anything for granted. Some of the measures that we have to take as theatre practitioners to make the public safe are way more constraining than a bar, a shop or even a tourist attraction.

Once you think you can cope with these challenges, you need to get the City of Edinburgh's public safety department involved. Malcolm Kennedy, who is responsible for public entertainment licensing, is a pivotal figure in this respect, so much so that he won a *Herald* Archangel in 2010 in recognition of his work. With a background in building control, he took the job in 1982 when his predecessor showed him how to license venues. Every year, he and his team have to get round all 250 venues on the Fringe in addition to those in the other festivals. 'I license the venue and have no jurisdiction over the show,' he says. 'Every production has to do its own risk assessment and send it in to my colleagues in the fire department to make sure it complies with them.'

As a basic requirement, he expects a venue to have toilets, at least two means of escape (for an audience capacity greater than sixty) and, as a rule of thumb, space for one person per square metre. It must also have emergency lighting, seating attached together in groups of four and a floor that can take the weight of the lighting rig. There is, however, room for manoeuvre as long as you can demonstrate you have taken health and safety seriously. 'Even the British Standard which recommends the amount of knee room there should be between rows is only a recommendation,' he says:

If the participant has a better idea then we will talk about it. We start off with the premise that it's your gig, how are you going to make it safe? If you want to have the audience in total darkness being harangued in Icelandic by a mad monk – which has happened – well, basically there was nothing to go on fire, it was not pitch dark so you could always see where the curtain was to be able to escape, so it wasn't unsafe.

Judith Doherty recommends becoming as knowledgeable as you can before you talk to the health and safety officer:

You want to prove you've taken steps to understand what you need to do and to come up with solutions, because then already they're thinking, 'Well, they're serious about what they want to do and they respect the fact that we need to be safe.' Sometimes rules seem too stringent, but if you have shown that you understand why they're there and how you can achieve things, then there will be room for manoeuvre.

As well as Malcolm Kennedy and his team at the City of Edinburgh's public safety department, you have to consult the Lothian and Borders Fire Brigade and quite often the City of Edinburgh's environmental health department if there is a lot of noise or if you are serving food. 'It's always good to be proactive,' says Doherty:

It's better to make an unnecessary phone call six months in advance and to make sure you've got all the forms and you know all the departments you should be hearing from. It's much less work for them to stop you doing something wrong in advance than to have to give you that twenty-four hours to get it all right. They really want all the shows to open. Edinburgh is a really special environment. We've toured site-specific shows to different countries and cities, and because this council is so geared up to almost everything becoming a performance venue, it's a lot more straightforward and they're a lot more open-minded about it.

Doherty's view is borne out by talking to Kennedy. Dispelling the image of the pedantic health-and-safety official hell-bent on shutting down anything that conflicts with the regulations, he says the ones he enjoys assessing the most are site-specific venues and those never designed for public entertainment. However willing he is to find a way for venues to work, sometimes nothing can be done to make a building safe. To perform in a second-floor tenement flat, for example, would be allowable only if the stairway was fire-proofed with one-hour fire resistance and all the doors, including those of neighbouring apartments, had half-hour resistance.

It is rare for a show to be cancelled because of health and safety concerns, but the council is vigilant about ensuring companies keep to the terms of their licence. Having passed a venue, Kennedy's team makes return visits during the festival to check nothing has changed. Sometimes a company will be tempted to add extra seats if its show is selling out; it might still be safe, but the council needs to be told. Sometimes someone might put a gel over a fire exit sign to stop it being so bright, rendering it less safe in the process. 'If it's totally unsafe, I get in touch with my licensing section to say they're in breach of their conditions of licence and they get in touch with the police to say they're now operating without a licence,' says Kennedy. Needless to say, that is an outcome you should do everything you can to avoid.

7. The Accommodation
Rooms for Improvement

YOU WOULD THINK IN a city that doubles in population during August that finding accommodation would be a major headache. Two factors mean it does not have to be. The first is to do with the city's housing stock. For the rest of the year, Edinburgh is home to a large student population whose absence in the summer makes available a lot of communal flats – plus university halls of residence – that are an ideal size for many Fringe companies. The students leave at the end of term, the landlords make improvements in June and July, then everything is set for the Fringe influx in August. In addition to this are many hostels, hotels and guest houses, which may be within your budget for a shorter stay, as well as the homes rented out by those local residents who choose to take a summer holiday elsewhere. Even at peak periods, the city's hotels have not been known to rise above 98 per cent capacity, so nobody should be turned away.

The second factor is geographical. Unlike many British cities, Edinburgh is designed for people to live centrally. Even on the tourist trap of the Royal Mile there is plenty of private accommodation alongside the shops, bars and hotels. It is a city of tall tenements, where people live closely together. This means many Fringe performers end up living within walking distance of their venues and hardly any will be more than a short bus journey away.

More likely to give you a headache is cost. Many Edinburgh landlords take advantage of the increase in demand by charging high rents in August, making living expenses a major part of your budget. The Fringe Office estimates the cost of renting is at least £100–£150 per person per week and that might still require sharing a room. As a nightly rate, it is much cheaper than a guest house or hotel, but for even a small company it can add up to thousands of pounds. 'If someone is coming to the Fringe for the first time they ought to try and befriend someone in Edinburgh that they can stay with,' suggests Tommy Sheppard of the Stand Comedy Club. 'The biggest single cost is probably going to be accommodation and if you can get a floor or a couch to sleep on, that's going to help enormously.'

That is not possible for everyone, of course, and some find themselves taking drastic measures. 'I met some students who were living in a caravan six miles away – and walking in because they couldn't afford the bus,' says Holly Kendrick of the National Student Drama Festival. You can see how this might happen, but you should try not to go down the same route; even if you can put up with the inconvenience, it is unlikely to be in the interests of your show. 'It's the one thing you don't want to save on,' says Sam Gough of the Edinburgh International Conference Centre. The stresses of performing are great enough without the additional hassle of living in out-of-the-way or substandard accommodation, whether that be putting up with the weather and inconvenience of living in a tent in a peripheral campsite or sharing with strangers in a hostel.

It is the one time of year when you will really value your privacy, home comforts and the chance to wind down. Indeed, some performers value these things so highly they go to the opposite extreme. Comedian Nick Doody knows people who rent two flats: one for themselves and one for their family. 'It seems ludicrous until you understand what it can involve,' he says. 'You can be doing a show that finishes at 7.30 p.m., so technically your day is finishing at 8.30 p.m., but it's not at all. You then have to go and be seen by as many audiences as you can at all the late-night shows, some of which go on as late as 3 a.m. or occasionally later.'

Just as you would with any rented accommodation, make sure you know if there is a washing machine, if bedding and towels are provided and if there are any extra costs for use of gas and electricity. In the era of the mobile phone, your company might not miss a landline, but this being the era of the laptop, they are likely to demand Wi-Fi. If your flat does not have all mod cons, you need to do your research into local launderettes and internet cafes.

Keeping everyone on side

If you are coming as part of a larger company, you should talk in advance about your ideal living arrangements. Would you like the whole company to live together in the same apartment? It is likely to be the cheapest and most practical option and it could be great for the ensemble spirit, but it could also make things worse when the inevitable tensions arise, especially if you are sharing bedrooms. Working, playing and living together for three weeks can be tremendous fun, but it does mean there's no escaping each other. By contrast, living separately could be lonely. You could have a similar debate about how near or far from your venue you would like to stay. Whatever you decide, it is in everyone's interests for the whole company to be comfortable. 'If you're bringing actors up, you have to be able to give them their own room, because they're here for the best part of a month,' says director Renny Krupinski, who works with professional actors. If, however, budget accommodation and sharing are the only way you can afford to come, you should explain this in advance. 'Make sure your cast understands what the deal is,' says Kath Mainland, chief executive of the Fringe Society.

One way to keep company tensions in check and spirits high, suggests producer Chris Grady, is to follow the lead of Three's Company and rent an extra bed space. 'They would offer the bed space to their mates for free to come up and spend two or three days at the festival in return for helping them do a couple of hours of flyering,' he says. 'So that throughout the festival they were getting fresh blood, people for whom Edinburgh was still exciting and the rain was a novelty. That really helps.' Take care to choose your friends wisely, however. You should prioritise those who wash their own dishes, keep the noise down and don't start drunken rows at 3 a.m.

Economising

Renny Krupinski inadvertently did something similar when, having booked well in advance to save money, he found he had rented two more rooms than his company needed. In his case, it turned out to be a financial benefit. When friends came to Edinburgh, he charged them £25 a night and clawed back nearly £1,000. Before you try this yourself, double-check you have the landlord's permission and that it is in the terms of the lease; as long as this is the case, there should be no obstacle to subletting. Indeed, the festivals would not function as they do were it not for students and other tenants subletting their property.

There are other things you can do to try to cut costs. One is to turn to the Fringe Office. Although it does not get directly involved in sorting out accommodation, it does collate a register of flats and rooms for rent and will send it exclusively to Fringe participants on demand (email participants@edfringe.com with 'accommodation register request' in the subject line). The merit of this list, updated weekly, is that landlords are not permitted to advertise rooms that cost more than a certain amount – in 2010 it was £150 per week per person. That could still impose a sizable dent on your budget, but the cap is a way of discouraging extortionate rates.

It also pays to follow Krupinski's lead and book accommodation early enough to get last year's prices or early-bird discounts. If you do not manage that, the Fringe Office recommends you start looking for accommodation as soon as you have confirmed your venue. You should also explore the market. 'If you're willing to walk a bit further it can be cheaper,' says Christabel Anderson, the Fringe's head of participant services. 'Don't take the first offer – shop around.' Bear in mind, though, that moving out of town could turn out to be a false economy if it introduces other expenses. A single bus fare in Edinburgh is £1.30. A company of ten taking two journeys a day would spend £182 a week on fares and potentially even more on eating out. That's before you start accounting for late-night taxis. Spending the same amount of money differently might allow you to stay more centrally.

Landlords and agents

As an alternative to finding accommodation directly, you can call on the services of a dedicated letting agency. There are several in operation, including Factotum Letting, which has a twenty-five-year history of renting property ranging from one-bedroom flats to seven-bedroom mansions. Fringe participants get in touch from as early as the autumn, but the company's work starts in earnest from about March – not least because that is when student property starts coming back on to the market – and reaches a peak in June. 'July isn't too late to book, but it can be a little bit fraught, particularly for the larger flats,' says director Chris Boisseau.

> It's fine if you just want a two-bedroom flat and you're not that worried if it's not absolutely bang central. Then you're in a buyer's market because there's always property left over that isn't let. If you do need a bigger flat, then you need to book early.

> As with your venue, if you can see your accommodation in

advance, you will have a good idea of what you are signing up for. If you get a friend to search for you, make sure they understand what you need. Boisseau says:

> One of the nightmares we have – and it particularly happens with bigger names – is that they employ someone to go round and make trouble. It's not a good idea. We show them all the flats, which is great because it avoids that problem of choosing flats sight unseen, but if the person doing it has no idea, you're better off putting your trust in the agent. An agent will straight away say, 'What age are the group?' and ask all the pertinent questions.

If budgets are tight, he reckons it is always worth negotiating with an agent or a landlord, but he also sounds a note of caution.

> If you negotiate down, you end up with a crappy flat. So you need to know what you want and then negotiate. The difficulty we get into is that we're constantly knocked back on price and inevitably they end up with a flat that's not as nice and then they complain.

In the time Factotum has been in operation, the whole market has become more disciplined and problems are relatively rare. 'You hear some ghastly stories,' Boisseau says, explaining that when the company started it was with the simple intention of marrying landlord and tenant:

> In principle it was all fine, but then you'd get landlords misbehaving and tenants misbehaving. Landlords would demand twice the money on the doorstep, tenants would leave the place trashed. It worked through a process of osmosis to demand good behaviour from all parties concerned. Our terms and conditions have altered as people try and find a

way round them. But the horror stories are so few and far between now compared with twenty-five years ago.

Today, most disputes are to do with cleanliness – either the tenants think the landlord has saddled them with a dirty flat or the landlord thinks the tenants have left it messy. In an era of mobile phones, there are fewer rows about the phone bill, but more conflict about failing or non-existent broadband. And if you are thinking of having a cast party, do remember Edinburgh is a city of tenement flats and people are living at close quarters. 'We do get calls from neighbours at 4 a.m.,' says Boisseau.

It's not as bad as it used to be. A lot of people are coming in after a show at 2 a.m. or 3 a.m. and they sleep through till 12 p.m., so the flats aren't really used much. We had one American lot who were young kids who were quite rowdy, but again they were reasonable when we phoned them up and said, 'Oi! Go and apologise to your neighbours tomorrow,' and they duly did and made the peace. Take them round a bottle of wine. So much is resolved by people actually talking to each other.

With such a competitive market, there are occasionally more serious issues. There are, for example, the unscrupulous agents who will take an inordinate cut of the rent for themselves and pass on relatively little to the landlord. And there are the scammers who advertise a bogus flat and disappear with the money. Boisseau says:

One thing about using a reasonably reputable agent is to avoid arriving in Edinburgh to find the person you gave the money to doesn't own the flat at all. You also need to make sure the agent doesn't give all the deposit money to the landlord. We hold all the funds as an agent, so if the ceiling collapses the tenants are going to get their money back and if the tenants leave a mess, there'll be money coming out of the deposit.

For these reasons, you should make the effort to study your contract, he says:

It's the old, old thing: 'I can't bear reading the small print,' but it's what we survive on and if ever there's any bother, we retreat back to our terms and conditions.

Once you've decided what balance you want to strike between saving money and staying somewhere convenient and once you've agreed with your company about the kind of accommodation you would all like, you should survey the market and hold out for the best deal. Book early to save money but not so early that you restrict your choice of properties, read your contract and be a good neighbour.

8. The Law
Rights and Wrongs

Accessibility

THE FRINGE SOCIETY TAKES accessibility seriously and wants to exclude nobody from the world's largest arts festival. In Scotland, the Equality Act 2010 ruled that people providing services must not treat disabled people less favourably than non-disabled people and must make reasonable adjustments to their premises to allow disabled people access. The makeshift nature of many Fringe venues means such adjustments are not always 'reasonable', but you should make every effort you can to make your show accessible to all. This includes backstage and on stage as well in the auditorium. For up-to-date advice email the Fringe at equalities@edfringe.com.

Contracts

'You can tell a venue manager who has been doing it for a long time because the contract will have every single clause in it,' says Barry Church-Woods, the Fringe Office's venues and companies manager. 'It'll be a six-page document. Other people are using a cut-and-paste template from the internet that might leave the venue open to the company doing this, this and this.'

The key thing to remember is a contract works in both ways. It gives you not only rights, but also responsibilities. Your venue has to keep its side of the bargain and you have to keep yours. For this reason, it is important that you read and understand the small print.

It might seem an unnecessary chore when you are busy rehearsing your show, but if you find yourself fighting over box-office returns in September, you will wish you had paid more attention. If you have concerns over certain clauses, you should raise them with your venue manager. It could be they have copied the contract from the internet, as Church-Woods suggests, and never thought to question it themselves. Your input could strengthen the contract for both parties, so you should not be afraid to query it. The same is true of any other contact you sign, such as with your landlord or letting agent.

As well as the contract with your venue, you should also consider a contract between the members of your company. This may seem inappropriately formal, something that flies in the face of the friendly and collegiate spirit of your company but, like a pre-nuptial agreement, it could save a lot of recriminations later on. It may be your company's intention, for example, to devise a play, perform it for three weeks on the Fringe, then disband. If, however, that play catches the attention of a producer who wants to send it on a spring tour, you could find yourself dealing with thorny questions about ownership. Some of the actors might not be available in the spring, but as co-creators, they could have a case for claiming writers' royalties for subsequent performances. That, in turn, could lead to disagreements. Better to sort it out with a contract from the start.

'Who owns the work if you're devising it?' says Church-Woods:

> If you take elements of it on tour, is it a different show? You need a strong agreement written about what the future of the work is and what sections of the work can and can't be used. Does the company own the entire thing or do four different people own parts of it? There's no right or wrong answer; the recommendation is to think about what you're doing.

Copyright

In the UK, an author (or their estate) retains copyright for an original written, theatrical, musical or artistic work for seventy years after the end of the year they died. This applies to artists including novelists, poets, playwrights, lyricists and composers. Musical recordings are also subject to copyright, but in this case, it applies for fifty years after the end of the year the recording was made (the law is changing and this is likely to be extended to seventy years). Additionally, performers have rights over recordings, films or broadcasts of their performances.

If you intend to perform a work that is still in copyright, you must get the written permission of the author or their representative, most likely a literary agent or publisher. You need to get specific permission to perform the show on the Fringe, even if you have been given permission to perform it somewhere else, and will probably have to pay a copyright fee. It is one of the terms and conditions of signing up to the Fringe Society that you will have the rights to perform your show.

This is also the case if you want to use material that is still in copyright as part of your show – for example, the screening of a scene from a film or the reading of a poem.

Publishers such as Samuel French routinely check through the Fringe Programme when it is published and complain if companies have not requested a licence to perform their work. Such instances are usually resolved amicably with a payment of the requisite fee, but occasionally companies are forced to cancel the show altogether. A copyright holder could have good reasons for turning down your request to perform their work: perhaps they have already granted exclusive rights to a commercial production or perhaps they are protective of an author's legacy and do not like your proposed reinterpretation. Whatever their reasons, you do not want to find yourself without a show to perform, so you should secure the rights as soon as possible.

See 'performing rights and music' below.

Journalists, including photographers, and publishers also hold copyright over their work. Copyright exists in a newspaper's layout and typography, as well as in the words and pictures themselves. That means if you want to photocopy a favourable review or reproduce it on a website, you should seek permission of the journalist and publication. In all likelihood, they will give permission, but you should not assume it. You do not need to seek permission, however, if you are using less than a substantial part of a work. The law does not define 'substantial part', but quoting a sentence or two of a review is accepted practice in the arts world, and provided it is accurate and properly attributed, should not be a problem.

For more details see the Intellectual Property Office website: www.ipo.gov.uk

Exceptional performance requirements

For the most part, you can rely on your venue manager to deal with the City of Edinburgh Council's licensing department and to ensure the proper theatre or public entertainment licences have been granted. If, however, you want to include unusual effects, such as pyrotechnics, trapezes over the heads of the audience or cannons firing confetti, these are likely to go beyond the remit of the licence and you must tell your venue manager, who will have further discussions with the council.

Malcolm Kennedy, who is responsible for public entertainment licensing at the council, says:

It's much easier to tell the fire department that you're going to use candles or any other kind of naked flame before the event rather than for them to find out through anecdotal evidence. We've got special forms that everybody has to fill in when they apply for a theatre licence; they also have to fill in a production form for the fire brigade. They also want to know what kind of fabrics are being used, whether they're flame retardant or made of shredded paper or anything like that.

Fly-posting

In Scotland fly-posting is illegal and controlled mainly through the Town and Country Planning (Scotland) Act 1997 and the Town and Country Planning (Control of Advertisements) (Scotland) Regulations 1984. In an effort to crack down on illegal fly-posting, the City of Edinburgh Council environmental department has introduced 900 sites where, for a fee, you can display your posters legally. They are run by City Centre Posters, which also has the job of removing posters placed without permission on walls, trees and street furniture. Contact the Fringe Office for up-to-date information.

Foreign Entertainers' Tax

If, for tax purposes, you are non-resident in the UK, you should submit an FEU8 form to Her Majesty's Revenue and Customs which will calculate how much, if any, foreign entertainers' tax you are liable to pay. The Fringe's participant services department will assist you through this process. Details at www.hmrc.gov.uk/feu/feu.htm

Health and safety

Under the Health and Safety at Work Act 1974, venue managers have legal duties to ensure you have a safe working environment. Equally, it is your responsibility to abide by your venue's health and safety procedures. Make sure you know what those are.

Illicit or controversial content

Until 1968, the Lord Chamberlain's Office was the official state censor of theatre in the UK. Edinburgh's Traverse began its life in 1963 as a theatre club partly to be exempt from the Lord Chamberlain's rule. Since 1968, however, live performance has been free of censorship although, like anything, it is still subject to the rule of law. It is possible for a performance to be prosecuted for being obscene, indecent or slanderous or for inciting racial hatred or encouraging terrorism. The contract with your venue is likely to include a clause in which you confirm the show is not in breach of the law and that you will be financially and legally responsible if it is. If in doubt, consult the Fringe Office for advice.

Licences

Your venue has to have a licence from the City of Edinburgh Council and will be inspected both before and during the festival. You must comply with the conditions of this licence. This means seeking permission before you make alterations such as adding seats, changing the seating arrangements or extending the stage. Acting without permission puts the safety of your company and the audience at risk. In theory the safety department could revoke the licence and notify the police. Keeping everyone informed is the wiser option. 'They could still be safe, but we just didn't know about it,' says Malcolm Kennedy.

Licensing laws

To sell alcoholic drinks, your venue must have a licence from the City of Edinburgh Council. It will have conditions about the hours and days that alcohol can be sold and the people who can buy it, as well as regulations to do with environmental health and weights and measures.

Performing Rights and music

With the rise of the internet, a generation has grown up who take file sharing and illegal downloading for granted. Even legitimate services such as web-based radio stations can create the impression that music is free. For this reason, performers do not always realise that using music in a performance can have a cost. 'It doesn't occur to them that playing music in front of people who have paid might be an issue,' says Christabel Anderson, the Fringe Office's head of participant services. 'That's not good for the people who create it.'

The Fringe Society works closely with PRS, formerly known as the Performing Right Society, which collects royalties on behalf of songwriters, composers and publishers when their work is used in public. It has negotiated a good-value bespoke deal for Fringe companies. You fill in a form in advance and the Fringe Society takes the money off your ticket income at the end of the festival. If you do not fill in the form, the Fringe Society will automatically charge you the full 3 per cent so, unless you want to spend time claiming a refund (and you have only two months after the end of the festival to do so), it makes sense to be upfront about what music you are using. See www.prsformusic.com

If you are performing an opera, ballet or musical with a specially composed score, this is considered a 'grand right' work – that is one where several copyrights apply, covering libretto, score and choreography – and you need to get permission directly from the rights holders. See copyright above. If you are using recorded music, you have to pay a PPL licence in addition to PRS (see below).

Phonographic Performance Limited (PPL)

Phonographic Performance Limited licenses the use of recorded music and distributes the revenue to the original performers and record companies. If you play recorded music in public, you will be infringing copyright unless you have a proper PPL licence. Where PRS (see above) covers copyright for lyrics and composition, PPL covers copyright for performance and recording. The Fringe Office will update you on how to make payments. See www.ppluk.com

Public liability insurance

In some cases, your venue manager will have a policy insuring against damage to property and injury to employees and the public. They may, however, insist that you take out public liability insurance yourself. *The Fringe Guide to Doing a Show* recommends that you do so. It also suggests 'adding an indemnity clause that allocates the risk to each party' and continues: 'While it is common for the venue to be indemnified against claims or losses arising out of your use of the space, take care that only those costs directly related to a claim or loss can be deducted from your box office takings.'

Smoking on stage

Since 2006, smoking in indoor public places has been illegal in Scotland. This includes smoking on stage and applies equally to herbal cigarettes. In England, exceptions can be made for artistic reasons if smoking is integral to the plot, but that is not the case in

Scotland. If your show involves characters who smoke, you need to find a way round it, whether that is using unlit cigarettes, fake cigarettes, mime or rewriting. Individuals who smoke in a public place are liable to a fixed-penalty fine of £50, while the venue manager is liable to a fixed-penalty fine of £200 if they have not taken reasonable action to prevent someone smoking.

Visa restrictions

Immigration regulations can change at any time, so it is important to check you have the most up-to-date information. If in doubt, consult the Fringe Office's participant services department.

Under current British law, the Fringe is considered to be 'permit free' for performers. That means actors, comedians, singers and musicians from overseas do not need a work permit and they enter the UK as an 'entertainer visitor'. Whether you need to apply for that status in advance depends on your nationality. It is the same system as visiting the UK as a tourist: some nationalities must apply for a visa in advance, others can enter freely. If requested, the Fringe Society will issue a letter to confirm you are performing.

'We have very few instances of people being refused,' says Christabel Anderson. You do have to be careful about timing, however. You cannot apply for a visa more than three months in advance, but if you leave it too close to your date of departure, there might not be enough time to process your application. The sooner you apply, the better. 'You do need to think of it in weeks rather than days,' says Anderson.

More complicated is if you are coming from outside the European Union with the intention of working in the UK. This applies to bar and catering workers, front-of-house staff, technical crew, flyerers and publicists. All these people require a work permit and will need an employer, most likely a venue, to be a sponsor under the UK's points-based visa system. 'It's not impossible, but it's never been that easy, even on a volunteer basis,' says Anderson. Further detail is available at www.edfringe.com

Working with animals

To work with animals on stage you need the permission of the City of Edinburgh Council and you should make a request as part of your venue's application for an entertainment licence. You need to follow guidelines laid out by the Scottish Society for the Prevention of Cruelty to Animals. The council does not allow animals to perform in any of its own venues, including school halls, and imposes conditions on private venues.

Working with children

It may be necessary to apply to your local authority for an entertainment licence if a child under school-leaving age is taking part in your show. This is to protect the child's education and welfare. If adults are working with children, they might need to be assessed by Disclosure Scotland or the Criminal Records Bureau. See www.disclosurescotland.co.uk and www.homeoffice.gov.uk/agencies-public-bodies/crb/

9. The Marketing Campaign
Sell, Sell, Sell

As with most aspects of this singular festival, marketing on the Fringe operates by its own rules. As publicist Claire Walker points out, 'You wouldn't stand on the Strand flyering for your show in the West End,' yet on the streets of Edinburgh, it is not only normal to see performers plugging their own shows, it is actually expected. In such a competitive climate, nobody is assured of an audience. Your show might be the most important thing in the world to you, but to your prospective punter, it is just one of dozens they could choose between. To get them to make the right decision requires all your powers of persuasion.

The good news is that many people are in town specifically to see shows. They are up for new experiences and willing to be persuaded your production should be on their list. In other cities, your marketing campaign might be directed at people who would otherwise stay at home, go for a meal or see a movie, sometimes people with no experience of live arts at all. In such cases, the tone of your marketing campaign would reflect that. In Edinburgh, although it is good to remember those people as well, it is safe to assume there are audiences out there who will be unfazed at the idea of seeing a site-specific comedy at 2 p.m. or an intellectual tragedy at 1 a.m. Your job is to let them know you are there.

The bad news is that, willing though they are, those audiences are finite. There are certainly a lot of them, but not quite enough to go round. A small percentage of shows do sell out, but most companies have to accept that even a half-full auditorium is an achievement. When you are up against 2,500 shows, competition for audiences is intense. Once again, the message of Chapter 4 rings loud: the more you believe in your show, the more committed you will be to persuading people to see it.

The audience

First let us consider what your audience might be thinking. Matthew Somerville, a web developer from Birmingham, could hardly be called a typical Fringe-goer, but he is exactly the kind of person you would want in your audience. When his sister moved to Edinburgh, he saw the opportunity for a cultural holiday. Willing to see everything from stand-up to street dance to musical theatre, he spent twenty-seven days on non-stop Fringe shows. By the time he returned to Birmingham, he had clocked up 136 – an average of 5.04 shows a day – and reckons he did it for less than £1,500. He describes his approach to selecting shows:

> I would take the programme with me if I was going to London for work and I would read through it on the train. The pictures were more important than I would have thought. When you're picking through 2,500 of them, if the picture grabbed your attention, then you'd be more likely to choose the show.

He found himself more receptive to titles the earlier they appeared in the programme, although he was unimpressed with those that shoved their way to the head of the alphabetical pile by beginning with the letters 'AAAAA'. The title alone could influence his decision making, for better or worse, and he found adverts often caught his attention. He took advantage of cheaper preview tickets at the start of the festival and booked some shows he thought would sell out later in the month, but otherwise left his schedule empty. Every evening, he would pick a morning show and plan the following day around it. 'I'd say, "Well, I'm at the Pleasance, so is there anything at the Pleasance soon after that finishes?"'

He went along the Royal Mile a few times and made a note of interesting flyers, which were sometimes instrumental to his decision making. 'In the queue for the Gilded Balloon, on the penultimate night of the Fringe, I got a flyer for Bec Hill – she was flyering the queue herself – and on the last day she was the last thing I saw, so that worked.'

The Fringe Programme

Somerville is unusual in the number of shows he saw, but he is typical in the flexibility of his approach. Every day, Edinburgh is full of floating voters, each of them open to persuasion that your show is the one they should see. As Somerville demonstrates, the Fringe Programme, with a print run of around 400,000 and twice as many unique web hits, is where your marketing campaign starts. 'It is the most used way to find a show,' says Christabel Anderson, the Fringe Office's head of participant services. She is thinking not only of audiences, but promoters, agents, programmers, editors and critics. This is your first chance to hook them and also your first chance to put them off the scent. Get it right and audiences will be more receptive to the subsequent marketing you do; get it wrong and you'll be playing catch-up.

Think, first of all, which section of the programme you want your show to appear in (the choice is: cabaret, children's shows, comedy, dance & physical theatre, events, exhibitions, music, musicals & opera, and theatre). As a general rule, do not try to buck the trend. The comedy section, for example, is the domain of stand-up comedians and sketch shows and not normally of funny plays. If you list a funny play under comedy, you might attract an audience looking for a laugh, but you risk being overlooked by the theatre audience – and that is more likely to be your core market. The Fringe Office's advice is to categorise your show according to form not content: a musical goes in the musicals & opera section even if it includes some dance.

Next, if your company is coming together purposely for the Fringe, think carefully about your name. If you want to be taken seriously, you should probably not call yourselves the Time Wasters Theatre Group or give yourselves the kind of punning title that is mildly amusing in March and positively grating by the time you are handing out flyers in August. Similarly, a memorable and self-explanatory show title will be easier to sell than something vague or obscure. The Fringe might seem a long way off at the time of the programme deadline, but decisions you make now affect everything that follows.

This is especially true with your forty-word entry (the forty words includes the title). These are the first words many people will read about your show, so you need to get them right. 'The forty words are very influential to me,' says Joyce McMillan, lead theatre critic on the *Scotsman*. 'Over the years, with experience, I've become quite good at reading between the lines of those blurbs to see what's good and what's not. One of the things I've noticed is you cannot waste your time trying to be funny. You have to make it crystal clear what your show is about.'

If you make exaggerated claims for your show or try to seem something you are not, the audience will almost certainly see through your deception. Being truthful is much easier. Miriam Attwood, former media manager at the Fringe, says you can't fall back on the idea that sex sells, for example, when you are competing against genuinely sexy burlesque shows. 'Trying to sell anything on the wrong kind of theme isn't going to help because audiences have got that elsewhere,' she says.

Take some time to look at a previous edition of the Fringe

Programme, noting the kind of entries that grab you and those that do not. Keep an eye open for the phrases that crop up repeatedly; if every other show claims to be 'innovative', 'unmissable' or 'hilarious', the reader will not be able to distinguish one from the other and the words will be wasted. If you avoid hyperbole and focus on your show's genuinely distinguishing qualities, you give people something to go on. That means being precise. You have too few words at your disposal to allow digressions, fancy poetic phrases, ego trips and in-jokes. People want to know what you are doing and why they should go. Make it easy for them. Use short sentences, familiar vocabulary and informative phrases. Refer also to the *Fringe Programme Production Style Guide*, downloadable from www.edfringe.com, which standardises spelling and punctuation in the interests of clarity and consistency.

Words and pictures

At the same time as focusing on your forty words, you should start thinking about the other marketing material you will need. Write your copy to three different lengths – perhaps at 60, 100 and 120 words – which you will then have ready to use in any publicity produced by your venue, on the longer entry on www.edfringe. com and on your flyers. The wording can also feed in to your press release (see Chapter 10). In this way, your marketing message will be consistent and each element will reinforce the others.

The same principle should apply to your artwork. The trick is to come up with a striking image and use it repeatedly. The more someone sees it – on adverts, posters, sweatshirts, underwear (it happens), newspaper articles and flyers – the more they will associate it with your show. If you change the image, they are less likely to make the connection with what they have previously seen. 'Once you see something three times, you begin to recognise it,' says Attwood. 'If you've seen that blood-splattered image of four cartoons for a sketch show in the comedy programme in June, then a member of that troupe comes up and gives you a flyer in August and you see their poster outside a venue, you will associate those things as one.'

Since 2010, every entry in the Fringe Programme has had a picture, so at an early stage, you will need to decide on an image that will be strong enough to carry your marketing campaign from start to finish. It should be arresting in itself and able to work at every size from thumbnail to poster. In many cases, your show will not even have gone into rehearsal at the time of the programme deadline, so you could be taking a leap in the dark when dreaming up the imagery to sell it. Don't be too worried about this. There should be some relationship between the tone of your image and the tone of your show, but beyond that, let the marketing work at bringing in audiences and don't fret if it is not a literal representation of the performance. As long as your marketing is not misleading and as long as your show is good on its own terms, nobody will complain if the two do not quite match up.

If you can, get your designer to come to rehearsals and to talk through your ideas; the more information you provide, the more creative the process will be. To help your show stand out from all the other shows, your flyer must stand out from the other flyers, your poster must stand out from the other posters, and your sweatshirt from the other sweatshirts. Channel the creativity you put into your show into the way you present it to the world. At the same time, you shouldn't feel obliged to emulate comedian Jim Smallman who had the title of his show tattooed across his stomach at considerable personal pain. 'The kind of image you need here is like hard news,' says publicist Liz Smith. 'What people are looking for is something to stare at – it's got to be clear, concise and it's got to say it all. It's the same thing with poster images.'

For more suggestions see *The Fringe Guide to Selling a Show,* downloadable from www.edfringe.com

Adverts, posters and flyers

At this stage, you might also take out an advert in the Fringe Programme – again using the same image and design style – and might consider an advertising campaign for the coming months. There is no shortage of publications eager to take your advertising, from daily newspapers to dedicated festival magazines and, increasingly, websites. Taking out a single advert is unlikely to be of value unless it is part of a coherent marketing strategy. To be effective, you probably need to take out several adverts, using them to reinforce the message of your flyers and posters. One advert in isolation is likely to be lost in the deluge of Fringe-related information.

A full-blown advertising campaign, then, could be an expensive business, one that would be easier to justify if you had more to sell than just your run in Edinburgh. 'There's no real point in advertising unless you have an objective which is beyond selling tickets for the Fringe,' says Tommy Sheppard. 'John Moloney is a case in point. He hadn't done the Fringe for ten years, he was only in a small room and didn't need to advertise for the sake of that. He sold enough tickets without it. But what was important for John was to be able to say, "Look, I've got a new show, I'm still here, I'm available." So he was putting himself on the radar for the industry.'

The official Fringe billboard sites around town are dominated by enormous posters of big-name comedians. In all likelihood, they are there not simply to sell tickets in Edinburgh, but to raise the performer's profile for the rest of the year. The agencies putting up these posters have sizeable budgets and go to considerable efforts to keep them visible. If you put your poster on top, don't expect it to be there for long. 'Posters have a half-hour lifespan,' says Marlene Zwickler and she is not entirely exaggerating. The Fringe Office estimates over 40,000 posters are stuck to its special flyer pillars on the High Street. Placed effectively, however, a well-designed poster – typically A3 size and 115 gsm weight – can help people recognise your show. Companies print between 100 and 500 copies and spend some time asking shops and local businesses as well as Fringe venues if they would mind displaying them – many refuse, but many enjoy being part of the festival atmosphere and are happy to oblige. Fly-posting is illegal and can land you with a fine.

There is still plenty of time after the Fringe deadline to print your flyers but, given the image will be the same, you should be thinking about design from the start. Don't cut corners: the less professional your marketing material looks, the less competent your show will seem. The advice of Marlene Zwickler, of MZA artist management, is to commission a good quality photograph or illustration and not to clutter the front of a leaflet with information (save that for the other side). 'It has to engage people and they need to get a flavour of what you're doing,' she says. 'Kai Humphries is a happy-go-lucky comedian, so we used a fluffier kind of font; with Daniel Sloss, we invented something that looked like a logo because he's a teenager; with Craig Hill it's the kilt because we always try and convey that it's going to be an hour of crazy fun.'

When printing flyers choose a decent weight of paper – say, 300 gsm – so they stand up well in display racks, make sure the ink will not rub off on people's hands and order them in sufficient quantity to avoid more expensive repeat print-runs. To help the environment, you should request sustainably sourced paper. There are a number of printers that specialise in Fringe work (some are listed on the business services directory at www.edfringe.com) and will be able to talk to you knowledgeably about what you need, as well as delivering direct to your venue. Prices vary considerably according to printer, paper weight and quantity – printing gets proportionately cheaper the more you order – so it is worth shopping around for quotes.

Ticket-buying patterns

We will return to the job of flyering later in the chapter, but first let us consider some other ways in which Fringe marketing differs from what you might be used to elsewhere. One of these is to do with the pattern of ticket sales. The central Fringe box office does not open until the launch of the programme in mid-June and at that stage, it tends to be the bigger, better known names that sell. In the first week of opening, the box office experiences an initial surge that tapers off until the festival approaches. Unless you have a particularly strong marketing angle, it is unlikely that audiences will have identified your show among the hundreds to choose from, so there is no need to panic if your sales are sluggish. Your friends and family may have booked to see you, but maybe few others. 'The top ten comedians will sell out for most of the weekend performances, but they'll still have tickets available for their weekday performances until people start coming up to attend the Fringe,' says José Ferran, the Fringe's box office manager.

Ferran observes that many of his regular customers will start off with tried and tested names – and in Edinburgh, that can mean names who have a good track record on the Fringe, even though they have little profile elsewhere – before taking a punt on a small show that has caught their attention. It means you are likely to start the festival with a good deal of uncertainty about how you will sell, but also a strong sense that everything is still to play for. Even once the festival is up and running, it can be hard to be sure of a pattern. 'On a Friday, you can sell 9 tickets; on a Saturday, you can sell 109 tickets and sell out the room; then on a Sunday, you can be back to 60 tickets,' says Alex Rochford, former programmer at Assembly.

The Fringe is a dynamic market that allows you to change strategy quickly if circumstances change. As long as you hold your nerve, all is not lost if you suffer a bad review or poor sales. 'If things aren't going as they should be, we'll review how we're marketing them,' says producer James Seabright:

The great thing in Edinburgh is you can go out and find an audience for anything any day; it's just a question of knowing where to find them. It becomes easier for us when we've got other shows to cross-sell through. Sometimes it's about doing discount tickets or taking a different tack with the flyering, such as identifying successful shows that would potentially appeal to a similar crowd and targeting their audiences, or committing some time to the Half-Price Hut where bargain hunters are in plentiful supply. In terms of emergency marketing, that's always much more effective than trying to print an advert somewhere or get a review.

Word of mouth

What is heartening for those on a low budget and perplexing for those with a big budget is that in Edinburgh, you cannot be certain that money will solve any of these problems. A big act cannot do without a substantial marketing budget, but that does not mean a substantial marketing budget can be guaranteed to work. 'You are not going to sell 800 seats a night in Edinburgh unless you are a big star or you have the most ridiculous marketing budget,' says Rochford. 'But then I know of people who had a £12,000 marketing budget and it did not translate into sales even in a relatively small room.'

Charlie Wood, co-director of the Underbelly, agrees:

You can spend a lot of money on advertising and marketing and, in the end, that can mean nothing. You can spend tens of thousands of pounds on advertising, have a really slick campaign, but if the show is not good enough and if you don't get good reviews and if the audience don't like it, you can't manufacture hype.

If they do like the show, it can be different. With the musical *Five Guys Named Moe*, which had 1,000 seats to sell every night in the McEwan Hall, the Underbelly spent the kind of marketing money Wood is talking about. In this case the investment paid off. 'If the show hadn't been any good then that money would have been lost,' he says. 'But the marketing still helped to build it up, because unless people have seen a poster or an advert, even if you have word of mouth, it will go into the back filter of their brain.'

At the other end of the scale, you can take advantage of the number of dedicated Fringe-goers in town to target your market directly and make the most of word of mouth. 'The joy of Edinburgh is that if you can get a few people in there, the word of mouth can spread pretty fast,' says Chris Grady, who set up the Music Theatre Matters awards. 'It is possible to do little publicity, but do it very carefully, so that word of mouth generates an audience of the right people who are going to be useful to you.'

Word of mouth is both persuasive and free, so how do you go about generating it? The first thing is to get people to see your show, even if it means giving away tickets. Take the example of *Slava's Snowshow*. Today this piece of elegiac clowning is a hit that has been repeatedly revived in mainstage theatres around the world, including a Christmas run at London's Royal Festival Hall at the end of 2011. When it first played on the Edinburgh Fringe in the early 1990s, however, it was an unknown quantity. 'I remember going down to London to see *Snowshow*,' says Liz Smith, a freelance publicist who for many years ran the Assembly press office:

> I thought it was the most incredible thing I'd ever seen. But then in the first week it came to Assembly, it hadn't sold and it wasn't being talked about. We absolutely papered it for the first four or five days and then the following week you couldn't get a ticket.

Fraser Smith had a similar experience in 2005 when he was

151

running the Gilded Balloon press office and had to sell an unknown comedian called Tim Minchin. 'Nobody knew him,' says Smith about the man who would go on to win the Perrier Best Newcomer Award:

> We did the same. We sold out the first five shows, but we were giving away the tickets to the right people. We went round and targeted who we thought would be his audience and they went and told other people and it worked.

He admits it is quite scary to give away your first 300 tickets' worth of income, but if the alternative is playing your first performances to audiences of three or four, you have nothing to lose. Whatever size your audience, you should take the chance to encourage them to tell their friends.

Smith's point about targeting the right audience is crucial. There is no point bringing in people who are likely to be indifferent or hostile towards your work. The same is true whether you are papering the house or selling tickets at top price. To help you in targeting the right audience, Chris Grady has a simple technique:

> Sit down and write a detailed analysis of the six people you want on the front row of your show. Give them a name, an age, a profession. Ask what do they do, why are they there, what do they want out of the experience and how did they find out about it? You lead yourself slowly to working out how to promote the show to get to those six people. If what I'm after is a journalist to be there writing a nice piece about the show, then what I do with my marketing is completely different from if I'm looking for a fantastic student crowd to whoop and holler.

Let them talk

Your attempts to generate word of mouth should not stop there. Everywhere you go, every person you meet, is an opportunity to talk about your show. Make sure everyone in the company carries flyers with them, ready to spread the word with every encounter. Better still, find ways of getting other people to testify on your behalf. Edinburgh is full of people asking each other what they recommend and they will always be more persuaded by a non-partisan opinion. Miriam Attwood, former media manager in the Fringe Office, says:

> If you have a good show, other performers that you meet will start to come to see it and then, if they're flyering, they'll say, 'Here's my show and here's an honest recommendation.' By the end of the festival there'll be thirty or forty shows that are selling out because performers from companies they'd never met before have been giving people their tips.

It is one reason for inviting fellow performers in your venue to see your show. Some venues, such as Hill Street (until 2011) and Forest Fringe, make this communal approach part of their philosophy. 'When Little Bulb, or whoever, are out in bars, they're talking to their friends, saying, "You should definitely come and see this other show, it's great,"' says Andy Field, co-director of Forest Fringe. 'It happens organically, but we do encourage them to see each other's shows and consider themselves as part of this community.'

It was a principle that worked for *Invisible Atom* by Novia Scotia company 2b which was championed by David Leddy, a Glasgow-based director who was also staging a show at Hill Street Theatre. Whenever Leddy bumped into the journalists and opinion-formers he knew in the Scottish media, he would rave to them about the show. Because it was not his own show, his recommendation carried weight. Keith Bruce, arts editor of Glasgow's *Herald,* took him at his word, saw the show and fast-tracked it for a *Herald* Angel Award. 'The quality of the work is what shines through: that's what people are attracted to and that's what makes them talk,' says *Invisible Atom* producer Sarah Rogers.

You will be hoping to reach ordinary Fringe-goers, but on the Fringe, there are some people whose word of mouth is especially influential and therefore especially worth cultivating. A critic, for example, might not have space to write about your show, but if they see it and like it, they will talk to a lot of people – many of them influential in their own right – and their opinion will spread. The same is true of producers and programmers. Comedian Nick Doody says:

> My agent pointed out that Kate Copstick, the *Scotsman* comedy critic, constantly talks to people. It's impossible not to hear an opinion if you're talking to her. You could do a lot worse than have someone who knows about the subject bigging you up every chance they get. It's like Twitter; it's an endless cross-pollination of opinions and experiences.

To kick-start this process, the Fringe encourages companies to opt into a two-for-one ticket deal for two days at the start of the festival. It is a way of generating interest while the festival is still gaining momentum and is particularly popular with local audiences, a market that should never be underestimated. You can also choose whether you would like to be part of the Friends of the Fringe scheme. In return for making a charitable donation to the Fringe Society, audiences can receive special offers – typically two-for-one deals – on selected shows. You have to weigh up the potential advantage of being seen by an interested audience – an audience that could go out and tell their friends if they enjoy the show – against the possible loss of giving away a ticket that someone else might have paid for. Given that relatively few shows sell out, it is a risk many companies think is worth taking.

A recent innovation is a smartphone app called Theatre Ninjas. A couple of hours before your performance you can upload free tickets which users can claim using a secret code. It brings you an audience that you wouldn't otherwise have attracted, creates a better atmosphere in the venue and increases the chances of word of mouth spreading. See www.theatreninjas.co.uk.

You can also reach Edinburgh audiences via the Cheaper Fringe for Locals website (www.cheaperfringe.com), which allows you to offer discounted tickets for some or all of your performances.

Flyering

And so to that most visible of marketing strategies on the Edinburgh Fringe: flyering. With so much paper printed (anything from 5,000 to 20,000 flyers per show) and so much effort gone to, can it really be worth it? The evidence is that it can. There was, for example, a student at the University of Edinburgh who was employed to flyer for a comedian, an established name in the USA but unknown in the UK. It felt like a thankless job until she realised the hard way quite what a difference she was making. In the middle of the festival, she locked herself out of her flat, leaving all the flyers inside. She was left with no choice but to take the day off. That's when she had to explain to a perplexed comedian why he had suddenly been faced with a single-figure audience.

In the Fringe Office, Miriam Attwood gives the example of a very successful cabaret act returning to the Fringe for a third year after enjoying two sell-out runs and high-profile press coverage. Despite the acclaim and despite every review being at least four stars, they were still out flyering every afternoon before their show and frequently contending with single-figure audiences. 'They had to get out and push that buzz,' she says.

The sight of people handing out flyers, especially in key areas such as the Royal Mile, the Mound and Bristo Square, is one way the people of Edinburgh know the Fringe has started. It is probably not what you are used to when performing anywhere else, but if you do it properly, it works. 'If you can go up to someone on the street and engage with them, they'll trot off and buy a ticket,' says publicist Claire Walker:

> You are the best advert for your own show. And as soon as you see five people that you spoke to for five minutes sitting in the audience laughing, you recognise the benefit of it and you'll go out and do it again.

It's early evening on the Cowgate and Marlene Zwickler is standing outside the Underbelly handing out flyers. You might think someone with her own artist management company would have enough on her plate, but that is not the Fringe way. 'You're not too big to flyer,' she says:

> Unless every seat is sold, what are you doing sitting there having a drink and the show hasn't gone up yet? It makes a difference. You will get those extra four sales that will make it a nicer house for your client to work in.

It would be wrong, however, to give the impression that flyering is some kind of marketing panacea. Not only does it require discipline, energy and the kind of self-belief we discussed in Chapter 4, but it works better for some shows than others. Neil McKinnon, the Fringe's head of external affairs, asks:

> Are you flyering in the right place at the right time? How are you flyering? Good flyering is about more than standing there handing out flyers to as many people as you can. What really works is engaging with the public and giving them some sort of sense of what the show is about.

Before launching into a flyering blitz, think clearly about the nature of your show and the kind of people you want to attract. If it's a lively, family-friendly musical taking place in the early afternoon at a central venue, then you would probably do well pitching to the crowds on the Royal Mile. If, on the other hand, you are performing a troubling drama about racism, you need a different strategy. Producer James Seabright says:

> It's about thinking about where that audience might be and going to find them rather than thinking everybody's on the Royal Mile. You should do as much thinking in advance as possible, so when you arrive in Edinburgh you know that these shows are going to be good crossovers. Also you can get in touch with other companies and arrange flyer swaps or mentions in programmes: that sort of recommendation and cross-pollination is what the Fringe is all about.

Anthony Black, doing a one-man play about global economics, felt it was pointless competing with the exuberance of the Royal Mile and concentrated instead on the area closer to his venue, Hill Street Theatre in the New Town, and the Fringe's Half-Price Hut on the Mound Precinct:

> I figured out a way to do it that maintained my pride and allowed me to be who I am. The game is not to give away as many flyers as possible, it's to sell tickets, so I'd rather have ten conversations than give away a hundred flyers. Does it convert into sales? Absolutely. You can elbow-grease your way into an audience here. We saw tangible results when we flyered.

Drumming up a crowd

It is a damp morning in the final week of the Fringe and Zoe Walshe is standing on the Royal Mile with a book on her head. She is promoting *The Fever Chart*, a play by Naomi Wallace about conflict in the Middle East. The company from the University of Warwick has been drawing audiences of between 20 and 40 at the Radisson Hotel, a short distance down the Royal Mile, in a room with a capacity of 55. Attendance has been increasing each afternoon and the company, subsidised by the university drama society, has already broken even. 'Maybe something we're doing on the Royal Mile has been working,' says Walshe. 'It's raining now and it's still a bit early, but after 12 p.m., the whole place is storming and there are a lot of bums you can get on seats.'

Nearby, her colleagues are bouncing a massive see-through ball filled with feathers, a visual link to the feathers on the poster. An actor with a book on his head is playing the guitar. Walshe says:

Firstly, it's a gimmick to get people's attention. If you have a book on your head and you smile, people double-take at you so you have the moment to sell the show. It's a serious piece of visual theatre about people caught in the crossfire, so we had to think of a way of selling that on the Royal Mile. You do need gimmicks. The feathers and the books are all part of the aesthetic, so we've tried to pick out the memorable bits of the set, something that will grab people's attention, and then you have to try and sell the show as quickly as you can.

Sometimes the ball can work too well. It tends to attract children and Walshe has to explain that a political piece about Middle Eastern conflict wouldn't be for them. The key thing, she says, is not to hand out flyers indiscriminately but to engage in conversation:

You want audiences who are actually interested. I've met

quite a few people who have been to the Middle East or have personal connections to the issues there and they have been very interested to have a chat, come to the show and give us feedback afterwards.

Having learnt from a previous run on the Fringe, the producers have been careful not to overstretch the company, asking them to commit to three hours' flyering before lunch, plus a half-hour session in costume immediately before the 3 p.m. performance. Walshe again:

You need a cast who are really up for it. You need people who are confident, enthusiastic and also happy about the show. You have to have an incredibly organised producer, so everyone knows their flyering hours and when they're doing what.

Using your wit and imagination need not be expensive to be effective. Magician Paul Daniels was struck by one example in particular in a year when he was performing:

I bought one of those four-wheeler two-pedalling bicycles, put my publicity all around it and employed a couple of students to ride around. But the best bit of publicity I saw was much cheaper. I really took my hat off to the attractive girl who slipped a note to me as I was walking up the Royal Mile. It really looked handwritten and it said something like, 'I know you might think this is forward of me, but I saw you across the street and I've been following you because I feel strangely attracted to you. Would you like to meet tonight in such-and-such a venue?' And it was the venue for the play she was in.

Sometimes you can hit on a brilliant marketing ruse by accident. The King's Players from King's College, London, spent a dispiriting couple of weeks flyering for a production of *Waiting for Lefty*, a political drama by Clifford Odets at the Pleasance. Nobody seemed interested in the flyers and it was hard to keep the energy levels up. Then one sunny day, when the cast were all in sunglasses and wearing their brown overcoats from the show, they just happened to stand in a line. When they raised the flyer, with its close-up of a woman's lips, up to their own mouths, everything changed. Company member Daniel Smith says:

> Suddenly, tons of photographers came and took photos. We realised the picture of the lips and the sunglasses actually made a striking image. That gets a lot more attention for you. People know of your play just through the image. We didn't realise at the time how good the image could be when we used it to get people's attention. We've had so many people coming up to our line of flyerers, holding it up to their own face and having photographs taken. We never offered to do that, they just wanted to do it.

It turned their trips to the Royal Mile into an enjoyable experience, although not one without its frictions:

> We've had a couple of issues of people not turning up, which has created a lot of drama. Living in a little flat with twelve people for a month causes tension anyway and something like flyering increases that. Some people will leave early to go and see shows whereas others will be completely committed and stay for the whole time. If we had done it again, it would have been good to have some kind of rota – 'Today you can have a day off flyering' – so there's no argument about it.

Taking a short walk up and down the Royal Mile in front of the Fringe Office, we find a woman in a flat cap sitting on a picnic blanket, a man dressed as Elizabeth I, a youth theatre group carrying trays of barbiturates, a woman in a 1920s flapper dress, a company in dinner jackets, someone in a toga and a woman looking like a torture victim sitting on a bed with mouth gagged and hands tied. All are trying to catch attention in a way that links to the theme of their shows. They are not only competing with each other for audiences, but also with street theatre performers who draw big crowds all through the day.

It does help if your show – or some aspect of it – lends itself to outdoor performance. Director Renny Krupinski observes the way week-one enthusiasm turns into week-two indifference as people grow tired of the bombardment of flyers. On the other hand, when his actors demonstrated their fighting skills – and Krupinski is a professional fight director, so they were good – people would actually request flyers:

> Doing very bad singing on the Royal Mile doesn't help you, nor does just saying, 'Come and see my show.' You have to do something that is a little spectacular, something that creates a crowd. We do two or three minutes of punching, get a crowd, flyer them, then stop, leave it for five minutes, then do it again. Once you've got your crowd you need them to move away.

Krupinski understands that flyering should have a clear purpose: to sell tickets. The more appropriate your sales pitch, the better chance you have of doing that. At the Pleasance Courtyard, a man is handing out flyers shouting, 'Daniel Sloss: tamer of cats . . . Daniel Sloss: inventor of sticky tape.' Passers-by repeat the surrealist joke and the message starts to sink in. By contrast, back on the Royal Mile, there is a company dressed in orange Guantanamo Bay prison uniforms, some with hoods over their heads. One of them tries to give a leaflet to a child in a pushchair. The parents might be interested, of course, but as a marketing technique, it looks indiscriminate.

As well as people selling their own shows, there is a small army of professional flyerers. You could end up using some yourself, either directly or via one of the bigger venues and agencies. However dedicated these people may be, they will be far more effective if they know and care about your show. 'Get to know your flyerers,' says comedian Nick Doody:

Get them to see the show early. The difference is enormous between somebody flyering for somebody they haven't actually heard of and somebody flyering for a show that made them piss themselves laughing on the first night of the festival and then they had a drink with the performer – they feel a lot more connected to it.

Using your imagination

It isn't only amid the exuberance of the Royal Mile that you find examples of imaginative marketing. They range from the mainstream to the maverick, as you might expect from a festival created by people who pride themselves on their creative prowess. To promote her show *The Naked Brunch*, Australian performer Natalie Bak got sponsorship in kind from the bakery at Henderson's restaurant and handed out toast and chocolate spread with the name of her show toasted onto the surface. 'We went around the whole of Edinburgh in the first week and wrote '*Thunderer*' in chalk everywhere,' says actor David Finn, referring to the name of a show in PBH's Free Fringe:

People then think they've heard of the show. There have been loads of times when I've given someone a flyer and they've said, 'Oh, I've heard about this.'

Claire Walker admires the enterprising publicist who took a

life-size cut-out of veteran performer Nicholas Parsons around the tourist spots of Edinburgh for photographs that ended up in all the papers. 'You have to be careful with scams because they can upset people,' she cautions. 'But a bit of gentle fun is all part of the spirit of the Fringe. In Edinburgh, it's all fair game.'

When Renny Krupinski bought a case of wine in an off-licence on the High Street, he charmed the staff into taking a pile of flyers, despite their no-flyer policy (and he knew he'd drink the wine). 'Last time I was here I did all the hamburger stands and invited them all to the show,' he says. 'They talk to people and they put posters on their stands. They're a good source of free marketing.'

You should also look out for opportunities to perform extracts of your show or a tailor-made routine to entice new audiences. The Fringe website at www.edfringe.com carries details of opportunities to give free performances.

Thinking local

When you are surrounded by other performers, it is easy to get locked into a Fringe bubble and forget Edinburgh carries on perfectly well without the festival for eleven months of the year. Any marketing you do should take into account that around 60 per cent of Fringe audiences are local. This means that, in addition to all your Fringe-specific techniques, you should also use conventional marketing methods.

It pays to think creatively. If, for example, you are putting on a children's show based on the work of a favourite author, you might get a better rate of return to pay for the author to tour Edinburgh schools and bookshops than to take out some less well targeted adverts.

Promoting the acrobatic and non-verbal spectacle of the *Controlled Falling Project*, producer Aneke McCullough spent time thinking about the kind of residents to whom the show would appeal:

I contacted gym clubs, circus organisations, theatres, schools and hearing-impaired organisations. Having lived here, I thought about all the ways I would promote a show at any time of the year, plus the Fringe ways. I think it worked: we did get a couple of groups from gym clubs – we made them special offers.

Similarly, the team behind *Hooked*, a musical set in a nightclub world of adultery, lap dancing and drug addiction, arranged to perform ten-minute sets in various casinos around town. They reasoned that was where they would find their most sympathetic audience. 'That comes from coming up the year before, walking round the city and seeing where your audience hangs out,' says Chris Grady.

New media

The advent of social networking gives Fringe participants even more potential to build audiences at very little cost. You can use services such as Facebook and Twitter not only to inform would-be audiences but to make them feel involved with your show. Publicist Claire Walker says:

Comics can find their own audiences much easier than they ever could before. I look after Matt Green, for example. He has a huge following on Twitter and he's brilliant at it, so his fans just come and see the show because they want to. That's something that a publicist can't do for you. You have to engage with that yourself.

With an eleven-strong cast in her staging of *The Tempest*, Claire Wood had a head-start in getting the message out:

The advantage of having a big cast made itself felt because they spread it far and wide though Facebook. We got a few followers on Twitter, so I talked feverishly about how few tickets we had left in the hope of spurring people on.

In addition, you should consider building a website to give audiences, promoters and journalists a fuller picture of what you are doing. Beware: this can work against you as well as in your favour. A badly designed website displaying a selection of blurry rehearsal shots and a poorly written synopsis will not reflect well on your show. The same is true of YouTube videos. Live performance often translates badly to film – rehearsal footage even more so – and it can work against you. On the other hand, a purpose-made movie can have tremendous immediacy.

There are so many shows to choose from, people look for reasons not to see something and it doesn't take much to put them off. Get it right, by contrast, and you have a tremendous chance to convey the atmosphere, excitement and character of your work in a way that forty words in the Fringe Programme never could. Spend time looking at other websites, blogs and clips, judging what you like and what you don't like, and design your site in a way that does justice to the show and is consistent with the imagery, typeface and style of the rest of your marketing material.

Then get out there and sell.

10. The Media Campaign
Read All About It

So SIGNIFICANT IS THE relationship between the Fringe and the media that a Louisiana sociologist once published a whole book on the subject. In the course of writing *Fringe and Fortune* (Princeton University Press, 1996), Professor Wesley Shrum immersed himself in the festival, even turning his hand to reviewing, believing there was no better place in the world to measure the effect of press coverage on ticket sales. The book was subtitled 'The Role of Critics in High and Popular Art' and it concluded that the popular end of the market was little influenced by critical opinion, while the highbrow end had a strong correlation between attendance and what the reviewers said.

Perhaps if Shrum did a similar study today, he would find the relationship harder to measure. The proliferation of personal blogs and review-based websites coupled with the declining influence of print-based media means on the one hand, an ever greater amount is being written about the Fringe and on the other, individual writers and publications have less authority than they once did. Fringe-goers can find it hard to know which reviews to trust.

Things may be in flux, but there is no doubt the media still has a major role to play and that Fringe participants value coverage highly. A lot of people spend a lot of time trying to get as much of it as possible. As we saw with marketing in the last chapter, media coverage on the Fringe operates by its own rules. Liz Smith, who works as a year-round press officer, says it feels like a different job. 'All the theories about how you do things go out the window,' she says. 'You've got to think so much on your feet.'

Fame, fame, fatal fame

With all this effort being put into getting media coverage, it is easy to lose sight of why you wanted it in the first place. Go back to Chapter 4 and remind yourself of your motivation. If you don't have a good reason for wanting your show covered – if, for example, you are concerned only for your ego or the thrill of being written about – then you could put in a lot of time and effort for relatively meagre rewards. If, however, you are clear about why you want media attention, you will find it easier to focus on getting what you need. Miriam Attwood, the Fringe's fomer media manager, says:

> It totally depends on what you're coming to the Fringe for. Some people are coming because it's an arts marketplace, they have a fantastic show and they need those reviews to go to theatres, promoters and festivals around the world and say, 'Look, at the Edinburgh Festival Fringe we got three four-star reviews from credible arts journalists; we should be performing in your space.' That can be invaluable.

The most likely reason for you wanting coverage is to drum up audiences. With 2,500 shows vying for attention, the more you can do to highlight your production, the better. 'I got a really good review for my debut solo show from Kate Copstick in the *Scotsman*,' says comedian Nick Doody. 'It came out on the third day of the Fringe and I sold out my run. It was the first really good review about anybody so I then got loads more reviews and it set the tone for them.'

Like word of mouth, media coverage is a free form of advertising and, for that reason alone, is much desired by Fringe companies. Playwright Ella Hickson says:

> The press is essential if you don't have a big marketing budget. It builds word of mouth. If you're a low-budget Fringe company, having the press on your side and knowing how to work the press are incredibly important.

Reviews

One of the most useful forms of media coverage is the review. If an independent commentator enthuses about your show, it is not only great for your morale, it is also a valuable marketing tool. The more credible the publication, the more valuable the recommendation.

As Doody acknowledges, reviews are often most useful to you after the festival has ended:

> If you don't win an award (and you're 99 per cent certain of not winning an award), what do you have to show for it? Well, hopefully a really honed show – and, if it's a stand-up show, probably some new material – and reviews. You have something that adds to your profile.

This is not just for your vanity. If you leave Edinburgh with a clutch of positive reviews from credible sources, you are on your way to persuading programmers and agents that you have something valuable to offer. The Fringe offers this possibility arguably more than anywhere else in the world. 'Ant Hampton of Rotozaza has said that, regardless of all the other big things they have done at BAC, the South Bank Centre and so on, they've never got more press than when they came to Forest Fringe,' says Andy Field, the venue's co-director.

For many performers, the Fringe presents one of the few times in their careers when there is a chance of any publication reviewing them. Comedians, for example, rarely get reviewed in the British national press unless they are launching a major tour. American comedians frequently comment about the shock and pleasure of finding their work being discussed seriously in the press. Likewise for relatively unknown theatre companies or musicians, there is little opportunity to be noticed by anyone apart from their local press.

The benefit of a journalist seeing your show might be indirect. Like everyone on the Fringe, journalists bump into people. A well-connected journalist is likely to spread the word about a good show to other journalists, to promoters and to award judges, so even if they don't manage to write anything themselves, they can be an invaluable person to have on side. Thinking in the long term, a journalist who enjoys your show this year is more likely to write about your work in future and more likely to do it with understanding.

Every year the Fringe Office accredits about 1,100 journalists, of whom around 600 are reviewers. Publications with a high profile on the Fringe include the *Scotsman*, *Guardian*, *Herald*, the *List*, *Edinburgh Festivals Magazine*, *ThreeWeeks*, the *Skinny and Fest*. There is also substantial coverage in newspapers such as *The Times*, *Independent* and the *Daily Telegraph* and the Sunday titles, as well as websites including *Broadway Baby*, *Chortle*, *Edinburgh Guide*, *Festival Previews*, *Fringe Guru*, *Fringe Review*, *Hairline*, *onstagescotland*, *TV Bomb* and *A View From the Stalls*. Throw in radio and TV reporters and journalists from specialist magazines and foreign publications, and it feels like the world's media is on your doorstep. Even in these sorts of numbers, however, there are still more shows than the journalists can get around. 'A more common complaint than bad reviews is, "I can't get reviewers to see me",' says Doody. 'When you look at the number of shows, well, of course you can't: just do the maths – there aren't that many reviewers in the world.'

Reviewers

So how do you get reviewers to choose your show? First, you should decide which reviewers would be most beneficial to you. That depends on the nature of your show and what you want to use the reviews for. A publication that exists only for the Fringe, for example, could be great for generating audiences, but less useful to market your show after the festival. Alternatively, if you have ambitions to tour internationally, it could be advantageous to get a quote from a non-UK publication.

Having decided who you would most like to see your show, you can then set about trying to get them in. The best way to do that, says Brian Logan, comedy critic of the *Guardian*, is to have an interesting show:

> You need to understand the journalistic mindset and have a show that a journalist will think, 'Oh, that's write-able about,' be it something topical or be it that your credentials make it obligatory to see you. Journalists on the Fringe want to find something interesting to write about and they want to make this year's big discovery. So I guess we look for novelty. We look for somebody who's doing a show about something we haven't seen a show about before. If you can say it's 'comedy about [blank]' or 'a combination of comedy and [blank]' and that sentence makes you go, 'I hadn't thought of that before,' then you're already ahead of the pack.

He gives the example of New Art Club, a comedy double-act who are also trained dancers:

> I hadn't even seen the show, but I knew it was a sellable article because it makes you go, 'Comedy and dance?' I'm hesitant to suggest everyone has such an obvious gimmick, but there is something in having an idea that catches the imagination,

171

although novelty does not necessarily indicate quality.

Since appearing in a student show on the Fringe in 1994, Logan has returned every year either as a journalist or with his theatre company, Cartoon de Salvo. At the end of July, he will go through the Fringe Programme and the press releases he has been sent ('so you can already gain yourself an advantage if you've got a press release either done by a PR or by yourself') and devises a longlist of the shows he would like to see:

> When I come home, half of that longlist hasn't even been touched. You come up to Edinburgh and you find there's a buzz about a show that isn't even on your longlist. Then you get a call from the arts desk asking you to cover a show you're not interested in. So there's no guarantee, but the real way to get a review is to have an interesting show.

Logan's colleague on the *Guardian*, Lyn Gardner, became a theatre critic straight out of university and has been writing about the Fringe since the early 1980s. Her principle when navigating the festival is to keep herself open:

> I'll have certain things in my diary, like shows at the Traverse, but then I keep the days free in order to be flexible and to respond. I respond to a mix of things. I will see six or maybe eight shows a day and I spend a lot of time in queues and a lot of time on my own, so therefore I make a point of constantly asking people what it is that they've seen and like.

She recommends targeting specific journalists on the basis of what they are interested in. If a critic has written several articles about their dislike of TV spin-offs, you will only irritate them if you write and suggest they see your production of *Downton Abbey: The Musical*. If they have published a book on Harold Pinter, they will feel patronised if you send a letter carefully explaining the cultural significance of *The Caretaker*. Gardner continues:

> You need to know your critic. I would suggest you send a one page of A4 press release with all the basic information on one side, but with that you might do a more personal covering letter – flattery always gets you a long way – to give a sense you know something about the kind of work the critic might be interested in. It has to be genuine. It can't just be generic. Bear in mind that critics do talk to each other and can see through these things.

When pitching to journalists, you need to strike a difficult balance. You do not want your press release to get lost in the deluge of emails, but neither do you want to pester the journalist to the point of irritation. Even outside festival time, Gardner receives 100 emails a day – and that is on her *Guardian* account alone. At the same time, she has an enthusiast's desire to see good work and if you are doing something special, she wants to know about it:

> It's about conveying their own passion for their show to me. A very good thing is to follow up the press release with an email, perhaps about three weeks before the festival begins. It is worth then reminding me during the festival at some point in the first week about your show, without harassing me.

However experienced you are as a Fringe-goer, you can never predict where the exciting shows will emerge from. Like Logan, Gardner keeps herself open to the unexpected, an attitude that means as long as you believe in your show, you should have every chance of being taken seriously:

> You have to be able to respond to those other things that come up. It could be anything. Who knows whether it might

173

be a musical or a piece of physical theatre? I have no agenda
in terms of the sort of theatre it is that I'm going to see. I'll
go and see anything – I'm a complete slut.

Joyce McMillan, chief theatre critic on the *Scotsman*, echoes
Logan's observation that critics gravitate towards shows with
intriguing content. In McMillan's case this is especially true
because of her central role in judging the Fringe Firsts. These awards
champion new plays and, by extension, new ideas. As someone
who reviews year round, she is, of course, interested in all kinds
of theatre, but if you are staging a conventional production of a
classic play, however competently you do it, you will find it hard to
distinguish yourselves from all the other companies doing the same
thing. McMillan, who has been reviewing the Fringe since the late
1970s when she remembers seeing Emma Thompson, Stephen Fry
and Rowan Atkinson for the first time and being bowled over, says:

The way to attract attention is to really have something to
say in your show and a belief in its significance as a piece
of cultural work. You should make the core of that clear in
your forty-word blurb so that it has that ring of urgency and
connectedness.

The Press Release

McMillan's remarks are a reminder, as we saw in the last chapter, of
how important your entry in the Fringe Programme can be. What
you write in March will affect people's decisions in August. Your
next opportunity to make a difference is with a press release. If
you have never written one before or simply need some additional
support, you should call up the media manager at the Fringe Office
for advice as well as the media team at your own venue if it has one.
Think back to Chapter 4 and your reasons for appearing on the

Fringe and focus on the characteristics that distinguish your show from everyone else's.

As James Seabright explains in his book *So You Want To Be a Theatre Producer?*, your press release should be engaging and informative but should not resort to 'marketing speak'. Journalists are on the lookout for attention-grabbing content, not empty hyperbole. They need facts and stories and will make up their own minds about whether something is interesting or not. 'Press are pretty well clued up at reading the messages between the lines as well as the lines themselves,' says Laura Mackenzie Stuart of Universal Arts. 'So if a press release says, "Come and see me because I'm great," I'm guessing it might go to the bottom of the priority pile.'

Producer Aneke McCulloch agrees: 'You need to tell them what it's about and why they should come and see it.'

In short, you need to answer the five questions that are a journalist's stock-in-trade: who, why, what, where and when? This is not to say you should undersell yourself. The Fringe press release that began with the phrase 'Although not one of his best plays . . .' was taking honesty a little too far. Like the forty-word entry in the Fringe Programme, you need to say simply, clearly and confidently what distinguishes your show from the rest. Joyce McMillan says that elaborate press packs are 'redundant':

> Because of the sheer volume of information, people should really try to be brief. It's a hiding to nothing to write a press release that's more than about a page and a half of A4. The first paragraph should say what the play's about. The second paragraph should say who's in it and who the artists involved are. The third paragraph should say where to get hold of you – and that is it.

It is hard to predict what will grab a particular journalist's attention, so the best you can do is present your information clearly and succinctly. That way, if your show happens to fit in with a theme the journalist has spotted or if it happens to be about a subject they care about, they will be more likely to follow it up with you. There's a lot of luck involved. If you are staging one of three plays set in a nudist camp, you can be sure there'll be a spate of articles about nudist camps. Come back twelve months later, and nudist camps will be last year's thing.

Think not only about the show itself but also about the people involved. Did your writer go through a harrowing ordeal that inspired the play? Are any of your performers famous or related to someone who is? Did the company go to extraordinary lengths to get the show on? Have you triumphed in the face of adversity? If you find yourself telling a story about your show to a friend, perhaps a journalist would like to hear the same story. 'Often in a press release it will be something just tiny that I will spot,' says Lyn Gardner. 'It might be just a tiny connection.'

Emailing journalists is both efficient and cheap and many of them prefer email. Some don't, however. You can forget an email once it has moved down the inbox and journalists do not always find it easy to retrieve them at a later date. A printed press release could have more impact and is harder to lose, although, of course, it costs more. To be on the safe side, some publicists send both and use one to remind the journalist of the other. Lyn Gardner says:

> I still insist on press releases by post. Edinburgh in particular
> is a really good example. Because I'll take a very small laptop
> with me, I actually want to have a physical piece of paper. It
> may save PRs a lot of money not to send you something by
> post, but it doesn't save me, because I have to stand there
> all day downloading it and printing it all off. And it's much
> easier to lose emails.

Talk to the media department at the Fringe Office or at your venue about getting the names and contact details of journalists. Make a plan about when to send out press releases and when to make follow-up calls. Getting the timing right is a fine art. Too soon in the year, and you lose the journalist's interest; too late, and someone gets in there before you. As a rough measure, use the publication of the Fringe Programme as your guide unless there is some special reason a journalist might need to know before that, such as a rare chance to see the show in advance. Getting in touch a week or less before the opening night is fine for a news story, but hopeless if you want preview coverage. The point in June when the Fringe Programme is launched is when most journalists are receptive to ideas.

The press night (there isn't one)

When it comes to getting reviewers to see your show, the sooner they see it, the sooner the review is likely to be published and the sooner word gets out. There are many factors influencing what shows they choose to see first (or which ones their editors choose for them), but it will be an advantage if you are performing in a prestigious venue, if you already have a reputation and if your show has some newsworthy or novelty value. In such an overheated market, it is difficult to attract a critic's attention with a faithful interpretation of a classic, however accomplished the performance.

Let's assume, though, you're about to get them through the door. If there is any danger of your show not being ready, putting it in front of a critic is a risk. Equally, this is not Broadway and you cannot afford the luxury of a long preview run. If you turn away a critic, it could be the first and last time they are available. 'It's so important for your show to be ready,' says publicist Claire Walker. 'If you're charging the public to go in, then the press should be allowed to go in and review it.'

Jonny Ensall, editor of the *List* magazine, agrees:

If your show is a shambles then don't open, but critics will not be able to pick up on most of the things that you think are wrong with it. Tweaking it will not change the production as a whole. So don't worry too much about the difference between the preview shows and the main run.

Either the Fringe media office or your venue will be able to tell you when reviewers have booked tickets. If you know in advance, you might want to make special efforts to fill the theatre, even if it means giving away tickets. Once they have seen the show, however, the uncertainty can continue for some time as Neil Mackinnon, the Fringe Office's head of external relations, says:

> The question we get possibly more than any other is: 'A newspaper was in six days ago and the review still hasn't appeared, what can we do?' Depending on the show and the publication, you can sort it out. You can very gently ask the arts editor when the review will appear. The Fringe-based media, such as *Fest* and *ThreeWeeks*, are perfectly happy to be involved in that kind of enquiry and things do get lost in the system because of the sheer volume they're dealing with.

Even then, there can be complications. The Fringe is as disorientating for reviewers as it is for performers and the most experienced writer can take a while to find their Fringe feet. Claire Walker says it can go both ways:

> It can go for you or against you. If you get a journalist in early and they've got nothing else to compare it with that year, they can be laughing like a drain and then only give it three stars because perhaps it wasn't as funny as something they saw last year that they remember through rose-tinted glasses. Or it can go the other way and they think it was absolutely brilliant and then go on to see something better.

A reflexive critic will be attempting quite subtle assessments not only of the experience of watching your show, but also of the very particular conditions in which it is taking place. They will know that a performance that seems delightful in a church hall on a wet Wednesday afternoon might appear less substantial if it were in a proscenium-arch theatre at 7.30 p.m. They will worry that a show will lose its sheen once the excitement of discovery and the atmosphere of festival hype have worn off. Sometimes, they will wonder if the production would be better if it were seen in different circumstances. Such suspicions are hard to quantify, which means the Fringe critic, more than most, must make as many educated guesses as definitive judgements. Lyn Gardner agrees:

> One of the things you're balancing all the time is the context in which you are reviewing. Am I reviewing only within the bubble of those three weeks in August or in the wider context of stuff I see over the entire year? There's no science to it. I verge more on the cautious side on the basis that a lot of the shows will make their way to other places and there is something rather odd when a show arrives in London – a show you liked but is very small and very fragile – and then looks exposed if you've given it too many stars.

What the reviews mean

Just as the Fringe has a profusion of shows, so it has a profusion of reviewers. In established, year-round publications, the writing and critical opinion is of a reliable standard. There is also a lot of lively, well-informed commentary elsewhere, but with so many reviewers, it can be hard to know who to trust, who to take seriously and whose quotes to use on your posters. Comedian Nick Doody:

> I read a review that started, 'I went into this show with

a sinking heart because I hate stand-up comedy.' Well then, you should not be reviewing it! It's not allowed for the genre to be a negative point. Because of the need to review an impossible number of shows, there's an ever-growing number of reviews written by the clueless or the uninterested – that's their assignment today but normally they're the architecture expert.

Doody, though, admits to the power of flattery:

If they give you four stars, it's amazing how quickly you will reassess their skills as a reviewer: 'Actually, it's quite perceptive.'

Once again, the Fringe is intensely competitive and even with a five-star rave or positive preview coverage from the *Scotsman*, you would be unwise to sit back expecting the audiences to pour in. With luck, you might get a blip in sales for a day or two but, when audiences have so much information to choose from, you cannot assume they will see, still less remember, your glowing review. Even after *Controlled Falling Project* made the front page of the *Scotsman*'s daily festival supplement (see story below), producer Aneke McCulloch had to keep up the pressure:

We sold really well for the first couple of days so I definitely think it worked, but it doesn't last for very long. It was such a good morale booster for the start of the season, but we had to keep on working at it.

While the memory of a good review is still fresh, now is the time to reinforce your message. Perhaps you will get flyers made up, quoting some or even all of the review (although if you want to reproduce the whole thing, you should obtain the permission of the copyright holder, remembering that copyright exists in the layout and typography, as well as in the words). Perhaps you will paste the star rating on top of your existing posters or staple it to your existing flyers. Even if the review is not a rave, it might include a favourable line you can quote – just as long as you do not quote so selectively that you risk breaching the EU's unfair commercial practices directive by misleading audiences. If it says 'not the most fantastic show in town,' you must resist the temptation to cut out the word 'not'.

With a little imagination, however, it is possible to capitalise even on the coolest review. Misleading or not, you could only admire the late comedian Jason Wood who, in 2004, turned his one-star review in the *Scotsman* into 'A star: The *Scotsman*' and emblazoned it across his publicity material. Other performers have run their bad reviews alongside the good ones to draw attention to what they regard as the inconsistency of the critics. Claire Walker says:

> There are other things you can do. If you get a bad review, you can focus away from the critics and try and find other places in the media for them: 'my favourite restaurants' or 'my health' or whatever these columns in the papers are. You give them some time to let their show run in before you let the critics back in.

Feature coverage

As Walker points out, the tendency is to focus on reviews, but there are many more avenues open to you, a lot of which are better at raising your profile and encouraging interest. From soon after the launch of the Fringe Programme, newspapers, magazines, websites and radio and television programmes start running interviews, comment pieces and profiles inspired by the events in August. Dedicated publications such as the *List*, *Edinburgh Festivals Magazine* and *ThreeWeeks* are the obvious ones, as are arts-orientated newspapers including the *Scotsman* and the *Guardian*. The field is much broader than that, however. A comedy routine with a scientific theme could end up on a technology page; a play about health care could be interesting to a society supplement; a musician with an emotive true-life story could make an ideal subject in a women's magazine. 'Journalists in Edinburgh do look for interesting stories,' says director Toby Gough, who has provided journalists with human interest tales from teenage survivors of the Asian tsunami and young dancers who have emerged from the favelas of Brazil. 'They don't just get seduced by names. If you do have a good idea and a story that needs to be told, it will always find its way out.'

At the *List* magazine, which covers over 500 shows in four weekly issues, editor Jonny Ensall says he is always on the lookout for interesting angles. He gives the example of the strongman from Circus Trick Tease who cycled the 400 miles from London to Edinburgh and kept a diary of his journey. Not every idea makes a major article, but it might be enough for a side bar or a quirky top five list:

> The shows that are most difficult to get excited about are those where they give you a flyer and it's got a man and a woman sat on a chair opposite each other and they say it's a play about relationships. Well, that pretty much describes a significant proportion of the Fringe output. The more simple or intriguing you can make your PR campaign, the more likely it is to be picked up by somebody.

In an effort to make their press releases stand out, many companies send accompanying novelty items ideally with some thematic connection to the show. If they are sufficiently original or amusing, they might even make a magazine story in themselves. 'This year people sent us a small menagerie of plastic animals, a miniature tractor, a set of his-and-hers underwear, a range of hats, various types of food and a hip flask,' says Ensall, who has been hooked on the Fringe since his first visit in 2003:

> It's less the branding that you send than the interest that you have in the object, so a jar of pickled onions went down well because you could eat them. Occasionally we'll get a symbolic object that'll arrive beautifully packaged in boxes that people have handcrafted as press releases. The more special and individual, the more likely we are to look at them. It's probably not more likely to be reviewed, but it is more likely to be previewed. Reviews do tend to be based on an objective assessment on whether the show is likely to be good and whether it fits into our criteria of what is an important show.

He recommends attending the Meet the Media event at Fringe Central, an opportunity for participants and journalists to come together at the start of the festival. Competition is still intense, but being there could make a difference:

> Of the people that I met, I picked out about three or four whose shows I thought were worth reviewing that I might not have been aware of otherwise.

Picture perfect

Publications such as the *List* and the annual *Edinburgh Festivals Magazine* place a high value on photography and the better your image, the greater the chance it has of being used. For this reason, as we discussed in the last chapter, getting a strong photograph is invaluable. Even daily newspapers with minimal Fringe coverage will have slots for memorable images and could be willing to run with yours. In publications that give more space to the Fringe, there is often a need to illustrate listings pages with good pictures. Even if a publication does not use the photograph you provided, the picture editor might like it enough to commission an original shot and an editor might be intrigued enough to find out more about the show. 'If you've got a good image it will be used everywhere,' says Liz Smith.

For those shows that are particularly photogenic, it can be worth inviting the press to a special photo call during the festival. Working with the Australian acrobats of the *Controlled Falling Project*, producer Aneke McCulloch decided to stage a trick at an iconic Edinburgh site:

> I don't know why I first thought of Greyfriars Bobby, but I spoke to a few people about it and some said, 'Oh, you can't do that,' and others laughed. I thought I've got to do that because it gets a reaction.

Ignoring the rain and cold, she persuaded the performers to do handstands on the head of the famous statue:

> We stopped traffic because there were so many photographers on the street wanting to get the right shot. It was an awesome flyering opportunity as well because it's the most photographed statue in Edinburgh and people would stop and want to know what was going on. I got a call at midnight that night to say we were on the front cover of the *Scotsman*. I thought, 'That's all right, the day before we open.'

The press will insist on your pictures being jpegs with average compression and high-resolution, at least 300 dpi, although it may be more convenient to email lower resolution images initially. If your show is new, your initial images will have to be set-up shots that capture the flavour or theme of the performance. As soon as the show is on stage, you should also distribute production shots, making sure you send them to the media office at the Fringe and, where applicable, your own venue. You should send images to picture desks rather than individual journalists (the Fringe press office will supply you with a list of contacts), making sure they are clearly labelled and properly credited with the names of performers and photographer. Send two or three of your best shots, using horizontal and vertical orientations, indicating that more are available on request.

Bringing in the professionals

Dealing with the media can be a job in itself and you need to weigh up whether it is something you can do on your own, perhaps in conjunction with your venue's media office, or whether you should employ a professional publicist. To start answering the question, go back to Chapter 4 and remind yourself why you are performing on the Fringe. Then consider whether a publicist is likely to help you fulfil your aim. If you are here simply to have a good time, the answer is almost certainly no; if you are aiming to have a television career by the autumn, the answer is almost certainly yes. Any position in between will require a more nuanced analysis.

Canvassing opinion, you hear every side of the argument. An obvious case that illustrates the value of a publicist is that of David Benson's *Lockerbie: Unfinished Business*. Responding to the bombing of Pan Am flight 103, the one-man play cast doubts about whether Abdelbaset Ali Mohmed Al Megrahi, the man convicted for the atrocity, was really to blame. At the time it was staged, the Scottish government had recently allowed Megrahi to return home to Libya on compassionate grounds, provoking harsh criticism from the USA. It meant that, irrespective of the play's merits (it happened to be very good), Benson was sitting on a hot news story. Producer James Seabright had to set up photo calls at 9 a.m., the only time the venue was free:

We went through a phase in the middle of the festival when we had a different film crew every day. It's difficult because you want to help the press out as much as possible, but also you need to balance that with the interests of the production and the audiences. Sometimes you have to say no to very good and interesting press opportunities because they might tip the balance in the wrong direction. We had one film crew that wanted to leave halfway through the show because they had to go to something else. We had to say, 'No, you either see all of it or none of it.'

In this instance, it is hard to imagine Benson dealing with the media on his own. Even if he could spare the time, would he have had the nerve to turn down interview requests? His investment in Seabright's publicity service was surely money well spent, not least because one of his aims was to raise awareness of the issues. Most of the media interest from abroad would have had no impact on the box office, but in this case, Benson was interested in more than ticket sales.

Lockerbie: Unfinished Business is atypical, however, and most shows do not attract a fraction of the attention. What is hard to assess is whether those that do attract the attention would have attracted it anyway. 'I would discourage anyone who was coming for the first time to waste money on hiring public relations support,' says Tommy Sheppard, artistic director of the Stand Comedy Club:

Everyone knows there are only a certain number of shows that are going to get reviewed and everyone knows your likelihood of getting reviewed is directly related to your general career profile and TV exposure. Any paper can't afford to ignore a show on the Fringe if the performer is familiar to its readers.

Actor, director and producer Guy Masterson agrees. He prefers to rely on his own reputation – which, on the Fringe, is good and long-standing – and only to take on a publicist when he has a bigger show:

> When you spend £2,000 on a publicist, you can't tell what you've generated from your own reputation and what they've generated from getting on the blower. You cannot make £2,000 of added value for a show on the Fringe unless you're playing in a 600-seat theatre.

Masterson has been a Fringe fixture since 1994, understands the system and is adept at doing his own publicity. Your perspective might be different, according to Nica Burns, artistic director of the Edinburgh Comedy Award, if you're going for the first time and you don't know what the system is:

> You might find someone who costs you £1,000 – that's quite a lot of money, but it's not £10,000 – and who will write you a press release, make sure it gets to everybody and get on the phone to hassle the journalists a bit. They'll also know which journalist is most likely to be interested in this particular piece of work. If you get one journalist in and the show is good, you're likely to get others.

No publicist can guarantee they will get you coverage – that decision lies with the editors alone – but they can commit to putting in the legwork and promoting the show confidently on your behalf. Claire Walker, who works with high-profile comedians including Ed Byrne, naturally defends her profession:

> An act has quite enough going on for that month in Edinburgh. It's a high-pressure situation for a comic. You're putting yourself on the line and you're being judged by your peers, the press and the public. It's quite a raw, emotional

time. So the less you can think about, the better. If you've got somebody else – a manger or a publicist – dealing with all the crap for you, you'll turn in a better show.

What Sheppard and Masterson say seems to be in direct conflict with what Burns and Walker say. The reason for this, as comedian Nick Doody explains, is there are so many variables in play:

The money goes out either way. You can't form a control experiment; you can't go back and do the same festival without a PR and see if you got the same amount of press attention. They can make a minimal difference and you can really resent that cash. But if they do a very good job, you won't be sorry you spent it.

Matters are further complicated because of the number of publicists who do not have a proven record on the Fringe. 'It's a real jungle,' says Martyn Jacques, lead singer of the Tiger Lillies. 'You get bad promoters, bad PR people, bad journalists. You can turn up there, you pay some PR person to promote your show and they just don't.'

'There are too many publicists who aren't actually publicists and just call themselves that,' says Fraser Smith, who has run the media offices in the Gilded Balloon and the Underbelly:

They're allowed to cause havoc and damage with young companies. If you want a publicist but you don't know who to hire, I would check with the venue's publicist and ask them if they could recommend someone.

You could also try asking a journalist. They are the ones who deal with the publicists and will know their reputations. If a journalist does not know the name, you can assume the publicist is not doing their job. From the journalist's point of view, a good publicist is the source of reliable information, a useful intermediary who can set up interviews, arrange tickets, deal with any follow-up questions and can be trusted to talk honestly about the work. The better established the publicist, the more likely they are to be promoting high quality shows and the more likely journalists are to trust their recommendations. On the other hand, a journalist will not penalise you for producing your own press release, says Lyn Gardner:

Yes, I will see things that have a PR agency attached and therefore I get a press release from someone I know and, of course, that helps. But you shouldn't spend lots of money on PR agencies. It's a job companies can do very well for themselves as far as I'm concerned.

Joyce McMillan says she values publicists as long as they understand the Edinburgh environment:

If you've got a press person who is not very experienced in the Edinburgh Fringe, they're useless because it is a completely different media landscape from any other situation. The competition for the time of all journalists, even the youngest student journalist, is intense. You need press people who know the writers involved, know what they're likely to be interested in, who don't waste your time, who are succinct, who know how difficult it is to programme something in at short notice, who get the timing right . . . the only way you're going to get that is by taking on a publicist who has a lot of experience in Edinburgh. If you can afford it, that is worth it, but if you get the wrong one, you might as well not spend the money.

If you choose to pay for a professional publicist, you should find someone who you get on with and who will work hard on your behalf. For that to happen, they must believe in you, says Claire Walker:

189

The first thing is to find a PR person you can be absolutely honest with and you can trust. Unless you have that honesty, the relationship just falls down. I spend quite a bit of time hanging out with people before deciding if I will work with them, to see what kind of relationship we're going to have. From my point of view, I have to really like their comedy; I'm hopeless at selling somebody I don't believe in. That plays to my favour because it means journalists trust my opinion that I'm not selling them a lemon – or at least they know that I genuinely like it.

The publicist's role extends further than securing preview coverage and getting reviewers in. They can be a protective barrier between you and the press and they can divert attention when things don't go according to plan. Walker freely admits there are people for whom a publicist would be an unnecessary expense. If you are a professional whose show is not quite ready, your career could be damaged by the premature publicity. And if you are performing on the Free Fringe, it is unlikely to be a priority. 'If it was posters or publicist, I'd go for posters,' she says.

There is also a middle way. Aneke McCulloch decided a publicist would be too expensive, especially if it was someone who didn't know her show, the *Controlled Falling Project*. Instead, she did the job herself but with the help of a publicist friend in Edinburgh:

I decided to spend just a bit of money on paying her to be a consultant and to use some of her contacts, but I'd do all the work. It worked really well.

When talking to publicists, you should ask if they have a sliding scale of services and can offer a package that best suits your budget and your needs.

Going it alone

The good news is that if you want to do your own publicity – and the vast majority of companies do – there is a lot of support available to you. Many of the larger venues run their own press offices as does the Fringe Society itself. The more you engage with the people working there – and the earlier you do it – the better your chances of getting your message out, says Miriam Attwood:

> There's something really cool about the fact that somebody can come to Edinburgh and not really know what a press release is, you help them write their press release and discover they are putting together something quite impressive. They get in touch with the right people and their name starts to crop up, this buzz begins and they realise they are doing it all themselves.

If you are running your own media campaign, one of the greatest challenges is to get a sense of perspective on your work. The interests of performers and journalists overlap, but they are not exactly the same. You might be desperate to talk about your show's finer aesthetic subtleties only to find a journalist cares only about your famous uncle. When you care about your work, it can be hard to accept the adage that all publicity is good publicity.

This is true wherever you are performing, but the Fringe brings with it additional pressures that make it hard to know when you are sitting on a story, as Attwood explains:

> You may be incredibly involved in your show, the exhaustion of flyering, going to bed really late, getting up early after sleeping on the floor, performing your show and doing it day in, day out, with audiences of five people and forty people and everything in between. In the Fringe media office, we try to get people into a sensible place, where they can sit

down calmly and think about what's going on. You need that fresh perspective. Diary stories are a mystery to performers because it's just not what is important to them at the time. You'd be amazed by the things people come up with that they hadn't thought of as press stories.

The key, says Attwood, is understanding what you are selling and telling people exactly what that is. You cannot second-guess what the press and, in turn, audiences are going to be interested in, but you can help them make their decisions:

Be clear about themes, about the company and what kind of performance it is. The amount of times people will send through a press release which is 250 words long in which they don't actually describe what you're going to see on stage. What's this show going to look like? What should audiences expect? It's one thing people often miss and it's because they're too involved.

Having decided why you want media coverage and the kind you would like to get, you need to think of the things that make your show and the people involved interesting to write about. Doing your research about what key journalists are interested in will help in this and it will also make it easier to tailor your pitches to them. You need to accept that it's a huge festival and that not everyone gets the coverage they'd like. You also need to make the most of the coverage you do get: when you get a good review, do everything you can to spread the word; when you get a bad review, think of other publicity strategies. Remember also that, for many companies, media coverage is not the be-all and end-all. It's possible to have a perfectly good time without it, so if the media winds are not in your favour, don't let it get you down.

11. The Awards
I'd Like to Thank ...

THE DOUG ANTHONY ALLSTARS, an early-nineties musical comedy trio, used to return to their native Australia claiming, with typical comic outrageousness, to have been 'winners of the Edinburgh Fringe'. Their Australian audience knew no better and might well have believed the whole event to be one big competition. It is nothing of the kind, of course. Not only are many people given awards, but even those who go home empty handed can still see themselves as 'winners'.

'I don't have a problem with the Edinburgh Comedy Awards as a competition,' says comedian Ed Byrne, who was nominated for the Perrier, as it was then known, in 1998:

> What gets me is the way people act like if you don't get nominated when you're supposed to, then somehow the festival was a failure. That annoys me. My first one-man show in 1996 sold out every night, got great reviews, I had quite a lot of sex, I got picked up to go to festivals in New Zealand and Australia, I got asked to do the BBC *Stand-Up Show,* I got interviewed for some other TV shows – all these things came off the back of a show in Edinburgh, yet people would say, 'You didn't get the Perrier Newcomer award.' And when I was nominated for the Perrier in 1998, they would give their commiserations for not winning it. But things were

going really well. You can't say things are only going well if you win an award.

If you do win an award, however – or even if you get a nomination – not only does it do wonders for your ego, but it can be invaluable for your marketing. Capitalise on an award in the right way and you can boost your audiences in Edinburgh and set your post-Fringe career off to a roaring start.

Check the Fringe website for an up-to-date list of awards. Here are details of the major ones.

Amnesty International Freedom of Expression Award

To raise awareness of human rights abuses, this Amnesty-backed award celebrates plays that foreground the political struggle for freedom. Around sixty shows compete for the prize which, in previous years, has gone to plays about sex trafficking, miscarriages of justice, asylum seekers and the death penalty. You can nominate your own show for consideration, but need to make a convincing case for its contribution to the understanding of human rights issues. The judges are a mixture of professional theatre critics and Amnesty volunteers and consider artistic quality as well as political content. www.amnesty.org.uk

Amused Moose Laugh-off

Aimed at the next generation of stand-ups, these awards are for comedians who can perform a ten-minute set. The qualifying heats take place around the country in the months before the festival, with the final taking place in Edinburgh. The prize usually includes £1,500 and a commercial-standard promotional DVD. www.amusedmoose.com

Amused Moose Laughter Awards

Run by the London comedy club, these awards aim to seek out

unsigned stand-ups who are 'almost DVD ready' and on the cusp of making a breakthrough. It is for comedians doing a full-length show or appearing on a mixed bill for at least nineteen days of the Fringe. Material does not need to be new but should be 'original'. To enter, you have to submit a video of your show towards the start of July and need to be available to do short sets in the semi-finals during the Fringe. The prize is judged by an industry panel and audience voting and usually includes £5,000 to develop your comedy career and a commercial-standard promotional DVD. www.amusedmoose.com

Arches Brick Award

Glasgow's Arches theatre prides itself on supporting new generations of artists. Its Brick Award is designed to give a showcase to a breakthrough company on the Fringe. The judges are looking for a new piece of work or a radical re-staging of an existing text by a company that has produced no more than three shows. The production can be text-based, dance or physical theatre and should demonstrate 'experiment, risk-taking and a bold approach to the exploration of new theatrical languages'. With the £1,000 prize, the winner should be able to re-stage their Fringe show in Glasgow for between two and five performances before July of the following year. The Arches retains all box-office income for those performances, but can offer support such as rehearsal space and marketing. Applications should be submitted before the end of July. www.thearches.co.uk

Bank of Scotland *Herald* Angel awards

Selected by the critics of the *Herald*, one of Scotland's national newspapers, these awards are made every Saturday of the Fringe and International Festival and have no eligibility requirements. If the writers love what you are doing, you are in with a chance. Winners have ranged from a group of buskers to leading choreographers in the EIF. If they want to honour your broader contribution, they have a special *Herald* Archangel. The awards go to shows the critics are seeing in the normal course of their festival reviewing, so you should invite them in the normal way. The exception is with the Little Devil, an award given to artists who have triumphed in the face of disaster. If you have a story of survival against the odds, tell arts editor Keith Bruce about it. www.theheraldangels.co.uk

The Bobbys

New in 2011, this award by website Broadway Baby gives a sixth star to one of its five-star reviewed shows. If a reviewer likes a show enough, they can nominate it for the extra star which is awarded after a judging panel has seen it for themselves. Winners receive a Bobby trophy, modelled on Greyfriars Bobby, and a Sixth Star Award certificate. www.broadwaybaby.com

Carol Tambor Best of Edinburgh Award

New Yorker Carol Tambor first visited the Fringe in the early 1990s and has not missed a year since. A keen theatregoer, she was captivated by the diversity of new work in Edinburgh. 'I love to see work by people who see the world in a different way,' she says, sitting in the late summer sun in Princes Street Gardens soon after the ceremony to announce her latest award:

> I was so frustrated because for so many years I had seen things that were so wonderful and they never went anywhere. I realised I would be able to finance one production in New York.

She gave the inaugural Carol Tambor Best of Edinburgh Award in 2004, using four and five-star reviews in the *Scotsman* as her guide while keeping herself open to other recommendations. She sees around sixty shows, keeping an eye out for work that will somehow stand alone and encapsulate the spirit of the Fringe for a New York audience:

I never go into the season thinking, 'This is the kind of play I'm looking for'. I want to be surprised. I don't really know what my audience wants because I've brought so many different kinds of things and they seem to be receptive to something new. So I wouldn't tell anyone to try to adapt their art to suit me or anyone else. Don't do it for the critics, don't do it for anybody. You make art that is meaningful to you and hope that it strikes a chord.

www.caroltambor.com/award/

CSPA Fringe Award for Sustainable Production

Based in Los Angeles, the Center for Sustainable Practice in the Arts aims to 'reward ecologically sustainable practice in the production of a fringe performance'. It is for work that is not only created on green principles but designed to encourage audiences to question their own environmental impact. Applicants fill in an online questionnaire about materials used, transport links and artistic content, which makes them think about how environmentally friendly they really are.

www.sustainablepractice.org/programs/fringe/

Edinburgh Comedy Award

Known for many years as the Perrier Award until the title sponsor pulled out, the £10,000 Edinburgh Comedy Award is one of the most talked-about accolades on the Fringe. 'It's like a stamp of approval,' says Ed Byrne about getting nominated in 1998. 'It's like getting your degree.'

An awards team sees every eligible show of substantially new material, which can mean around 400 in the first ten days, in order to create a shortlist for the judges to see. The show needs to run until the final week of the Fringe and it must be in a full fifty-minute slot. To encourage fresh talent, the award cannot be won by TV names or previous winners. Beyond that, the field is open. Previous winners include Russell Kane, Al Murray and Daniel Kitson.

To be eligible for the £5,000 best newcomer award, you are allowed to have performed short sets on a mixed bill in previous years, as long as this is your first fifty-minute show. Sarah Millican, Tim Minchin and Josie Long are among the recent winners.

'The first rule is do not compromise your show,' says Nica Burns, the artistic director of the award:

> There are no rules about what makes a prize-winning show. You don't have to be polite about the sponsor, their product or anything like that: just do what you want to do. You can't set out to win an award.

The advantage, says Burns, is an invaluable publicity boost. 'And publicity brings attention to your work,' she says. 'That is all any artist wants. You need to capitalise on it very quickly. You're hot for that moment, so take every single opportunity you can.' www.comedyawards.co.uk

Edinburgh International Festival Fringe Prize

In an attempt to make more of the creative outpouring on his doorstep, Jonathan Mills, artistic director of the Edinburgh International Festival, introduced a prize for Fringe companies. A panel of judges selects one or more inventive theatre companies which are given £5,000 to stage low-key work-in-progress performances in the following year's EIF programme. www.eif.co.uk

Evening News Awards

Celebrating the best musical and best play staged by local and amateur companies on the Fringe, the *Edinburgh Evening News* drama awards are judged by a professional panel and the paper's readers. 'I look at it more as a PR thing than a prize (although I always hunger to win the prize) because you tend to get coverage in the *Evening News*,' says Claire Wood of Edinburgh Graduate Theatre Group. www.edinburghnews.scotsman.com

Fringe Review Outstanding Theatre Awards

The online website gives up to three of its teapot awards to theatre productions that have received a five-star review and are considered outstanding. There is also a Hidden Gem Award for great shows that haven't attracted the audiences they deserve.
www.fringereview.co.uk

Funny Women Awards

A number of awards designed to encourage new female comedians. If you can perform five minutes of comedy, you could be eligible for a cash prize, a comedy writing award or a variety award, with showcases in London to follow. There is a £15 registration fee and entrants must have been performing for less than five years. It is a national competition with several regional heats, four of them in Edinburgh. www.funnywomen.com

The Holden Street Theatre Award

Judges from Adelaide's Holden Street Theatre join producers and practitioners in working their way through around 600 productions in search of the ideal show to bring to the Adelaide Fringe. Shows must be of high artistic merit and not previously seen in Australia. The prize includes support for flights, visas, accommodation and other production costs. The panel works from the Fringe Programme, but you can also send details to the address on the website. www.holdenstreettheatres.com/edinburgh/award.php

Jack Tinker Spirit of the Fringe Award

Named in honour of the late theatre critic of the *Daily Mail*, this award goes to someone whom the judges feel epitomises all that is best about the Fringe. The winner is at the judges' discretion.

Malcolm Hardee Awards

There are three awards in honour of the late comedian and lover of anarchy: the Malcolm Hardee Award for Comic Originality, the

Malcolm Hardee Cunning Stunt Award for best Fringe publicity stunt and the Malcolm Hardee Act Most Likely to Make a Million Quid Award. There are, of course, no rules.
www.malcolmhardee.co.uk

The Mervyn Stutter Spirit of the Fringe Awards

With a twenty-year history, these six awards are given out at the final performance of Mervyn Stutter's Pick of the Fringe. They are aimed at Fringe companies who receive little or no financial support, but continue to entertain audiences through their talent and doggedness. Winners are at the judges' discretion.
www.mervynstutter.com

The MTM:UK Musical Theatre Awards

To qualify for these musical theatre awards, you need to be performing a long enough run for the judges to see you, which means playing weeks two and three at the very least. You cannot have given more than fifteen performances of the show before the Fringe. Eligible for professional and aspiring companies, the awards are for best book, lyrics, music, production and others. 'Stick to the criteria and think about why the award would be useful to you,' says Chris Grady, who set up the awards. 'They are looking for shows that have a long-term commercial life. That doesn't mean that they've got to be West End blockbusters, but it means a feeling there's going to be an audience demand for it.'
www.musicaltheatrematters.org.uk/awards

NSDF & Methuen Drama's Emerging Artists' Competition

In addition to its twelve-play event in Scarborough in the spring, the National Student Drama Festival runs a competition for the best original student work on the Fringe – whether a new musical, a devised drama, a new play or an adaptation – offering a £1,000 prize, guidance from a professional director and the chance of a transfer to the Pleasance in London. In any given year there are likely to be upwards of sixty eligible shows performed by those over the age of 16 who have been a student within the last year. 'In terms of student work, the competition for emerging artists is about new work,' says the NSDF's Holly Kendrick. 'They do manage it and come up with some extraordinary ideas. It's about imagination and ownership of ideas.' Application details at www.ideastap.com

Scotsman Fringe Firsts

Established by the *Scotsman* newspaper in 1973, the Fringe Firsts were designed from the start to encourage new playwriting. So successful have they proved, that today the newspaper's reviewing team can only just keep on top of all the eligible work. Your show must be an original play with less than six performances before the Fringe. If you are coming from abroad, the production should not be older than two years. It should be listed in the theatre, dance and physical theatre, musicals and opera or the children's section of the Fringe Programme. If you believe your show is eligible, you just need to say so on your Fringe show registration form. 'The awards are for new work on the Fringe that has some kind of dramatic content, which is quite widely defined,' says *Scotsman* theatre critic Joyce McMillan, who leads a small team of professional reviewers in making the weekly decisions. 'There's a slight bias towards texts, but only slight. The point is it should have some kind of narrative structure. And that's really it – it then just depends on what the various reviewers and judges have seen and like.' www.scotsman.com

So You Think You're Funny? Award

Created by the Gilded Balloon, this is an award for new comic talent, based on heats around the country in the months preceding the Fringe. Typically, there are 600 applicants for seventy places in the ninety-minute heats. www.gildedballoon.co.uk

The *Stage* Awards for Acting Excellence

Based on nominations by the *Stage*'s review team, these awards are given to Best Actor, Best Actress, Best Ensemble and Best Solo Show. www.thestage.co.uk

The *ThreeWeeks* Editors' Awards

Ten awards chosen by the team at the free festival newspaper for the events that 'make the Edinburgh Festival extra special'. www. threeweeks.co.uk/awards

Total Theatre Award

An important award in the physical theatre world, this one is designed to celebrate accomplishment in the work of professional practitioners of 'theatre, live art, visual performance, mime, experimental theatre, clown, circus, street arts, mask, cabaret and new variety, site-specific, dance-theatre, puppet-theatre and more'. The work does not have to be new but it does have to be pushing the art form in new directions. Awards are given for innovation, visual theatre and an emerging company. To qualify, you need to submit an application by the end of July. After it is seen by two initial assessors, it may be shortlisted and seen by a panel of twelve judges. www.totaltheatre.org.uk/awards

Zebra Awards

Promoted by Edinburgh's Dupliquick Digital Printing, these awards are for the effective design of posters, postcards and flyers on the Fringe. Applicants email an example of their intended publicity material, three members of the Dupliquick staff select a shortlist of twenty and an independent panel chooses the winners. All this is done before the start of the Fringe to give extra value to the first prize of £250 cash and £250 of printing, with similar runners-up prizes. www.dqprint.co.uk

12. The Show Must Go On
First-night Nerves and Second-night Wobbles

IT'S HAPPENED. YOU'VE BEEN planning for this moment for months, if not years. You have booked your venue, found somewhere to live, rehearsed your show, planned your publicity campaign and here you are in Edinburgh ready to give your all. Now the excitement can really begin – and so can the drama. There will be teething problems, glitches, full-blown disasters, unexpected triumphs and a whole host of opportunities opening up. Some things you can prepare for, others you just have to deal with when they hit you.

The first challenge is getting into your venue. The more ready your show is, the easier you will adapt to the venue's technical demands. You are likely to be working in a newly constructed space with an all-new production team, so you should be ready for things to move slowly at the start. The more efficient you are, and the more co-operative you are to work with, the more you will help everyone else. At the same time, be vigilant about getting everything the venue promised you. Producer Dana MacLeod recalls the time a company arrived to find the stage was exactly the size the venue had promised – great – except there was a grand piano on it – not so great. 'It's a situation where the artists are very vulnerable and they're dealing with a chain of people and no one quite knows what their responsibility is,' she says, extolling the virtues of taking on an Edinburgh-savvy producer who can speak up on your behalf.

British playwright Simon Stephens also sings the praises of producers, not least because he tried producing one of his own plays and, by his own admission, 'it was shit'. 'I didn't have the energy to get myself out of bed and go and tread the Royal Mile and hand the flyers out,' he says. 'I got really upset by it.'

By contrast, the previous year, 1992, when he had just graduated from the University of York, he had a much better experience:

> It was produced by a woman called Dody Nash, who was a powerhouse of organisation. We couldn't have done it if it hadn't been for her. We were all being arty and drinking too much and she whipped us into shape and got us good press and good publicity.

Make sure your company members are well briefed on what to expect at the Fringe. A first-timer will always find it disorientating, but you can lessen the blow. Explain what kind of commitment you need from everyone, both on stage and off. The less familiar they are with the Fringe, the more explaining you have to do. 'For companies coming from abroad it's a major culture shock,' says Laura Mackenzie Stuart of Universal Arts. 'As actors, their job is to be rehearsed, go on stage and deliver, but not to take their costumes home and wash them.'

Understandably, you will have been putting all the focus on your show, but one of the most important lessons you can learn from the Fringe, according to Alexander Wright, co-artistic director of Belt Up theatre company, is people management:

> Actors will do a hell of a lot for you, but you have to make it feel worthwhile and not take anything for granted, and not take the fact that people are rehearsing twelve hours a day for granted. You should really appreciate how much effort people will put in. They do it willingly, but we're so grateful to them and try our best to look after them.

Director Renny Krupinski says that to keep good company relations when everyone is living and working at such close quarters, you need someone keeping order:

> You have to be able to manage everyone, so whatever traumas they're going through – splitting up with their girlfriends, having problems with their bills, having to go and sign on – you have to keep everybody focused. It's difficult, particularly when you're facing huge losses, you've got problems of your own and you've got to keep on top of that. I go home and I do all the washing, because it has to be ready for the next day. You have to focus everybody daily and say, 'Tomorrow we're going to do this,' make sure they're there and be prepared to bollock people if they start slacking.

From this kind of attitude can emerge a well-disciplined company and a clear plan of action. Jethro Compton, another of Belt Up's artistic directors, recalls the time when a staged fight went dangerously out of control in a promenade production of *Romeo and Juliet*. Performing on the city streets, the actors playing Mercutio and Tybalt went off-script, doused themselves in fake blood and started throwing bins full of glass bottles at each other, much to the distress of passers-by. 'The advice from that would be, if you're coming to Edinburgh for a month, it's intense and emotional and you can only do it with people that you absolutely trust,' he says.

James Wilkes, another of the Belt Up team, agrees:

> You can do the most experimental risk-taking things, but you've got to have a lot of control. You can't wing anything. If you're doing unconventional work, you've got to replace the rules with another set, otherwise you cause so much havoc.

Human beings are good at adapting and it doesn't take long for people to get in the swing of things. Of all companies, Belt Up has a reputation for hard work; in 2010 it took over a whole floor of C Soco and staged its own productions back to back from midday to midnight. The artistic team got little sleep, but they coped. 'You get used to it,' says Compton. 'You always think in the first two days, "I cannot do this. I'm not going to last a month." But a couple of days in, it's exactly the same as having a shower and brushing your teeth in the morning. It stops being stressful, it stops being terrifying, it becomes part of your day.'

Coping with low audiences

Having worked harder than you ever have, you can find it particularly galling not even to get the validation of a decent number of people in your audience. Don't let it get to you. Audience numbers can vary enormously from day to day and you should be ready for the worst. Whatever the Fringe throws at you, it is important to maintain a professional work ethic argues Tomek Borkowy, Mackenzie Stuart's partner in Universal Arts:

> I've seen it a number of times when, after a two-star review and five people in the audience, a company collapses and they start to fight each other. My old teacher in Poland used to say, 'If you have one person in your audience, you have to be as good as if you have a full house.' We on stage are hired people who have to give the best, otherwise there's no point. Most Eastern European professional companies, it is the same whether they perform for two people or 200. They can cope with that because of the training. It is often a shock for them coming to Edinburgh, but the show is on the same level all the time.

Even with the most successful shows, audience numbers can be erratic and it takes discipline to adjust. Tommy Sheppard, artistic director of the Stand Comedy Club, says his venue hits an average of 60 per cent capacity over the festival. Averages, of course, disguise the fact that some shows sell out and others struggle, he explains:

> It's not a meritocracy. Your show could be really good, but that doesn't mean you're going to sell any tickets for it. That's one of the cruel things about the Fringe. There's no way that critics can go round every show, never mind audiences, and there aren't enough audiences to go round. My advice is to approach it as a bit of a laugh and try and keep a sense of perspective. If you take it too seriously it'll be a nightmare of an experience.

For a model positive frame of mind, look no further than actor and director Cora Bissett. She was the co-star of the internationally successful *Midsummer*, a romantic musical comedy by David Greig and Gordon McIntyre, and was the director of the equally successful *Roadkill*, a harrowing site-specific drama about sex trafficking. In her time, she has done everything from a promenade production in the Royal Botanic Garden in Toby Gough's *Linnaeus Prince of Flowers* ('running round the Botanics with blue hair, dressed up as a flower, getting chased by some guy with a big book') to Jim Cartwright's *I Licked a Slag's Deodorant* with Glasgow's Arches Theatre at the Assembly Rooms:

> I've played to roaring crowds and the legendary two men and a whippet. At the worst end it can be pretty grim. *I Licked a Slag's Deodorant* was getting great critical reviews and the people that did come seemed to love it, but we got some very small audiences. If you're not quite the hit show, you can just get missed. It's one thing playing an up-beat piece of daft Fringe stuff to two men and a whippet, but when you're pouring your heart out playing a crack addict and doing simulated sex off-stage every afternoon at 12 p.m. to two

people, you ask yourself a lot of questions! But you just get on with it. I don't even remember being that down about it. I just thought, well, it's swings and roundabouts.

The healthiest attitude is to think in the long-term and treat the Fringe as merely one stage in your career. Michael McIntyre, for example, is now said to be the most financially successful comedian in the UK, but his success was hard won. Had he been discouraged by his box-office figures on the Fringe, he would not now be playing stadium gigs. Fringe box office manager José Ferran worked at the Pleasance at the time and recalls a different comedian from the star we know today:

> I remember McIntyre, I think it was in 2000, not having the greatest summer in the Pleasance Attic. I remember him coming into the box office and saying, 'Is this usual?' We'd say, 'You just have to keep at it.' A couple of us would go and see his show on a quieter night – and he was pretty good then. It's just building the audience. It's incredible what the Fringe does not only for comedy, but for a lot of theatre companies that do grow and develop.

Faced with a small audience for the final night of his run in an otherwise successful year, Nick Doody came up with a novel solution. Instead of doing his show, he took his audience of four next door to see Matt Kirsten's show. He points out that low audiences are not the worst thing you have to deal with:

> I had a Glaswegian dock worker in my show three years ago and he just could not be shut up. As a result, the audience that night got to hear about half the show. He took up so much time, I had to slash and burn whole twenty-minute chunks. It was an electric experience, in some ways the best night, because it was just pure performance. There must be

times when that happens in other places, but Edinburgh's just a bit special that way.

On coping with pressure

To get an idea of the kind of intensity Fringe performers endure, talk to Mark de Rond. He is an anthropologist and ethnographer at the Cambridge Judge Business School who specialises in studying people working under pressure. His subjects have included students competing in the Oxford–Cambridge boat race, military surgeons in Afghanistan and comedians on the Edinburgh Fringe. 'They're people who are reasonably bright, putting themselves on the line and quite affected personally by what they do,' says De Rond, who watched a dozen performances by Terry Alderton, charting how the routines changed in reaction to the audience, as well as studying Catriona Knox, who was performing on PBH's Free Fringe:

> It can be very stressful. Looking at Terry day after day, some days he'd feel good, other days he'd feel terrible. Poor guy: you go to sit in the Brooke's Bar and you'll see whether things have gone well or not well as the audience come out and you can see from the whites of their eyes if they've had a good night or not. The comedians expose themselves to that.

He is reluctant to overstate the connection between soldiers and comedians – his studies are qualitatively different – but he admits there are some comparisons. This would be true for comedians at any point in the year, but performing thirty days in a row on the Fringe sends the tension levels rocketing.

> They do get tired – and tired of themselves as well, because cracking the same joke night after night and making it look

spontaneous is all part of the routine. There's something about being worn out by thirty consecutive performances and sick and tired of it that adds to the level of stress and exhaustion.

De Rond's picture is one comedian Ed Byrne recognises:

There's a relentlessness; you're in the goldfish bowl like you never normally are. If you're of a reasonable profile, then there'll be two or three members of the press and/or the entertainment industry every night. So every show is like a career breaker. There is the pressure to sell tickets and there is also a desire to get good press. Yes, there are some people who will sell tickets regardless of what press they get, but you go to Edinburgh, in part, for your career and good press is part of that. For most people in comedy, it's the only time you will ever get reviewed. So there's a lot of pressure.

Catriona Knox talks about the phenomenon of 'Brooke's eyes' to describe the way nobody can look each other in the face in the Brooke's Bar, a haunt for stand-up comedians in the Pleasance Dome, because they are always gazing over their shoulders in case someone more important is in the room. The combination of competition, personal investment and a fragile ego can mean an ambitious comedian will be made miserable by something as small as a dip in ticket sales or a less than complimentary review. At the Stand Comedy Club, artistic director Tommy Sheppard has seen what happens when a performer buckles under the pressure:

You do see people who are not 100 per cent committed to what they're doing on stage; they maybe haven't quite worked it out fully or something's not working for them. They begin to lose confidence in the show, then if they have a small house they would rather cancel than proceed with it.

You then get into a vicious circle. That happens occasionally – not very often, but I've seen it.

The best solution to deal with these stresses, says De Rond, is to have someone to talk to. 'You need a network of close friends,' he says. 'You don't need many of them, but at least one person you can talk to and who can reciprocate.'

It is a way of getting some perspective, a quality in short supply when everything seems so important. Mel Giedroyc agrees. She remembers getting audiences of one when she and Sue Perkins made their Fringe debut as Mel and Sue in 1993. They returned for several seasons before establishing themselves on TV and have been back since, notably when Giedroyc took a lead role in *Eurobeat: Almost Eurovision!* 'The best thing I ever did one year was I went to Portobello beach,' she says, referring to the seaside town that's less than half an hour on the bus from Edinburgh. 'I had a day that was totally non-festival. It's the best thing you can do. Or go to Glasgow for the night and get some reality.'

On coping with failure

If you are at the start of your career, you should relish the opportunity the Fringe gives you to learn and develop. With hindsight, you might discover success is not a five-star hit, but an experience on which you can build and come back stronger the following year. 'It was the making of my career,' says Simon Stephens:

I was really glad that *Bluebird*, which was my first professional production, was my eighth play and that I'd done all those Fringe plays and exercised the muscle of writing a play, putting it on, it plays for four nights at university and then you write another one. The Fringe was particularly important for me: it took me away from the comfort zone of a university environment and you're testing it with proper punters. The thrill of them enjoying the plays and staying, or the challenge of them walking out in the middle of the play because they were bored; as a writer, you really learn. How am I going to stop them from walking out? What am I going to do to make it better? I loved it. At the time it was really hard because one wants to thrive and be successful, but something I always try and tell my eldest son is you learn from failure, you don't learn from success.

'If you're in a show and getting bad reviews and it's only half-full every night, it can become real hell,' says Martyn Jacques, lead singer of the Tiger Lillies:

There are a lot of artists that really suffer. I spoke to an Australian performer who told me it was hell for the first two weeks; nobody was coming and it cost her $20,000 to come over here. She has this dream of becoming a cabaret star and it was really awful for her and she was utterly depressed. That happens to a lot of people. All you can do is commiserate and say, 'I've been there myself.' The only thing you can do is learn from your experience. You do learn a lot about yourself in Edinburgh.

If you are aware of the success of *Between the Devil and the Deep Blue Sea*, you will be surprised to learn it was a show borne of failure. The production, a series of gothic tales set in an animated landscape, won a *Scotsman* Fringe First, a *Herald* Angel, the Total Theatre Award, an Arches Brick Award and the Carol Tambor Best of Edinburgh Award, and was snapped up by festivals around the world. Twelve months earlier, however, the 1927 company had a different story to tell. Writer and performer Suzanne Andrade, before going on stage in her latest sell-out show at London's Battersea Arts Centre, says:

Paul Barritt and I had gone to Edinburgh the year before and had this massive failure of a show. One day no one turned up. It was a literary cabaret thing and the section Paul and I had done was similar to what we're doing now; I was stood telling very strange stories in among projections. We were really proud of what we'd done, so we never doubted the work and we got to meet such interesting people who we're still friends with now. It made us really determined to come back the next year and have a successful show.

Rather than be defeated by poor audiences, they set about making the most of the opportunity they had:

We went to see loads of shows and said, 'OK, we can feel what the Edinburgh audience wants, so let's go and make a show that they want.' It feels like people are hungry for something new in Edinburgh – they're looking for a different experience. So we made *Between the Devil and the Deep Blue Sea* with Edinburgh in mind. Because we'd done so many cabaret shows, we knew the audience were going to like it and that it was a good festival piece, but we didn't think for a second that critics would like it and it still surprises me when we get good reviews.

Coping with reviews

Be careful what you wish for, goes the saying, and in all the clamour to get reviews, you can forget that critics might not tell you what you want to hear. For many people in Edinburgh, this can be a double shock because it is the first time their work has ever been reviewed. Stand-up comedy is written about only sporadically for the rest of the year and in the other art forms younger performers rarely come under the critical spotlight. 'You really have to be prepared for harsh judgement at the festival,' says comedian Phil Nichol, on his way to the Stand Comedy Club to perform his latest solo show:

> It's more so than anywhere else because you're getting compared with every other act. Sometimes it goes your way, because you are a new act and people give you some leeway, and sometimes it doesn't. Reviewers are human beings who have good days and bad days. Critics can be quite harsh. You have to be prepared to get up here and realise that what you've got is not what you think you have.

How you respond to negative comments depends on your temperament. You can take it on the chin and try to learn from it or you can argue that a review is only one person's opinion. Miriam Attwood, former media manager at the Fringe Office, says you need to keep things in perspective:

> With bad reviews, people are often embarrassed, but it's not the end of the world. Think about how other areas are going. How are your audiences? How are you getting on with people on the street? Go back to your reasons for coming to the Fringe. Did you come to get reviews? Or did you come because you just wanted to perform your show? Go back to that ethos and, in the grand scheme of things, how does it really matter?

She gives the example of a musical duo who were unperturbed by getting several mediocre reviews because they were attracting an audience of thirty a night and people were enjoying themselves. The bad reviews made no difference to the good time they were having. 'We do meet people who are peeved about reviews, but we'll just sit them down and say, "Let's have a cup of tea and move on to the next thing."'

That is the approach that worked for producer Stefania Bochicchio bringing Compagnia della Quarta from Italy to make its Fringe debut with *Cento Cose*, a piece of physical theatre. It is the middle of the festival and, despite getting a review she describes as 'devastating' from Kelly Apter in the *Scotsman*, she remains undaunted. 'I took the Fringe as going to a crusade and, in that case, you've got to keep your eyes fixed on Jerusalem at the end of it,' she says at a time when, despite the mixed reviews, the show is attracting 75 per cent houses in a fifty-seater venue:

Anything that happens in between is just a matter of strategy. You shift your cavalry somewhere else. I'm firmly enjoying my stay here, maybe because I set out with the idea of making the most of it. Seeing how people deal with criticism is a bit of a filter: you see if you are really cut out for this job. Some performers feel attacked personally by bad reviews and maybe they lose the ability to put it into context. But some of the best performances came after bad reviews. When the adrenalin was flowing, they focused and gave some of the most intense performances I've seen them do.

It is hard not to let reviews affect you personally, but it can help to remember no review is definitive, says Chris Grady:

I've witnessed firsthand the sheer devastation there is to a performer who has given their all seeing that two-star review. And the sheer joy and elation that comes an hour later when the same show gets a five-star review in the *Metro*.

A negative review can be particularly bewildering for those who are not used to being written about and for those who have no professional aspirations. Directing the amateur Edinburgh Graduate Theatre Group, Claire Wood has to ensure criticism does not undermine morale:

215

It's fifteen people who are doing day jobs and then struggling to get on at 7.30 p.m. Most of them haven't had a chance to get something to eat, others are putting the kids to bed in this little gap. The commitment is crazy when you're doing it on an amateur basis. When you're doing it for fun, it's vexing to have people being very critical because maybe you forgot your lines and were a little bit fluffy one night. So I had to do rousing pep talks every now and again, all the classic management techniques to spur them on and cheer them up.

Publicist Liz Smith says there has been only one occasion in a long Fringe career where she felt a *Scotsman* reviewer got it so badly wrong that she was compelled to have a quiet word with the editor. On that occasion, her judgement was right: the editor saw the show, loved it and fast-tracked it for a Fringe First. This is exceptionally rare, however, and like it or not, a review will usually be a fair assessment of your work – at least from that one reviewer's point of view. Smith says you have to be realistic:

I think you have to be brutally honest. In some cases, you can say, Well, yes, it hasn't worked out the way you thought it was going to, there is nothing you can do about it now, but read the review and see if there are positive things you can take from it. It is heartbreaking for actors.

As ever, you should return to the first principles of Chapter 4, remind yourself why you are in Edinburgh and get back in the fight. If you are convinced of the merit of your show, you need to let people know, says Alex Rochford, former programmer and producer at Assembly:

You've got to get on the phone and get another reviewer in for your own peace of mind that what you're presenting is the best work you can present and that reviewer was wrong.

Watching other people's work, Simon Stephens knows how much opinions can differ, which is not to say you should dismiss every review out of hand:

> I saw one play this year that got a one-star review from the *Guardian* and I really enjoyed it. It was really thrilling and I wrote to the author. There will be somebody in your audience for whom your show is the best thing they've seen all year. But whether you're a writer, an actor, a designer or a director, the Fringe should be a moment on your career. For the writers, I'd say, 'Now, go write the next one.' If you've got a two-star review, get a three-star review next time. My Fringe plays were two-star reviews, occasionally a three-star review. Then the aspiration was to get a four-star review the time after. You keep going back. Don't stop.

Even highly experienced performers can benefit from the experience of performing on the Fringe and taking note of what people say. When a reviewer complained of not being able to make out the words of a Tiger Lillies gig, lead singer Martyn Jacques made efforts to focus on his diction. 'I've been doing this for twenty years, but going up to Edinburgh, you still learn things about who you are and your performance, so I enjoy it,' he says. 'The fact that it's not a runaway success sometimes can be good for you.'

This is the kind of attitude Charlie Wood, co-artistic director of the Underbelly, believes to be most productive. You should be careful about making alterations to your performance too rashly and you need to know whose opinions to trust, but it is a question of enjoying the creative experience and not being disappointed by unrealistic expectations:

> You need to love what you're doing, but if it doesn't happen, you use Edinburgh as another opportunity. You might have a terrible show, but you also have an opportunity in which you

can network, meet other people, see other shows, get other ideas for your next show. It doesn't matter if you lose money as long as you knew you were going to; it doesn't matter if the show doesn't transfer to the West End, because hopefully you've seen another show that's given you another idea or you've met another performer, writer or director with whom you're going to create your next piece of work, and you couldn't have had any of those experiences anywhere else but Edinburgh.

Coping with success

It is not only failure that takes its emotional toll. Learning to cope with acclaim, especially in the distorting bubble of the Fringe, takes some doing as well. By all means revel in the attention, but when the applause dies down, you should try to put it in perspective. If you start to believe your own publicity, you can come unstuck. 'For a lot of companies, it's the start of a journey,' says Lyn Gardner, theatre critic on the *Guardian*, who tempers her love of finding new talent on the Fringe with the knowledge that many companies produce their best work at a later stage. 'There is a danger that companies or individuals can become over-feted. You've got to go out and prove yourself in other arenas.'

Cora Bissett, who won the Stage Award for Best Actress for her part in *Midsummer* and won seven awards as director of *Roadkill*, learned at a young age that success can be illusory. When she was seventeen, her band Darlingheart landed a five-album record deal with Phonogram and supported Blur, the Cranberries and Radiohead on tour:

> I was told we were the next big thing. Even then, I was quite a sussed seventeen-year-old and I thought, 'Hmm, we'll see.' It went horrifically, quintessentially wrong and we

were absolutely not the next big anything. As much as it was devastating at the time, it did me a brilliant service in life really early on. People will acclaim you today and forget you tomorrow. You should take it all with a pinch of salt. They might mean it in the moment, but you're yesterday's news by next summer. You go into the Traverse the day after the Fringe has finished and all your *Roadkill* posters and all your five-star gleaming reviews are down – it's a new bar, a new play and a new story. Everybody likes to be appreciated, but I know I could be in next year's turkey. Enjoy the moment, be in the present, but know that it doesn't mean anything, you're just in a very good moment right now.

After she won a host of awards for her debut play *Eight*, it took Ella Hickson a couple of return visits to the Fringe to work out what her early success meant:

I can't say enough how lucky I was to have my first experience being *Eight*, but it's a very funny yardstick. The first thing I ever wrote I was in every newspaper on the Fringe. In the last week of the Fringe, people would stop me and say, 'Oh my God, you're a hit.' And that has never happened again and probably never will. I am slowly learning to embrace the much more humble, steady and quiet long-game. It is a work ethic that I respect more than I do that hype.

Looking after yourself

Preparing for the stresses and strains of the Fringe is important, but you should not forget it is also tremendously good fun. You are doing what you love in a city full of people who are doing what they love. The atmosphere is infectious. Many people rate the social side of the festival even higher than the artistic side. One conversation leads to another, one drink leads to another, one bar leads to another. That, of course, has consequences of its own. The fact that so many people perform during the day can compound the problem further. 'God forbid you're in a 2 p.m. show, because you're in the pub at 3.30 p.m.,' says John Clancy. 'You're sitting there because it feels like it's 9 p.m. Get yourself to Bar Napoli as often as you can, eat pasta and get back out.'

Ed Byrne remembers the time in 1995 when, as well as performing in *Young, Gifted and Green*, he was opening for Corky and the Juice Pigs. One afternoon, feeling the effects of the night before, he thought he'd have a quick nap. 'I woke up bang at the time when I was supposed to be on stage,' he says. 'It was one of the most unprofessional things I've done and it was a consequence of overdoing it.'

So too was an even more dramatic no-show three years later. 'One thing that a few of us do is go and play the Leeds and the Reading festivals,' he continues:

> You fly down in the morning, do the gig in the afternoon, then fly back to Scotland to do your evening show. In 1998, I was supposed to do that at Reading. I stayed up all night in Edinburgh, got to the airport, checked in, sat at the gate and fell asleep. I woke up at the gate five hours later, right at the point when I should have been on stage in Reading. My phone had been ringing the entire time.

It's fun to party, but you can have too much of a good thing. If the hedonism starts reducing your capacity to perform, you have got the balance wrong. In truth, when Fringe veterans tell you stories of their wild nights on the town, they are almost certainly not mentioning the many more nights when they went to bed early. 'You can't really complain if you don't have a full house or a successful career if you just come up here and party,' says artist manager Marlene Zwickler. 'It's the world's biggest arts showcase and you've got to find a mix of the two.'

Nick Doody says it is your responsibility to do the best show you can:

> We've all been guilty when we overdid it the previous night and you're a bit hung over. The last show I did had a lot of personal stuff about my mum dying and, because of that, I had a moment before every show where I thought you can't talk about this stuff half-arsed, you have a duty to yourself and everything you're talking about and this one hour has to be as intensely perfect as you can make it. You don't get a night that doesn't matter. Melbourne Festival might be sending somebody along to decide whether or not to invite you or the reviewer from the *Scotsman* might be in. It should go without saying – why would you give an audience a half-arsed show? – but we all have at some stage.

The way to avoid letting yourself down – whether through excessive pleasure or excessive work – is to pace yourself, says Kath Mainland, chief executive of the Fringe Society:

> It's a marathon not a sprint. It's three and a half weeks. It's really difficult when you're two weeks in and it's not going well, but I've seen companies who in the last week will suddenly get a review that they want and their audience will go up or somebody from the Sydney Opera House will come and invite them to do something there. So you have to treat it as a marathon and plug away.

You also need to keep things in proportion. The Fringe is all-consuming and it is easy to get a distorted impression of what is important, says Nica Burns, director of the Edinburgh Comedy Award:

Watch the alcohol intake, watch the substance intake, get some sleep and keep some sense of perspective. Edinburgh is a hothouse and three and a half weeks there feels like three months. Everyone's in each other's pockets. Everyone's asking everyone else how their audiences are doing. If you go up and you know nobody, you'll want to find out how everybody else in your venue is doing. All the groups are very aware of ticket sales and it is very easy to lose your sense of perspective and feel your life, your world, is coming to an end.

She is talking not only of your professional life, but your private life too. 'There's never a festival without a fair amount of tears and a huge amount of break-ups. Don't go with your partner!' she says, only half-joking:

You fall madly in love at the beginning of the festival, you cry during the middle of it and you've broken up by the end. It's very easy for the whole thing to get out of hand. Part of that is quite fun – I have very fond memories of dancing at 4 a.m., totally, er, stimulated – but you have to get on and do your job the next day. You have to be focused and do your best show every night. Keep the perspective: there is life after Edinburgh.

Even if you are being sensible with your alcohol intake, you can find yourself compromising your performance simply because you were straining your voice to be heard in a noisy bar. When Siobhan Redmond was starring in Liz Lochhead's Fringe First-winning *Perfect Days*, the part was so vocally demanding and she was having to do so many interviews for the play's London transfer that she consulted a voice doctor. He described acting as a cross between athletics and opera singing and suggested that if a house is three-quarters full, you should play as if it is three-quarters full. Redmond continues:

That's very hard to do, because nobody likes to feel that they're underselling something. I do take his point that you should be judicious about how you use your voice. You don't need to be using it at the very top of its register all the time. And if you don't need to, then don't. Do what you know will be heard and leave it at that. The other thing is just shut up – and actors are not good at that. 'Vocal naps,' he said. The worst thing is pitching your voice over other people talking. The problem is not being heard in a big auditorium, it's trying to order your drinks in the pub. It's those situations that push your voice.

It is an experience Cora Bissett recognises:

If you're hollering above the noise of 300 people and music, you're absolutely knackered the next day. I would only go out on a late one if I had a late start or a day off the next day. If I had a lunchtime show, I'd take myself off and go and see other shows. You've got to pace yourself. We're all a bit like children inside and it's like a birthday party every night of the week. You come out and everybody you know is there. Even with the best will in the world, you bump into five people you know and it turns into a party – which I love, but I know it can be a total downfall as well.

Redmond recommends Benylin Children's Chesty Cough Mixture for sore throats, while director John Clancy says his actors swear by Vocalzone, lozenges designed for singers and public speakers. Coming from the warmer climes of the USA, he also recommends bringing a couple of sweaters. Actor Nancy Walsh speaks from experience when she says actors should not smoke. 'You're performing every single day but one,' she says. 'When I smoked, I remember losing my voice in *Americana Absurdum*. I broke two blood vessels. Now I don't smoke any more and it feels like I'm a better actor. I've got a lot more energy.'

Phil Nichol starts even the most arduous of Fringe days with a run around Edinburgh's iconic mountain, Arthur's Seat:

> Mental, emotional and physical fitness does help. Comics often get caught in the trap of not pacing themselves or thinking themselves superhuman. Talking about me personally, I've been a bit of a show-off and wanting to be the guy who's the last up at night and first up in the morning and you just have to take care of yourself. In the end, it depends what you want to do the festival for. If you want to come and party and have a good time, it's there to do that; if you want to do a show, to enjoy performing and to genuinely do it for the audience, then take care of yourself. Neither one is right or wrong, but you have to decide which one you want to do.
>
> If you find yourself in week three with no voice, unable to do the routines that you love and the audience isn't getting it, you feel that you're letting them down and yourself down and it's really discouraging. There's a lot of industry pressure to produce a slickly packaged show and by the last week when the TV people roll into town, they're looking at stuff that you know you were doing really well in the first week and you can't hit that note or you're too exhausted or you come in having been up all night and it happens to be the day that the critic from the *Sunday Telegraph* is there, you screw your show up and you're devastated. So being really fit, eating well and taking care of yourself are important. I'm known as someone who burns the candle at both ends, but I also take care of myself. Give yourself some personal space, a bit of you-time, outside of the show and outside of the partying.

Practicalities: warming up

Keep your eyes open during August and you will spot all kinds of behaviour that would normally be considered odd. Down an alleyway, you notice a dozen people having a group hug; through the window of a second-floor flat, you see a company in the middle of a singing exercise; on the Royal Mile, you catch a physical theatre group going through movements that are half warm-up and half flyering opportunity. The pressure on space to perform has a knock-on effect on the available places for performers to prepare. Away from the Fringe, you will be used to getting to the venue in good time to ready yourself for the show. On the Fringe, you have to make alternative arrangements. 'You have to grab what you can,' says actor Cora Bissett:

> When we did the Vox Motus show *Slick*, we had a flat just up the road. We used to all warm up in the flat and then walk down to the theatre together. Otherwise there was no space to do it as a group. It's important when you're working in an ensemble to hit base with everybody before you meet on stage.

Even if you are doing a one-person show or for some reason you don't need to warm up, you can find it hard to get yourself into a performing frame of mind amid the hubbub. Bissett knows it can be difficult:

> At the Traverse, you can't get into your dressing room until thirty minutes before the show because someone else is in it. You've only just got time to get your costume on, get your make-up on and get on stage. Trying to find some moment of calm to focus your head is hard. I try and find nooks and crannies in the building beforehand just to get my head down and find a bit of space.

Chris Grady agrees:

It goes for any actor, dancer or musical theatre performer that you don't wander to the theatre having had a nice boozy lunch and go straight into a show. Warm up the voice, warm up the body and prepare for it. The chance is that the most important person in your life is the person sitting there that night in the auditorium – and they want to see the best performance you can possibly give.

On the Fringe, this remains true throughout the festival. It is not like other places where all the influential people turn up on a single opening night. John Clancy recalls how, a week or so into the run, his production of *Horse Country* was playing to an audience of six, including himself, when Joyce McMillan of the *Scotsman* saw it. The actors maintained their professionalism, gave a 'blistering' performance and earned themselves a five-star review, a Fringe First and eventual full houses.

A lot of big decision-makers wait until the end of the festival when all the reviews are in and the consensus is there, so they can see the five shows that have a buzz. So right at the end of your run when you're exhausted (whether it's a hit or not), that can be some of your most important shows. That's why you have to prepare yourself. You have to open strong and you have to close stronger. If you have to go out every night, sleep in.

Week two

The time to be particularly on your guard is week two. You sail through week one on a tide of energy, adrenalin and optimism.

226

Anything seems possible. But by the second week, the dust is starting to settle. Word is out about the must-see shows, the mediocre reviews are coming in for the rest, you are getting tired and, somehow, the Fringe isn't feeling quite as glamorous as it did a few days ago. Pockets of cynicism pop up all over town; reviewers despair at ever discovering the big hit show; programmers say last year provided richer pickings than this year; companies swear blind the bad/good weather (delete as applicable) has adversely affected their audience figures. With a little perspective, you realise they say this every year – because every year the story of the festival plays out in a similar way – but this knowledge will not help if your show is losing momentum.

It is a scenario with which John Clancy is familiar:

> The one thing I've seen over and over is an untested company coming up, opening strong, then the drinks are taking their toll, they did not get a Fringe First, they only got three stars, and the show begins to unravel right when it really should be as tight as it can be.

Alex Rochford refers to the grimmest day of the festival as 'suicide Tuesday', when the post-weekend blues are compounded by low mid-week audiences. If it has been raining, he says, the mood is more desperate still. He recommends finding support in fellow performers:

> That's when the venue mentality comes together and all the companies congregate in our club bar or the Pleasance courtyard or the bar at Universal Arts. They've all got this central area where the companies just have to come together. They help each other through the Wednesdays and the Thursdays.

Chris Grady agrees you need others to help you through it:

It's awful. I have graphs of it. You can see incredibly clearly the path of a show that gets not very good reviews and they begin to lose heart. It slowly stagnates and the gross at the box office slows down. It's not good for the health doing Edinburgh. The lows and the highs are extraordinarily exaggerated. Never be alone. You need a friend, somebody there who's supporting you. The week-two slump needs to be supported by someone coming and having a party with you, giving you great feedback and telling you you're wonderful. And go and support each other's shows. If you've got a low point, someone else will be having a low point as well.

In the back room of the Stand Comedy Club there is a wall planner to keep track of the festival reviews. In week two Jen Lavery, the press officer, has written in enormous letters: HUGS! 'That's when everyone needs a hug,' says Tommy Sheppard:

We do make a point here of saying to all our fifty comedians, 'Try and see each other's shows and support each other.' We have a family support mechanism here. Ironically, the bigger the venue the more lonely the experience of playing it because the more anonymous you are. Some people here if they aren't getting the houses and they might get a two-star review and they're beginning to feel miserable, I send them off to the other venues to have a chat with their mates and they come back refreshed because everyone's having a worse time. They get a sense of perspective.

At some venues, the performers make a commitment to supporting each other, as actor Anthony Black found at Hill Street Theatre:

We proposed a solidarity pact whereby we would endeavour to see each other's shows early in the run, to give each other a bit of an audience boost (even though they're comp tickets), just to feel a little support and also so we can spread the word about each other's shows. It was a good way to feel that we weren't alone in all of this.

All this helps you look beyond the immediate demands of your own show. That is important not only for your mental health, but also for your artistic development. Being in Edinburgh, you are at the heart of a cultural crucible and you have an unparalleled opportunity to see the work of some of the most accomplished practitioners in your field. It is an opportunity you should grab. As you meet fellow artists all over the city, make use of the facilities laid on at Fringe Central and engage in the work of your peers, you can set the course of your future career (more of this in the next chapter). At the same time, whether your show is a hit or not, you can only learn from the experience of performing. 'This is the best place in the world to perform, to show your work and to develop,' says Miriam Attwood:

You can perform twenty-one times in a row and see three shows every day, develop ideas and talk to other people about theatre or to other comedians, seeing what changes every night with a different audience. It's very exciting.

It is this excitement that will carry you through. Coupled with your careful preparation, good company communication and solid belief in your show, the thrill of being in the Fringe's artistic crucible will provide you with the extra reserves of energy you need. As long as you maintain a professional attitude, keep some kind of perspective and look after yourself, it's possible to have fun off stage and on. If you get a taste for it, the next chapter is for you.

13. The Next Step
Beyond the Fringe and Back Again

FOR MANY PEOPLE, PERFORMING on the Edinburgh Fringe is the beginning and the end of their ambitions. They are delighted to have had the experience and return happily to their schools, universities or day jobs. If you're one of them, you can skip this chapter. If, on the other hand, you are one of the great number of participants who hope the Fringe will further their career, read on.

Let's start with the good news: countless artists get their first break on the Fringe. Some of them have a high-profile hit, others get picked up by an agent. There are comedians who land TV deals and shows that go on to global acclaim. Check out the autumn and spring seasons at venues such as the Soho Theatre and the Pleasance London and just look at the number of post-Edinburgh shows. There are a lot. 'I've been going up for ten years actively looking for stuff,' says Mark Godfrey, Soho's executive director. 'We can always sort out quite a lot of the programme with a good trip to Edinburgh. There's always something that's going to surprise you that you haven't seen or heard of elsewhere.'

Every other year, the British Council invites international promoters to a showcase of theatre and dance. The organisation estimates £1.5m-worth of deals are signed each time. The Scottish government's Made in Scotland programme and seasons supported by Culture Ireland have the same aim. Some companies just get lucky. 'The Fringe made us,' says 1927's Suzanne Andrade, whose

Between the Devil and the Deep Blue Sea got a rave review from Lyn Gardner in the *Guardian*, kicking off a wave of sustained press interest:

> I can't even think what would have happened to us if we hadn't taken our show to Edinburgh. The success we had was phenomenal. We didn't expect that for a second. We had this huge world tour booked. Suddenly it was a whirlwind. You'd wake up in the morning laughing, thinking, 'What's going on? This seems absurd.' I can't think of a platform that would give us the kind of thing Edinburgh gave us.

Judith Doherty has taken her Edinburgh-based company Grid Iron to cities including Cork, Stavanger and Beirut:

> Grid Iron wouldn't have had all the experiences and wouldn't have the reputation that we have if we hadn't had exposure in the Fringe. It's the biggest arts market in the world. You have also those different festivals happening at the same time, so you have all those producers and promoters coming from all different levels of festival and venue and looking for product. You can be a tiny company with a really hot show and somebody from the Sydney Festival can have been told to go along and see you. It might take two or three years for them to get back in touch, but you're not going to get that anywhere else in the world.

There is no denying all of this happens. The caveat is you cannot guarantee it happening to you. In such a big festival, there are many shows that are never heard of again, many actors who don't get spotted and many comedians who return to their day jobs. There is no room for their stories in the rags-to-riches mythology of the Fringe. The reality is that few participants are overnight sensations, as Charlie Wood, co-artistic director of the Underbelly, explains:

There's no better place in the world to come and try your show, but please don't bank on it having a longer life. I would never try to persuade someone to come up to Edinburgh for the reason that their show will get taken on. The chances are it won't. The point is, you've got more chance here than you have anywhere else.

Although you cannot bank on a post-Edinburgh life for your show, you can make efforts to maximise the chances of being spotted and to be ready to act effectively. 'Being responsive to opportunity is as realistic as you can be,' says Louise Oliver, the Fringe's participant development coordinator. To do that, you have to be clear in your mind what your ambitions are, ready to sell your show to producers and prepared for success. How to achieve that is what this chapter is about.

Why tour?

Before working out how to be seen by the right people, you should question your motives. Just as you should have a clear idea about why you want to perform on the Fringe, so you should know why you want to take your show on tour. There are many valid reasons, but knowing what your reason is will help you make decisions along the way, as Louise Oliver says:

> Some companies say, 'We've got this show, we want to tour, we maybe want to go to Germany.' But they have absolutely no idea why they want to go to Germany or why their show might be right for Germany.

David Sefton, artistic director of the Adelaide Festival, recommends caution:

You hear young companies saying, 'Oh we've got a gig in Lincoln, Nebraska.' You could end up putting a huge amount of effort for the equivalent of taking a gig in Strathclyde and it just feels glamorous because it's America. Companies should think through why they want to be on the road, why they want to be booked and where they're going.

Whether you want to expand your horizons, discover new artistic possibilities, reach new audiences or build a national or international reputation, you should be certain your company is ready for it, says New York director John Clancy:

A very good question to ask is, 'Let's plan for success, let's say this will be very successful – can we tour?' Is this cast ready to pick up, leave their lives for even a couple of months and go around the world? You have to look at jobs, family, classroom commitments, so that you know in your head even if there is success, what it can translate as. Try to be objective and specific: 'What we really want is a sit-down in London,' 'We really want to go to Australia,' 'We just want some great reviews to build on next time we go,' 'We want to see a bunch of shows and see this beautiful city.' You're thrown into the ocean and you have to have some sense that the shore is that way or that we'll all meet back at the boat or else you're all just going to thrash around.

This kind of thinking will help focus your strategy in the run-up to the Fringe and once you are in Edinburgh. Mark Godfrey agrees:

Think beforehand what is your dream fit: a venue, an agent, a TV deal or whatever it is you're trying to get out of it. Then try and find out when those people are going to be in Edinburgh and then, not bombard them, but let them know you're there and invite them. Ideally, get somebody else to tell them and just get it on their radar. That buzz starts pre-Edinburgh. I don't necessarily book, but I think, 'Oh, yes, I know about that one.' It makes sense to be sitting down and researching, having a look at where you want to be and making a personal direct approach to them, which is much more effective than emailing a hundred theatres.

Ideally, these are questions you will have asked even before choosing a venue. Chasing promoters and agents is not so different to chasing audiences and critics: being in the right place at the right time can make all the difference, as Louise Oliver explains:

Look at where all the programming venues are geographically. Look at the other kinds of work they programme, do some research about the previous work they've picked up from the Fringe, compare your work with that and see if it is right. If you do that research nice and early, you can get in touch with them earlier in the year when they're not inundated with Fringe performers.

Getting the show seen

If you are serious about wanting a life for your show beyond the festival, you have to do all you can to ensure promoters are seeing you at your best. Louise Oliver again:

The first and most important piece of advice is to ask if your work is good enough. Is it going to work? Is it quality stuff? It really surprises me how often companies say to promoters, 'Yes, I've got this show, but it's not really the show I wanted to put on and there's this other show I want to get booked.' Why would you spend all this money and effort coming to what is the most fiercely competitive environment in the arts world and not put on what you think is your best work? That's madness to me.'

Tina Rasmussen, director of performing arts at Toronto's Harbourfront Centre, says it is important to have a sense of where your work fits in the Fringe ecology and what should be its logical next step:

Learning the best way to position your work is critical. That's how you can have leverage; otherwise, it's just a one-shot deal. If you understand where in the ecology you fit, you can lead a discussion around the work at the festival.

Rasmussen has been visiting the Fringe for a decade and routinely sees anything from forty to seventy-five shows on each trip. Because she is programming a season rather than a festival, she is on the lookout for shows that can stand alone and do not depend on the Fringe atmosphere:

If somebody is working hard to get me to see their show, I try to honour that. But do some research. If you're doing an outdoor water show, don't look for a presenter who runs a venue in a desert.

She also keeps track of interesting companies, which is one reason for you to make repeat visits to the Fringe. Overnight successes rarely happen overnight. You need to plan for the long term. David Sefton, who is unlikely to be persuaded by companies cold-calling him, says he looks instead for a demonstrable track record:

It's hard to go into Edinburgh without having done anything before. Of course, sometimes the word of mouth happens when they're in Edinburgh and there's nothing you can do to force that apart from doing a good show. When five or ten people say to you, 'Have you heard about blah?' that tends to get you to go.

An early date with the Fringe's participant development coordinator will help thrash out your most effective approach, as well as steering you towards promoters who might be interested. It is possible, of course, not to realise how good your show is until you arrive on the Fringe and find yourself dealing with a hit. If that is the case, it is not too late to capitalise on it, says Oliver:

> There are three weeks to plug away and make those connections and figure out what you're going to do. In an ideal world, you want to start thinking about that beforehand because it makes everybody's job easier if you've got a clear idea of what you are after. But if you have an unexpected success, don't worry, come in and speak to us. We've had a couple of companies come in and say, 'We've won a Fringe First, everybody's excited about our show and we don't know what to do.'

Networking

If the very idea of networking strikes fear into your heart, you are not alone. It is an activity that is neither entirely social nor entirely professional and that can make you uncomfortable. You feel awkward selling yourself and hypocritical pretending you are not selling yourself. If it is any consolation, the people with whom you are networking probably feel the same. Judith Doherty, producer of Grid Iron theatre company, has never got completely used to it:

> I still get really nervous in those big environments. If it's your first or second event, it's helpful to remember that everyone – even people like me that have done the festival lots of times

– can still be quite nervous and might not always be on form for the whole selling thing.

What you should not forget is that the Fringe lets you network more freely and more widely than anywhere else. Get over your nervousness and plunge in. Opportunities range from events at Fringe Central to informal encounters pretty much anywhere you happen to be, but in particular at promoter-friendly haunts such as the Traverse bar. Louise Oliver says it's a question of attitude:

The trick is being prepared, looking professional, being nice and not harassing people. You should listen and you should chat. Treat it like any other social situation. Don't be daunted. Everybody's there for the same reason. It's your job to get out there and promote your show. But be sunny. If you're going to be grumpy, don't go. Remember that it's better to have one really good conversation than to fly round an event with fifty cards, throwing them about like ninja stars, because you're more likely to come away with something.

As someone on the receiving end, Tina Rasmussen agrees:

There's a fine line between pestering, stalking and making people aware. Go to the bars where the presenters go. Introduce yourself and talk about the presenters, learn about what they're doing, the work that they're seeing, what they're excited about – because that's what we like talking about – and then follow up with, 'Come to my show.' Don't do a hard sell to the presenters.

Switching from actor to director, Cora Bissett had to deal with promoters for the first time when her site-specific production *Roadkill* became the talk of the Fringe, winning at least seven awards:

You know it's a cliché to say all the deals are done in bars, but it really is true. I'd been down to see the show, made notes, been in meetings all day and I got a call to say David Sefton really wanted to meet me in the Traverse bar, but he wouldn't be there till about midnight. So I'm drinking Cokes and Red Bulls and he doesn't arrive until 1.45 a.m. and I am sitting hanging off the edge of the table going, 'Oh my God, I know this could be really good for the show, but I just want to go to my bed.' And it was worth it, because we had a great chat.

'She can cope,' laughs Sefton, a couple of months later at the Dublin Theatre Festival. 'I have every confidence in Cora and I really liked that show.'

Bissett continues:

It is about building those personal contacts. Promoters like building up a good personal relationship with you because, as much as they may love your show, if they find you a bit of a pain in the arse, chances are they won't fancy working with you. Half your job as director is to make sure you get on well with people.

Her tip for networking is not to try to seal a deal:

In the first few times you meet someone, it's just about having a laugh, maybe talking about plays you've seen, kind of talking round it and seeing if you've got something in common. Only much further down the line do you go, 'OK, are you interested in having the show next September then?' It's like going on a date when you mustn't talk about the fact you're on a date: 'Do you like me? Are you into this? Is it happening?' You just wouldn't do that.

Sefton confirms it is the best approach:

Cora has a very good attitude which is that she doesn't talk about the work unless you do. It's good not to be too pushy. There's nothing worse than being collared at 1 a.m. by somebody who wants to talk about the prospects for their show. I'm prepared to have that conversation, but I'd rather someone said, 'Can we set up a time to talk about my show which I believe you are interested in?' It's hard, but it's good to pester only people who are actually interested in the show and not just blanket-pester 2,000 people. That can work against you in the end.

Eugene Downes, chief executive of Culture Ireland, has seen how you can bolster your relationship with crucial programmers by running into them several times during the year. In his case, that could be Edinburgh in August, the Dublin Theatre Festival in October and Under the Radar in New York in January:

With that rhythm through the year, you can connect with many of the same presenters. If you're seeing someone once a year it's OK, but if you are connecting with them three times a year in three different places it creates a much more natural, personal, rolling conversation which takes the pressure off. It allows everyone to get to know each other much better and get a sense of each other's tastes and interests, and of the arc of a company's work. Edinburgh is a critical link in that rhythm through the year.

The moment anyone shows an interest in your work, you need to be ready with your contact details so you can talk again later. Judith Doherty makes sure she is prepared:

What you want is for people to be able to take away

something that three weeks later they can go, 'That show was brilliant and now I want to carry on the dialogue.' People spend a fortune on getting big heavy packs of paper to give to promoters. They don't want that. They just put it in the bin. What you want is a DVD, if you've been able to have a bit of the show filmed, and your business card, so they can put it in their suitcase and travel away.

Brokering the deal

Being prepared means knowing the kind of questions a promoter will ask. When is it available? What are the technical requirements? How much will it cost? Will there be additional re-rehearsal costs? On the most basic level, it means agreeing who has the rights to the show – especially if it has been devised and there is no single author – and who is allowed to make the decisions. John Clancy says you should sort out these questions at the start:

It's very important to know from the beginning who owns the property and who is going to make the deal. If you have a deal, even if you're oldest friends, you should have some agreement so that someone is authorised to make those deals. You have to plan for success that way. It's much harder to do business with friends than business with strangers. With strangers, usually you're very careful: what are we talking about, what are the terms, when is the money coming in? With friends, you don't do that because you're friends. When something successful happens, suddenly you're not doing good business.

Having your own producer, whether it is someone already in your company or a third party, allows negotiations to take place with a degree of impartiality and level-headedness. 'This is near impossible, but the artist should not negotiate with the new producer,' says Nancy Walsh. 'It's such a danger. You need somebody who'll be a spokesperson for the company to talk to the producer.'

Producers come in various types, from general managers to those who get involved creatively in building a show from scratch. If you don't already have someone in that role to represent your company, you need to find a person who understands, respects and likes what you are doing. Their fee is unlikely to be less than £1,000 and could be ten times as much, depending on the workload. Producer James Seabright stresses they should be in it for the right reasons:

> I would always advise that people tread carefully in terms of making sure they're bringing on board someone who is sympathetic to what they're doing and isn't just there to fill a gap in their roster or make a quick buck. There are people out there who will do that and it's not good for either party if you end up with a mismatch of show and producer.

When word got out about *Between the Devil and the Deep Blue Sea*, Suzanne Andrade says she accepted some bookings but did avoid a couple of promoters who were 'really sharky'. It was then the company took on a producer to organise everything as the show toured to Korea, Singapore, Australia, Slovenia, South Carolina, Germany and elsewhere:

> Contracts are really hard work and when you've gone to Edinburgh knowing nothing about it, it is all quite overwhelming. Get a producer if your work warrants it. Make your work first and let that justify the producer.

Being prepared also means not saying yes to the first offer that comes along, says Oliver:

If somebody says, 'I want you to come to my venue in Australia,' don't go, 'Yes! Australia! That'll be amazing!' Instead you should go, 'OK, that'll be expensive, what are you offering, let's have a chat.'

This applies even more so if – as is the Fringe way – your first conversation is over a pint or two, as John Clancy says:

> Don't make deals in bars. You have negotiations in pubs – that's where they happen, of course – and if it's really looking good, it's very simple to say, 'Let's leave it until tomorrow morning for coffee and we'll sit down in the cold light of day to figure out what we're talking about.' The artist can get very carried away: 'This guy's buying me drinks, he loves the show, done, shake hands.' You wake up the next day and realise you're touring Tasmania for five months.

Any credible promoter would expect you to behave like this. It is not in their interests to rush into an agreement any more than it is yours. Exchange numbers and, if possible, agree on a time for a follow-up discussion. If you don't hear from them, the ball is in your court, says producer Nica Burns:

> Don't count on them calling you. They might have seen something they prefer, which is disappointing, but they are already a good contact. If they bothered to come and see you, they're serious. They didn't have to do that. So follow it up. If you get some reviews, email them straight away. Do not let the fish wriggle away. At least you made a friend if nothing else and you can invite them to your next show. In my case, there are people who have done exactly that and they keep writing to me and, even if I don't have anything, I always remember them. I've had people who I've seen who have come and done an understudy on a West End job; there's

someone in particular who I saw on the Fringe and they've now got a small part in the National. So any interest you get, grab it with both hands and never let it go. We expect that.

If you are lucky enough to have one promoter interested, you may find others follow in their wake. There is a relatively small pool of them, they all know each other and, if one likes a show, word gets around. Even if they are fighting over you, however, none of them is likely to do a deal on the spot. They want to find out if they can get along with you, establish a relationship and take time to assess the true potential of the show, says Eugene Downes of Culture Ireland:

In many cases, international presenters won't want to put their cards on the table. They need to let the dust settle and then focus on the show. For the artist to have the opportunity to make that face-to-face contact makes everything subsequently so much easier. It makes the Traverse like the agora, the Roman forum, where you can meet people bidden or unbidden.

Cora Bissett says this chimes with her experience as a first-time negotiator:

Talking about deals and tours, I felt quite out of my depth, although there was a huge support network. Nobody wants you to sign on the dotted line because they've got to go back and work out budgets. We had a blueprint for how much it would cost to take *Roadkill* on the road. We had one promoter who said on the night, 'I want it, I'll book it for my festival, no questions asked.' But other people, there's no way that they'd just sign something. So it's never as crazy as that. There was one point when I was in a state of sheer panic because there were too many offers coming in and I didn't know where to start, but for the most part it's a slower process.

As negotiations progress, you should make sure any deal works in your favour. John Clancy says, for example, you should hold out for a guarantee rather than a box-office split:

> With the best of intentions, you can get a split of the house and then go to Sydney and play to ten people. You're a long way from home and your money's gone.

David Sefton says most promoters are 'people sincerely wanting to do stuff' and are not out to rip you off. The worst that could happen is they overstretch themselves by taking on too much. Those to look out for are agents who appear more interested in money than art. 'You do have to be careful if someone says, "I can book you an American tour for eighty-five per cent of your gross box office,"' he says.

What is crucial is that you remain realistic about costs and practicalities, as Judith Doherty explains:

> You should never get your hopes up and don't agree to anything until it's all down in writing. Particularly if you're going overseas, there are a lot of hidden costs, freight costs, duties when you're taking things through ports, the regulations might be different, censorship laws . . . and are you going to be asked to change your show almost out of all recognition to be able to fit into their programme or hit their targets or please the audience they want you to appeal to?

The hype of the Fringe affects promoters as well as companies and, in all the excitement, they might overlook those aspects of your show that would be unsuitable for their audience. Do your research and find out about the place the promoter is from. Decide for yourself if your show sounds like a good match. Doherty's company performed on an island in Norway – and successfully – but only after careful thought:

After all that effort, excitement and money, you need the audience to like your work and your actors to stand on a stage in an island in Norway and be appreciated. If you feel in your gut that it's not a good fit, then you should stop because you're going to lose a lot of money, be heartbroken and exhausted – and probably a bit cold and dirty.

Beyond the Fringe

The Fringe is so consuming, it can be hard to make a clear judgement on the true potential of an Edinburgh hit. A company can watch people fighting for tickets on the Fringe, only to be received with indifference on a subsequent autumn tour. Some work suits the heady festival atmosphere, some is ideal for a short afternoon slot, some panders to a clued-up cosmopolitan audience. Take those factors away and long-term success is less certain. These are the questions that promoters are weighing up. Fortunately, a lot of Fringe hits prove to be more than just a flash in the pan and continue to be successful as they travel. Carol Tambor, who brings one Fringe show to the USA each January through the Carol Tambor Best of Edinburgh Award, understands the risks. 'Every time I have seen the first run-through in New York, I've been holding my breath,' she says. 'But somehow real talent just pops out and the reception has always been terrific.'

Producer Sarah Rogers of Montreal's Menno Plukker argues that to enjoy success beyond the Fringe, you should think bigger than the Fringe from the start. 'A lot of companies come here and they build a show to be a success at the Fringe,' she says. 'And then what?' She brought 2b Theatre Company's *Invisible Atom* to Edinburgh knowing it could never make a profit but gambling it would recoup the deficit in its subsequent life. She believed the show was good enough and her hunch proved right: it was quickly booked for the Sydney Festival and an Australian tour. 'We knew the company had a lot of potential, so it was a matter of getting people to see the work very quickly,' she says.

Your show has been tailored with the specific conditions of the Fringe in mind and it could be necessary to rework it once it goes beyond Edinburgh. If that is the case, you need to budget for making changes, says producer James Seabright:

> Often we'll revisit the show after the Fringe. With Barbershopera as an example, they always do their shows as an hour in Edinburgh, but we've been touring their second show as eighty minutes plus interval. It can be an expensive exercise to revise a show like that, but it made sense for Barbershopera. We do try with shows for which we're envisaging a future life that they're not just a flat hour because that does often prove problematic in terms of them going out to the arts centre circuit. We tend to go towards seventy/eighty minutes for those shows.

None of this should presuppose the Fringe is a jumping-off point to somewhere else. It is an end in itself and if you treat it merely as a stepping stone, your audiences in Edinburgh are likely to feel you are exploiting them. In addition to that, the Fringe can continue to support your career. Taking a hit-and-run approach could turn out less valuable than returning repeatedly. When Ed Byrne skipped the Fringe for a couple of years, for example, he came to realise how important it was to his career as a whole:

> I think that was why my career then took a dip. I wasn't getting asked to do things, the kind of things I used to be asked to do. Partly it was, 'Well, you've been around for a few years now, you've been on these shows, so you've done your time and we'll move on to the next thing.' But also you fall off people's radars when you stop coming to Edinburgh. When you do three or four good shows in a row

in Edinburgh, TV people think, 'Oh, this is the guy now.' I went back in 2003 and did a play; and from 2004, I did shows that got progressively bigger and put my career back up again. Unless you're a megastar, there's a lot to be gained still by doing the Edinburgh Fringe.

It is a pattern Karen Koren, artistic director of the Gilded Balloon, recognises:

Stewart Lee and Richard Herring worked together for a long time and they have always come back. Graham Norton did twelve years at the Fringe before he made it. It wasn't just one or two. Frank Skinner will come back. These people remember what the Fringe did for them. It is continually doing it for so many people. It's about constantly working and believing in your own craft.

At Culture Ireland, Eugene Downes gives the example of playwright Enda Walsh. He found recognition on the Fringe with *Disco Pigs* in 1996 and more recently had a particularly successful run of plays – *The Walworth Farce, New Electric Ballroom* and *Penelope* – which Galway's Druid Theatre Company brought to the Traverse. Having an Irish play at the Traverse is important in its own right, says Downes, but Enda Walsh makes a particularly interesting case study:

The Walworth Farce played at the Traverse and that opened the door to New York and Los Angeles. That, in turn, helped seal the deal for a coast-to-coast tour of the United States.

Promoters in Australia, many of whom had seen the show at the Traverse, were pleased to see the success of the USA tour, which smoothed the way for the next leg. All those promoters were naturally receptive to Walsh's next play, *New Electric Ballroom*, but by opening at the Traverse, it got an extra boost. By the time *Penelope* came around, the international bookings were in place before the Traverse run, but it couldn't have happened without the previous two plays. Downes says you have to keep working on these relationships:

> Saying you have a longer-term commitment to Edinburgh is really important. It's not just about doing it for two years and then reviewing it. You have to become part of the landscape so people expect there will be Irish work there and from year to year the awareness grows.

That is also the approach taken by Kate McGrath, who produces several companies for Fuel:

> It's about them getting to know us and us getting to know them. They see our work over a number of years and with a number of different artists. We start to understand what they like and what they don't like, and they start to understand the range of work that we produce and where we might make a connection with their audience.

In an era of instant Lottery millionaires and *X Factor* celebrities, this advice may seem frustrating. But to enjoy a career of any longevity, you need to build firm foundations for the future. You would expect this to apply to your artistic work, and it applies equally to your professional career. In both cases, the Edinburgh Fringe is where the sparks fly and the relationships develop. Wherever you end up, you will always want to come back.

14. The Money
Balancing the Books

In the early 1960s, when there were just two dozen groups performing, the Fringe Society produced a leaflet called *Fringe Without Tears*. It warned participants of the tough competition, of the many costs involved and of the near impossibility of making a profit. If that was true fifty years ago, how much more so must it be today in a festival that is so many times bigger?

The short answer is that unless you are one of the very few big-name acts who can command a sell-out audience in a 1,000-seat room, you should not expect to make money. Instead, you should focus on how to limit your loss. Kath Mainland, chief executive of the Fringe Society, makes this clear:

> It's about being realistic about what it's going to cost you. If you have a realistic plan and you budget properly, you can either raise the money before you get here or focus the spending on what you think is important.

As ever, you should go back to Chapter 4 and remind yourself why you are coming to the Fringe in the first place. As Charlie Wood of the Underbelly sees it, there are three possible reasons, each of which will make you think about the costs in a different way:

One is to have fun. In this case, you have to work out what your cost is, what you're going to make, what the difference is, and then ask yourself if that margin is a cheap or expensive holiday. The second reason is to make money. Be really careful about that because it's really difficult. Even established performers, comedians and theatre producers come up here thinking they've got a show that will sell really well and it doesn't. Even one man and a microphone, because that market is so competitive, can still lose £5,000 or £10,000. The third reason is because you hope your show will get bought and find a future life. It happens every year, which is why people keep coming back, not because it's a myth. It does genuinely happen, but be aware that it only happens to a very small percentage of the overall number of shows.

Proceed with caution

Whichever category you fit into, you should do your financial planning with extreme wariness. It is not uncommon for producers even of outwardly successful shows to run up debts they are still paying off three years later. 'Think of a worst-case budget, add 25 per cent and try to stick to it,' says Nick Read, head of hire and events at Northern Light. 'It does always cost more; it's like moving house.'

When drawing up a budget there are many costs to remember in addition to the obvious expenditure of travel, accommodation and venue hire. 'There are the sundries that go on top that you forget,' says director Renny Krupinski. 'Insurance, Performing Right Society, Fringe box office taking six per cent off your tickets . . . all those things add up.'

In addition to this, you need to have a contingency fund of, say, 10 or 15 per cent of your total budget for the less predictable costs. 'You need to be prepared to spend a lot of money,' says Alice

Williams, part of a company from Reading University performing *The Talented Mr Ripley* and *Shakers*:

> I don't think we realised how many flyers we would get through and just little things, like we got a review for *Ripley* and printing off all of those and stapling them to our flyers is time-consuming and costs more money.

Fringe veterans will tell you that, however fantastic your show, however brilliant your marketing, however prudent your financial projections, sometimes things just don't work in your favour. William Burdett-Coutts, artistic director of Assembly, has been coming to Edinburgh long enough to see a pattern:

> I have a rule that every seven years you go bust. It's for no particular reason except inevitably running anything like that you can't expect it to work every year. You don't know going into the festival if all the shows are going to work or not, you don't know if there's going to be a downturn in the audience. A lot of my grey hairs are through keeping it all going.

Burdett-Coutts, of course, is running a whole venue and therefore dealing with more uncertainty than most. The lesson of caution, however, applies to even the smallest show. If your budget is unrealistic, you can find yourself being sucked into a deeper and deeper hole. 'There's nothing worse than looking over your shoulder for the whole month,' says Alex Rochford, former programmer at Assembly:

> With your budget set out, you say, 'We have to sell twenty tickets a day.' Then you fall short, so you say, 'It's all right, we can sell twenty-five tomorrow.' It falls short again and you say, 'We'll sell forty the next day.' You'll have the most horrendous month ever.

Getting the balance right is a fine art. With his twenty-year track record as a Fringe producer, Guy Masterson may appear to have got it sussed, but he freely admits he has made many miscalculations along the way.

I've learnt by mistakes – and I have made lots of mistakes, artistically and financially. I've not spent on marketing when I should have spent on marketing; I've overspent on marketing when I shouldn't have spent on marketing.

To complicate matters, Fringe finances frequently don't make sense. After reaching the finals of the So You Think You're Funny? competition in 1994, comedian Ed Byrne came back the next year as part of a triple bill of Irish comedians with Andrew Maxwell and Kevin Hayes:

We made money in that first year. The show sold about eighty per cent of its tickets and we probably got paid about £400 or £500 each. I was reasonably happy about that. I went up the following year and did my first solo show. It was a fifty-seater venue, it sold out every night and I still lost £500. The promoter said he would absorb that £500 and I thought, 'Too right you will because who budgets for a hundred per cent sell-out that loses £500?' My advice, if you have a promoter, is ask to see projected figures for how much you will lose or make, depending on how many tickets you sell.

Byrne points out that some costs, such as hiring a PR, remain constant irrespective of the size of your venue. He lost out because many of his overheads were the same as they would have been even if he had played a room twice as big, yet he had no way of increasing his box-office revenue to cover those costs. In his case, he would probably have done financially better in a 100-seat venue, but that is easy to say with hindsight. For a comedian at the start of his career, a bigger room would have been a bigger risk and a flop could have lost him even more.

The stories are not all negative, however. 'We make money now,' says Martyn Jacques, lead singer of the three-man Tiger Lillies, just home after a sell-out run of seventeen nights in a 150-seat venue at the Pleasance with a top ticket price of £15.

> For me, now it's perfectly legitimate to do it, which makes me happy. I feel it's part of our year's work. It's not an enormous amount of money, but it's all right. And we sell CDs which we sign after the show, so we make money from that as well. We're very lucky in that respect and it took us fifteen years of hard work.

This, however, is a rare sell-out show with ticket prices up to twice what many companies charge. A sell-out Tiger Lillies performance, assuming all tickets being sold at full price, would have a gross daily box-office figure of £2,250. That sounds like riches, but if you took the advice of publicist Liz Smith that 'you should never budget for more than thirty per cent – maybe forty per cent if you're really confident,' the picture would change dramatically. It's a projection in line with the Fringe Office's own recommendations and, in this case, your maximum takings would be more like £675. If your tickets averaged a more typical £10 (still on the high side), that gross would shrink to £450. Once the venue took its share of the takings, you'd be left with £270 and you would still have to account for production costs (costumes, set, props), accommodation, subsistence, travel, artwork, publicity, programme fee, Fringe box-office commission, public liability insurance and VAT. If there was anything left after that, it would surely evaporate once it was divided between the company members.

There are some costs that won't apply to you and some things you can do yourself, but you will find yourself paying for at least some of the following:

- Venue hire and/or box-office split
- Other venue charges such as staff, marketing and storage
- Fringe programme fee (roughly £300 for early-bird registration or £400 regular, including VAT)
- Fringe box-office commission (6 per cent of face value plus VAT)
- Wages for company and crew
- Administration costs
- Rehearsal room hire
- Costumes, props, set
- Equipment hire or purchase
- Public liability insurance (£120)
- VAT (20 per cent)
- Copyright
- Music licence fees
- Accommodation (£100–£150 per person, per week)
- Travel to Edinburgh
- Travel around Edinburgh
- Food and drink
- Company press officer
- Photocopying and distribution of press releases
- Company producer
- Design of adverts, flyers, posters, programmes, CDs, DVDs and T-shirts
- Design of website
- Internet domain name and web space
- Internet trailer
- Photography: advance publicity and production shots
- Advertising
- Printing of flyers, posters, programmes and T-shirts
- Copying of CDs and DVDs
- Distribution of flyers and posters

To get the clearest sense of your likely outlay, consult the *Fringe Guide to Doing a Show*, which is available for download from www.edfringe.com. This document gives a set of up-to-date sample budgets that take into account shows and venues of different sizes.

Getting the most from your venue

The standard financial arrangement between companies and venues across the Fringe is a 60/40 split. Simply put, this means the artist takes 60 per cent of the box-office returns and the venue takes 40 per cent. It isn't quite as simple as that, however. The venue is also likely to demand from the artist a guaranteed amount of money irrespective of ticket sales. This is known as a box-office split with guarantee. If you fail to attract an audience, you still have to pay the guarantee. In many cases you will be expected to pay some of it up front as a deposit.

The arrangement puts the venue in a more secure position. It will cover its costs even if the show is a flop and it will profit from a runaway hit by taking 40 per cent of a sell-out house. This sounds one-sided – a case of heads I win, tails you lose – but a box-office split can work for you as well. The deal means the venue has a vested interest in selling your tickets because it profits from you doing well. That, in theory at least, gives it an incentive to promote you.

A more established artist, such as a well-known comedian, can sometimes negotiate a more favourable deal – perhaps as high as a 90/10 split – because of the kudos and audiences they attract. This applies to a very small minority of performers, but whatever your level of fame, you will find different venues offer different deals. It is well worth investigating which works best for you. Rocket Venues, for example, charges you a fixed amount for rental and lets you keep all box office money until it exceeds 2.5 times the rental fee. Only after that point – when you would be close to selling out – does the 60/40 split come into play. Some venues will offer you a straight hire, others will have a box-office split from the first ticket sold, still others will take a communal approach with all the companies sharing the revenue between them.

Two venues offering 60/40 deals could start to look very different once you realise one offers an hour-long get-in and automatic press support, while the other insists on a fifteen-minute turn-around and charges for every extra with the opportunism of a budget airline. Look carefully at the way the venue calculates your deal; if, for example, audiences have to pay commission for booking by credit card, you need to know if the box-office split is worked out before or after it takes the commission. One reason comedians like playing the Stand Comedy Club (see Chapter 6) is it offers a deal that means they should not lose money even on a poorly selling show. Director Tommy Sheppard draws up a budget of every cost, such as room hire, registration with the Fringe Office, staffing costs and publicity. That figure has first call on the box office. He says:

> It takes between twelve and fifteen tickets a day to cover those costs. Anything above that, we split 80/20 in the performer's favour. Anything under that, we pick up the tab and don't charge the performer. People know that if they do a show with us and it's good and successful, they're going to make money, but if it's not good and they have a terrible time and they don't sell tickets, well, at least they're not going to lose any money. In other venues you have a terrible time only to leave and receive a spate of invoices.

It is an approach borne of an egalitarian ethos and a love of the art form, which is why a comedian such as Phil Nichol has returned there repeatedly. Playing at the Stand, he spends between £4,000 and £6,000 on a show and comes home with money. The comedians who might not be so keen on this arrangement are those with a guaranteed audience and who do not require services such as marketing and press. That it exists at all, however, reminds you of the value of shopping around for the deal that best suits you.

Charlie Wood, co-director of the Underbelly, says the field is open:

> There's no such thing as one deal. We do different deals for everybody. We do help produce and take some risk; we'll always help promote and sell the show with the press office. There are different degrees of how much we like the show, how much we want it and how much we think we can support it. If we really like a show, then we will go out really hard to get it.

When talking to your would-be venue, you should ask not only about what you will have to pay and what you get for your money, but also about the price of tickets and the revenue you can reasonably expect to earn. Find out the box-office figures for similar shows that played in the same time slot in previous years.

Anecdotally, you will hear various figures quoted about average attendance – usually along the lines of 'three people and a dog' – but there is no statistical truth in them. For an average attendance figure to be meaningful, it would have to reflect total capacity as well as total sales. That is because you would be very happy to have an audience of fifty in a sixty-seat venue and rather less so if it were fifty in a 600-seat venue. Using 2010 figures, you can do a straight division of the total number of tickets sold by the total number of performances and end up with an average of forty-eight people per show. Those figures, however, include everything from the site-specific show *Roadkill*, which had a daily capacity of twelve, to comedian John Bishop, who had a potential audience of 1,000. It would make no sense for either Bishop or *Roadkill* to have budgeted for forty-eight people and it is unlikely to make sense for you.

A better bet would be to talk to your venue manager about how similar shows have done at similar times of day in previous years. The more information you have, the more confidently you can draw up your budget. Producer James Seabright says:

> You have to look at the contract and analyse it fully. Ask the Fringe Office, ask people who have done Edinburgh before, for advice to make sure, when you're budgeting and working out what your potential is, that you're doing so rationally and reasonably.

Choosing a venue that charges you for every square metre of storage space, every microphone stand, every technician and every press release needn't be a problem as long as you include all the additional items in your budget. Following this advice should mean that you contain your costs and stay within the budget you set for yourself. Anthony Alderson, artistic director of the Pleasance says:

> If you were in a fifty-seater for twenty nights at £10 a ticket, that sum of money is not that unachievable. In the last five years, I can't think there are many companies that have left Edinburgh needing to pay us their guarantee. They've all made more than that. They're not having to mortgage their houses. Whether they've capitalised and paid for their own production – probably not – but they will at least have afforded to put the show on stage.

The pros and cons of performing in Peter Buckley Hill's Free Fringe or the Laughing Horse Free Festival are discussed in Chapter 6. The chief advantage, of course, is you have no venue hire costs to worry about. This does wonders for your budget, especially if you are able to attract an audience that is generous with its donations. The possible downsides are not to do with balancing the books, but with production values and establishing your reputation. How you weigh up those things will depend on your reasons for coming to the Fringe – Chapter 4 again.

Performing in an alternative space

Some combination of the pressure on space and the desire for novel artistic experiences means the Fringe is awash with productions in unlikely places. There have been shows in public toilets, in stationary camper vans, in moving cars, on open-top buses, in an out-of-hours department store and on the streets. Many of these have been among the most talked about shows, ideal for an audience in search of the new, but you should be cautious about choosing an alternative location if your primary motivation is to save money. In many cases, it can be the more costly option. The money you save on venue hire can quickly be exceeded by the cost of health and safety measures, for example, and depending on the space, you can find yourself with a very low audience capacity and therefore limited revenue.

If you are playing to small numbers, you might find it even harder than normal to raise sponsorship money. Judith Doherty of Grid Iron theatre company, presenter of many site-specific shows in Edinburgh, has seen this firsthand:

> You don't often have the audience capacity that makes it attractive to a company to give you a couple of grand. You don't have the nice, warm, fancy bar to schmooze your sponsors and, because you have a limited capacity, you're probably doing a more restricted print run that people would put their logos in.

She points to the expenses that accrue as soon as you step outside the comfort of a theatre. Put your audience on a bus and you might have different insurance to pay. Ask them to cross a road and you might need to employ ushers. Bring them into your bedroom and you'd better get the floor stress-tested by a structural engineer. And what about your front-of-house arrangements?

261

Where are you going to have the tickets taken? Are you going to have a float? Are you going to be able to sell tickets on the door? Is the person taking the money going to be safe? Do you need to put them in a taxi back to where your box office is?

When York's Belt Up Theatre Company programmed C Soco in Chambers Street with eight of its own shows and one co-production, it managed to do it on a shoestring despite the scale of the operation. Dominic Allen, one of the company's four co-artistic directors, explains their ethos:

> If professional companies have got some money, they budget to buy things. But we never have that money, so all of our set has been completely free. We've depended on favours and we hit some really good deals, whereas if we'd had money, we'd have bought it. That makes a huge difference, because you can get things for free so easily.

All the same, to take over a whole venue has unavoidable costs that serve as a reminder that such ventures are not a cheap option, as fellow director Jethro Compton found:

> The thing we spend money on is not the thing people see. This is our biggest budget for a show ever, but it's all for fire exits, scaffolding, electrics, fake walls, deliveries . . .

The lesson is that it should be art and not money that drives you to do something different.

Day-by-day budgeting

Keeping track of income and expenditure is your next challenge, not least because it all happens in a very concentrated period of time. One of the most frequent questions addressed to the Fringe Office in July is about how tickets are selling. For companies that have little profile, sales tend to remain sluggish until the festival begins. That can be alarming, but all you can do is trust your publicity campaign will be effective once you get to Edinburgh (see Chapter 9).

After that, everything happens so quickly, you need to make special efforts to keep up to date with box-office figures, adapting your marketing strategy as you go. 'Even while the sales were on track and we were getting good houses, it wasn't until the last few days that I knew we hadn't lost money,' says Aneke McCulloch, producer of the *Controlled Falling Project*. During the festival, you can see how your show is selling at the Fringe's box office by checking the online reports. It is possible your venue will be using a web-based version of the same system, which allows you to sell tickets, keep track of your inventory and report on sales.

Venues supply the Fringe's central box office with at least 25 per cent of their tickets – these are subject to a 6 per cent commission plus VAT – and sell the rest through their own box office. The exception are those that do not have their own permanent box office. They prefer the Fringe to hold all their tickets until an hour or two before the performance when they can be sold on the door. It is quite possible for a show to sell well at the Fringe box office and poorly at the venue or vice versa. If a show appears to be sold out at the Fringe box office, it could mean merely that the 25 per cent allocation has gone and the remaining 75 per cent are still unsold. You could lose audiences this way so you should monitor the online reports and adjust the Fringe's allocation accordingly. You can sign up to receive scheduled reports by email, giving you updates once or even several times a day. 'They can log in from anywhere in the world and see how their sales are doing,' says Fringe box office manager José Ferran, remembering the days when every request for a report meant another computer printout. 'They're a lot more in control than they used to be.'

The scratch nature of many Fringe companies can take a toll on bookkeeping. In the Fringe Office, Ferran commonly gets calls from companies trying to trace their money. Even though participants now register with the Fringe Society online, entering their bank details electronically, they can forget what details they gave between the programme deadline in April and the payout time at the end of September. 'We give them the number and they say, "That's not my bank account," says Ferran. 'This year, we've had, "That's my mother's bank account number," and "That's my partner's number."'

Such confusion will eventually be resolved, but it is better to get it right in the first place. So too is remembering to fill in the PRS form (see Chapter 8): unless you say otherwise, the Fringe Office will assume you owe royalties for using music in your show. If you forget to explain that you have not used any music, you have until the end of October to claim a refund.

Professional rates

It is the nature of the Fringe to embrace everyone from amateur dramatics groups to major-name comedians, professional theatre companies and student improvisers. Everyone in this mixed economy will have a different idea of financial success. If a group of amateur musicians cover their costs and have enough left over for a drink at the end of the night, they will be happy. By contrast, a professional company will be satisfied only if it raises enough money to pay its cast and crew union-sanctioned wages as well as covering their subsistence and accommodation costs. Needless to say, it is a lot harder for the professionals than the amateurs.

Brian Logan of Cartoon de Salvo takes the professional approach:

> We're assiduous in paying ourselves. If you're ever tempted to bend that rule, you can only do it if only the core members of the company were performing in any given show. Usually we've got some recruits and we can't not pay them. Sometimes Alex Murdoch, the artistic director, and I have waived our fees, but when you're thirty-seven it starts to get undignified.

The question of exploitation is a fraught one, but those who do choose to work voluntarily sometimes find they are at an artistic advantage. Nobody was paid, for example, in the early days of Out of the Blue and the Bongo Club, which grew out of the Fringe together in the late 1990s and became, respectively, a year-round arts centre and a nightclub. Producer Dana MacLeod was one of the volunteers in a building they occupied for a nominal rent because it was about to be demolished and she relished the freedom:

> Everybody worked for free – it was just a brilliant community thing – and then suddenly we started having bar income. We used to use the income for creative projects, so we were able to be adventurous and entrepreneurial with ideas. It meant there was a certain amount of freedom to be able to just take projects on without years of fund-raising and planning and setting up formal structures.

More recently the Forest Fringe has taken a similar approach. Paying no rent and receiving some philanthropic support, the organisation is run by volunteers and does not charge for tickets (although audiences can make donations at the end of the performance). By taking money out of the equation, it allows artists to concentrate on aspects they regard as more important, says co-director Andy Field:

Rather than spending £30,000 and trying to recoup £30,000 to break even, we're saying, 'Spend £200 and you might make £50 back.' You can accommodate making a £150 loss, because of other values to do with your profile as an artist – generating audiences, trying out new work, meeting other artists and getting bookings. You've got the real potential there for meaningful value for your career and your work. We wanted to create a space that focused on those potential values rather than money. That has its own liberating effect in terms of what you're willing to do.

Where you see yourself on the amateur/profit-share/professional spectrum will make a huge difference to the way you create your budget.

Raising money

It's a Saturday night in February and twenty people have gathered in an Edinburgh living room. They know each other through work or the playground or the book group and they have turned up tonight for a rather unusual gig. Standing behind a microphone in a glittering dress with a flower pinned to her hair, jazz singer Becc Sanderson welcomes them to the inaugural performance of her *Passion Flower Lounge Tour*. 'We're going to be playing a few tunes from my album *Passion Flower* – which is also available for sale if you have £10 – and we're going to start tonight with a very well-known standard,' she says, launching into *Bye Bye Blackbird*, accompanied by guitarist Graeme Stephen and, later in the set, trombonist Chris Grieve.

Sanderson's purpose is twofold. In this musical equivalent of an Avon party, she is able not only to raise money towards the costs of putting on her debut Fringe show (as well as album sales, everyone has paid to be here), but also to raise awareness of that show. Over the coming weeks, she will repeat the performance in other living rooms, building her audience as she goes. By the time the festival comes round, all the people who have seen her at these parties feel they have a vested interest in her show.

This is an example of a performer thinking creatively about raising money. As we have seen in this chapter, a lot of money has to be raised. According to one newspaper, it can cost the student actors of the American High School Theatre Festival over £3,600 each to make the trip across the Atlantic. Some spend two years fund-raising. You can imagine all the sponsored walks, jumble sales and benefit nights they will organise.

It takes a lot of effort, but it can work. Bringing *Cento Cose*, a three-person physical theatre piece from Italy, producer Stefania Bochicchio devised what she calls a 'micro-philanthropist' scheme:

> People, by giving €10 or €12, would get a certificate, a badge and a discount card, so that if they come to five shows, they get the sixth one for free. I think it's very important to get people involved in the process. We raised the whole budget of €15,000 from doing this and holding benefits.

This kind of crowd-sourcing has become common through internet sites such as www.wefund.co.uk ('where people offer perks in exchange for pledges'), www.kickstarter.com ('the largest funding platform for creative projects in the world') and www.indiegogo.com ('the world's leading international funding platform'). Such sites give you a space to describe your show, say what support you need and explain what you can give donors in return. If enough people like what they see, they need only contribute a few pounds for the money to stack up.

Getting public subsidy can be difficult in the UK where arts councils often choose not to support festival shows. You might get lucky with other trusts and foundations, however. For members of theatre companies between the ages of 16 and 25, for example,

267

Ideas Tap (www.ideastap.com) is an arts charity designed to help artists at the start of their careers, not only with money but also with advice and support. Every year its Edinburgh Fringe fund provides one winning company with £20,000 and one runner-up with £10,000.

Depending on where you live, you might be able to draw on other funds. Escalator East to Edinburgh supports artists who have a connection to the east of England; Made in Scotland allows professional Scottish dance and theatre companies to present work; Culture Ireland promotes companies from the Republic of Ireland at all the Edinburgh summer festivals; and national agencies such as the British Council, the Adam Mickiewicz Institute in Poland and the Goethe Institute in Germany sometimes offer support. 'Ten years ago, no one knew about Korean arts; now we do, because the national agency realised that this is the place to show their culture,' says Tomek Borkowy of Universal Arts.

These schemes are nearly always for professional artists and are selective in their support. Your chances might be higher seeking private sponsorship, although potential sponsors might worry that your show – and their investment – will be lost in a sea of Fringe competitors. On the other hand, they might like the idea of getting a logo on your flyer. You are handing out publicity material to a global audience of culturally minded people who could be just the customers a sponsor wants to reach. Tell them how many flyers you are printing and the kind of people you will be handing them to.

Otherwise, you are most likely to have success appealing for direct funding from individuals, organising benefit nights in your home town and asking for support in kind. 'Individual fund-raising is more realistic,' says Kath Mainland.

Thinking long-term

If so many people are losing so much money, how is it possible for the Fringe to maintain its position as the world's largest arts festival? There is little doubt Fringe participants are the biggest subsidisers of the event, so why do they keep coming back? One reason is that, although it makes no financial sense in the short term, the Fringe can start to add up in the long term. 'I've never broken even,' says comedian Nick Doody, whose venue sizes have ranged from sixty seats to 140:

> I don't think it's possible. If you're funding your own show and every part of that – renting a room, paying a techie, paying flyerers, paying a producer, paying a PR, paying for photography, producing posters – the overheads are immense. You're also paying a month's rent wherever else you live and you're not working for a month. But there's nothing else that does what Edinburgh does. I have had tangible financial rewards from Edinburgh.

Some people never make money on the Fringe, but would not be able to sustain a career for the rest of the year without it. There are those who see it as the equivalent of research and development, and those who treat it as a way of marketing themselves. Like spending money on a business card or a website, it allows you to let people know you are there. 'I've learned it's not about returns,' says playwright Ella Hickson. 'Out of *Hot Mess* I got three commissions, so it's career development. I got my first piece of work out of it in the first week, which meant I'd already broken even.'

You cannot guarantee those rewards, but if you envisage a life for your show beyond the Fringe, you can justify a budget that includes more than just August. What you spend in that month can pay financial or artistic dividends later in the year or even in years to come. Comedian Phil Nichol says he does not regard the money he has spent in Edinburgh over twenty years as a loss. 'I see it as an investment into the growth of my career,' he says. 'If you're going to spend all that kind of money, then you do a show that teaches you and expands your range.'

Charlie Wood considered the Underbelly's large-scale production of *Five Guys Named Moe* to be a success because it met its box-office targets, which justified the amount the venue had spent on marketing. That is not to say the show made a profit, however:

> We knew it would lose money. *Five Guys Named Moe* is a classic example of a producer using Edinburgh as a springboard. Even if we sold every ticket in Edinburgh, which we didn't do, and in Stratford East [where the play transferred to], we would still lose money. We are a very large and arguably very foolish version of the producer who understands Edinburgh is a beautifully benign environment because you are effectively gifted an audience. That benign environment is not a bad place to start a show, because you've got that audience and you've got the UK's press on your doorstep.

Guy Masterson took a similar approach when he produced Tim Whitnall's *Morecambe,* a one-man show about the comedian Eric Morecambe. In Edinburgh, it attracted sell-out houses and ecstatic reviews; in London, it went on to win the Olivier Award for Best Entertainment. Yet from the start, Masterson knew he could not earn at the Edinburgh box office what he needed to spend:

> We knew we had to tour the show afterwards. I booked a sixty-stop tour of an unwritten show before we'd even started rehearsals. It was a strong idea, strong reputation and that was it. We knew we could throw enough money at it in Edinburgh to make the show wow people production-wise and we knew we'd get out money back on tour.

Like Masterson, producer James Seabright returns year after year knowing he will not make money:

> The flat we rent as an office in Edinburgh costs more than our office in London costs for a year. So in some ways, the economics are crazy, but it remains the place to try out a new show and to sell it to the touring market. You get more press attention and promoters' attention than you would trying to open a show on that scale in, say, London.

If you are thinking of your career as a whole, then you could decide to spread your costs over a number of years. You could regard each return journey to Edinburgh as another step up the ladder. The investment you make in year one might pay off a considerable time later. 'You have to look at Edinburgh as a three-year plan,' says comedy publicist Claire Walker:

> It's pointless going for any less than three years on the trot. Make a big splash in the first year, capitalise on it in the second year and the third year you'll be getting somewhere. Of course people lose money, but people do make money as well. Ed Byrne, having put the years and effort in, makes money in Edinburgh.

The message is to make a sober estimate of your income and expenditure, then make sure you can afford the difference between the two. Whether you do this by fund-raising, cutting costs or absorbing the shortfall into a bigger annual budget will depend on your circumstances. There's no denying the riches you will find in Edinburgh are cultural not financial, but with prudence, you should be able to make the figures balance.

15. The Coda
A Final Thought

YOU'VE GOT A LOT on your plate. As if your show wasn't enough to worry about, there's the venue, the publicity, the accommodation, the timing, the morale and the budget. Dwell on these things for too long and it can seem overwhelming.

On the other hand, if you stay focused and take it one step at a time, you'll find it surprisingly manageable. Just think of all the people who've managed it before. And remember all the people who are there to help you – at your venue, in the Fringe Office, all over town.

Many thousands of people did the Fringe last year, many thousands more will do it in years to come. They will not do it because they have a love of bookkeeping and unduly stressful situations. They will do it because the Edinburgh Fringe is the most exhilarating place on Earth. They will do it for the sheer love of it. And the following year they will come back and do it some more.

You will too. So put the book down, get out there, and prepare for the time of your life.

Index